LIBERATING THE SOUL

A GUIDE FOR SPIRITUAL GROWTH
Volume One

By
Shaykh Nazim Adil al-Haqqani

Foreword By
Shaykh Muhammad Hisham Kabbani

ISLAMIC SUPREME COUNCIL OF AMERICA

Published and Distributed by:
Islamic Supreme Council of America (ISCA)
1400 Sixteenth Street NW, #B112, Washington, DC 20036 USA
Tel: (202) 939-3400
Fax: (202) 939-3410
Email: staff@islamicsupremecouncil.org
Web: http://www.islamicsupremecouncil.org

Publishing Office:
17195 Silver Parkway, #201
Fenton, MI 48430 USA
Tel: (888) 278-6624
Fax: (810) 815-0518

First Edition, July 2002
Library of Congress Control Number: 2002109747
ISBN: 1-930409-14-1

On the Internet, please visit http://www.islamicsupremecouncil.org for more titles in Islamic spirituality and traditional scholarship.

Head of the world's largest Naqshbandi Sufi spiritual order, Shaykh Nazim (right) is known for his life-altering lessons in how to discipline the ego, reach a state of spiritual surrender, and achieve true liberation from the bondage of worldly distraction and pursuit. Shaykh Hisham Kabbani (left), Shaykh Nazim's deputy and spiritual heir, accompanies the venerable shaykh on his many visits to various regions of the world, where they meet with political and religious leaders, media, and throngs of common folk.

table of contents

FOREWORD

Bismillah ir-Rahman ir-Rahim
In the Name of God, The Most Beneficent, The Most Merciful

All praise is due to God the Exalted for the endless blessings He bestows on each of us, both what we see and know, and the infinite blessings that are unknown to us.

In these days of struggle and challenge - when people are scattered and human relationships are weak, and hearts are left searching for inner peace – through these pages we are blessed with immediate, tangible guidance which, at the very least, leads us away from the darkness of doubt and replenishes our inner strength and confidence.

Liberating The Soul is a thoughtful series comprised of transcribed lectures of the head of the world's largest Naqshbandi Sufi spiritual order, Shaykh Nazim Adil al-Haqqani. His timeless teachings are heavenly wisdom for all, reaching beyond ethnic, cultural, and religious barriers, like illumined arrows penetrating the heart. His divinely inspired words are special gifts to one who has devoted his heart and life to The Almighty for more than sixty years.

The series presents more than three hundred of Shaykh Nazim's lectures, which cover broad topics of interest to a spiritual seeker living under these contemporary, stressful times. Taken all together, these talks form a unique handbook of instructions, wisdom, guidance and support for seekers of any spiritual path.

I have been honored to follow Shaykh Nazim since my childhood in Beirut, where he often visited my family. At the tender age of ten years, Shaykh Nazim took me under his wing. He later introduced me to

Grandshaykh Abd Allah ad-Daghestani in Damascus, who, from our first meeting, became a grandfather figure - always loving and patient.

For more than forty years I have witnessed Shaykh Nazim's furtherance of Grandshaykh Abd Allah's teachings, and the vast audiences from around the world that gravitate to him, always seeking his healing guidance, his heartfelt advice, and encouragement to serve The Almighty.

The perpetual, oft-reaching, and miraculous power of their guidance has changed individual lives and households, and indeed, entire communities. I have seen countless numbers of seekers - people of all walks of life, from common citizens to heads of state - refer to Shaykh Nazim's healing words as they navigate the challenges of their daily lives. Many have been healed of physical and mental illnesses; most have been blessed with a rekindled spirit.

Thus, I consider it a distinct privilege to present their teachings to you, and I pray you receive the benefit of all four volumes of the series in your personal quest to "liberate the soul".

Shaykh Muhammad Hisham Kabbani
Chairman, Islamic Supreme Council of America
Washington, D.C.

ıntʀoԀuctıon

The late afternoon sun, subdued and filtered through the high, lead-encased panes of an old church in southeast London that now serves as a mosque, shines down upon an extraordinary group of people. It is not uncommon to see semi-circles of ethnically-diverse men and women of varied ages, clustered around an elderly turbaned, white-bearded man who could have stepped straight out of the Bible or the Quran.

Addressing their hearts, he bathes them in a sublimely eloquent discourse in his own unique style, punctuated by many flavorful examples and endless humor, about the necessity of a seeker emptying his heart of everything except God.

A newcomer to the group is likely to feel both awe and love for the possessor of that luminous face with its large, expressive blue eyes. They are touched by his speech and warmed by the graciousness of his welcome. And to his tens of thousands of followers now spread throughout the world, this simple, humble but supremely luminous, saintly man is the most revered and loved of all people on earth. He is their teacher, counselor, guide and living example of the faith of Islam in its fullest embodiment, their beloved "Shaykh Nazim".

As a *murshid* (spiritual guide) of the Naqshbandi Sufi order, Shaykh Nazim is an inheritor of the past fifteen centuries of the highest Islamic knowledge, both of the external and spiritual sciences. Among the elements that make him so unique is the fact that, although he is a man of the East, he speaks to his Western followers in English – his own inimitable, flavorful brand which reaches straight into the heart, punctuating his talks with unfailing humor and moving anecdotes.

Since the beginning of human history, God Most High has conveyed His revealed guidance to mankind through His prophets and messengers, beginning with the first man, Adam (a). The prophetic line includes such well-known names as Noah, Abraham, Ishmael, Isaac, Jacob, Joseph, Lot, Moses, David, Solomon, and Jesus, peace be upon them all. It was a descendant of Abraham, namely Muhammad (s), the Seal of the Prophets, who brought the final revelation from God to all mankind.

But although there are no longer prophets upon the earth, the Most Merciful Lord has not left His servants without inspired teachers and guides. Awliya – holy souls or saints – are the inheritors of the prophets. Up to the Last Day, these "friends of God," the radiant beacons of truth, righteousness and the highest spirituality, will continue in the footsteps of the prophets, calling people to their Lord and guiding seekers to His glorious Divine Presence.

One such inspired teacher, a shaykh or murshid of the Naqshbandi Sufi Order, is Shaykh Nazim Adil al-Qubrusi. A descendant not only of the holy prophet Muhammad (s) but also of the great Sufi masters Abdul Qadir Gilani and Jalaluddin Rumi, Shaykh Nazim was born in Larnaca, Cyprus, in 1922 during the period of British rule of the island. Gifted from earliest childhood with an extraordinarily spiritual personality, Shaykh Nazim received his spiritual training in Damascus at the hands of Mawlana Shaykh Abd Allah ad-Daghestani (fondly referred to as "Grandshaykh"), the mentor of such well-known figures as Gurjieff and J. G. Bennett, over a period of forty years.

Before leaving this life in 1973, Grandshaykh designated Shaykh Nazim as his successor. In 1974, Shaykh Nazim went to London for the first time, thus initiating what was to become a yearly practice during the month of Ramadan up to the present time. A small circle of followers began to grow around him, eagerly taking their training in the ways of Islam and *tariqat* (spiritual path) at his hands.

From this humble beginning, the circle has grown to include thousands of murids (disciples) in various countries of the world, among whom are to be found many eminent individuals, both religious and secular. Shaykh Nazim is a luminous, tremendously impressive spiritual personality, radiating love, compassion and goodness. He is regarded by many of his murids as the *qutb* (chief saint) of this time.

The shaykh teaches through a subtle interweaving of personal example and talks ("associations" or *sohbets*), invariably delivered extempore according to the inspirations that are given to him. He does not lecture, but rather pours out from his heart into the hearts of his listeners such knowledge and wisdoms as may change their innermost beings and bring them toward their Lord as His humble, willing, loving servants.

Shaykh Nazim's language and style are unique – so eloquent, moving and flavorful that not only do his teachings seem inspired but also his extraordinary use of words. His *sohbets* represent the teachings of a twentieth century Sufi master, firmly grounded in Islamic orthodoxy, speaking to the hearts of the seekers of God of any faith from his own great, wide heart, in a tremendous outpouring of truth, wisdom and divine knowledge which is surely unparalleled in the English language, guiding the seeker toward the Divine Presence.

The sum total of Shaykh Nazim's message is that of hope, love, mercy and reassurance. In a troubled and uncertain world in which old, time-honored values have given place to new ones of confused origins and unclear prospects, in which a feeling heart and thinking mind is constantly troubled by a sense of things being terribly disordered and out of control, in which the future seems forebodingly dark and uncertain for humanity, he proclaims God's love and care for His servants, and invites them to give their hearts to Him.

Shaykh Nazim holds out to seekers the assurance that even their smallest steps toward their Lord will not go unnoticed, nor neglected. Rather than threatening sinners with the prospect of eternal Hell, he offers hope of salvation from the Most Merciful Lord, and heart-warming encouragement and incentive for inner change and growth. As one who has traversed every step of the seeker's path and reached its pinnacle, he offers both inner and practical guidelines for attaining the highest spiritual goals.

All the books in this series are based on talks given extempore, as Shaykh Nazim never prepares his words but invariably speaks according to inspirations coming to his heart.

In keeping with the shaykh's methodology - the methodology of the prophets, particularly of the Last Prophet, Muhammad - of reinforcing vital lessons by repetition and reiteration, the same themes and anecdotes recur again and again. The talks seem to come in unannounced clusters, centered on a primary theme, which develops and evolves according to the spiritual state of the listeners. Thus, Shaykh Nazim may cite the same verse or a *hadith* (holy tradition), or tell the same tale on different occasions, each time reinforcing a slightly different aspect of the eternal message of love and light, which is embodied in the Islamic faith.

The shaykh's talks are interspersed with words and phrases from Arabic and other Islamic languages, which have been translated either in the text itself or in a footnote the first time they occur. A glossary has also been provided. Quranic verses mentioned in the text have been referenced for easy access.

Every attempt has been made to retain the shaykh's original language with minimal editing. However, some inadvertent errors may have found their way into the text. For these, we ask Allah's forgiveness and your kind indulgence. May your heart be filled with light and love as you read and reflect upon these inspired words, and may your soul be "liberated".

publisher's note

Shaykh Nazim is fluent in Arabic, Turkish and Greek, and semi-fluent in English. Over three decades, his lectures have been translated into twenty or more languages, and to date have reached the furthest corners of the globe. We sincerely hope the reader will appreciate the author's unique language style, which has been painstakingly preserved in this work.

As some of the terms in this book may be foreign, to assist the reader we have provided transliterations, as well as a detailed glossary and a table of the Islamic months and commonly observed holy days.

notes

Quotes from the Holy Quran are referenced in brackets, i.e. (3:127), indicating the third chapter, verse 127. Quotes from the Hadith (holy traditions) are referenced by narrator and transmitter.

Dates of events are characterized as "– AH", which infers "after Hijra (migration)" on which the Islamic calendar is based. A table of Islamic months and holy days is provided.

Muslims around the world typically offer salutations upon speaking, hearing or reading mention of Prophet Muhammad, other prophets, his family, his companions, and saints. We have used the following international standard:

(s): for *sall-Allahu 'alayhi wa sallam* or "God's blessings and greetings of peace be upon him," following the names of the Prophet.

(a): for *'alayh is-salam* or "peace be upon him," following the names of other prophets, male members of the family of the Prophet, angels, and Khidr.

(a): for *'alayha as-salam* or "peace be upon her," following the names of female members of the family of the Prophet, and Mary, Mother of Jesus.

(r): for *rady-Allahu 'anh* or "may God be pleased with him/her," following the name of a male or female companion of the Prophet.

(q): for *"qaddas-Allahu sirrah"* or "may God sanctify his secret," following the name of a Saint.

In the Name of Allah, The Beneficent and The Munificent

This, my English, is strange English. Not everyone can understand because, *subhanallah*, meanings are coming to my heart, and when running in my heart to give to you, I am using any means – from here, from there - bringing any word which may be useful.

I am like a person waiting for water to run out from the faucet. Then, when suddenly it comes, and he knows the water is going to be turned off, stop running, he may take any container – with a no-good shape, broken on one side, or anything he may find there – quickly bringing them to take that water and store it. Therefore, when meanings are coming to my heart, I am trying to explain with any word, which you may understand or not. But you *must* understand, because we have a saying, "Listeners must be more wise than speakers." Therefore, when inspiration comes, we must explain.

They are living words, not plastic – bananas, plastic; apples, plastic, and grapes. Even if the shapes are not much, they are living, real. When you are going to arrange them in measures, good system; when you are going to be engaged by outside forms, you are losing meanings. ▲

1: at the beginning…

In the name of Allah, All-Mighty, All-Merciful, Most Beneficent and Most Munificent, the Lord of the worlds, the Lord of the sons of Adam, the Lord of the heavens, the Lord of the angels, the Lord of every creature.

Subhanallah, glory be to Allah Almighty, making bodies of earth – going, coming, eating, drinking, speaking, thinking, doing everything! Who can do this except the Lord of the universes, Allah Almighty? And we are sufficiently proud to be His servants.

That is the eternal honor that we have been given: that He accepts us as His servants. And we are His servants from pre-eternity up to post-eternity. We are not servants to anyone else, we are *His* servants. ▲

2: the owner of this universe

We are living in a world and we are surrounded by a universe. We are in such a center that, from every direction we are surrounded by a universe. Some part of it we can see and some part we cannot.

We say that there is space. In space we are seeing lighted dots and we are saying that those are stars, suns, galaxies, and between each one there are huge distances. What do scholars and scientists say – are the distances in between, huge distances, empty or full?

We are looking and saying, "It is empty." Then I am saying, "Empty? If it is empty, is it *something*, or not?"

We are seeing only some dots of light and black darkness. *Is it something or not?* If it is empty, it means it is nothing. And if it is nothing, how are so many galaxies and stars and suns standing or running or spinning in *nothing?* And if it is nothing, everything in it must be nothing, also.

Something in nothing – how can it be? I am thinking about it so many times, but what is the answer? Therefore, it is a strange thing; a surprising universe, this universe. How are galaxies running in *nothing?*

Allah Almighty, the Lord of the universes, is calling people to believe in the Unseen. We must believe in unseen worlds, in unseen universes, in unseen creatures, and in an unseen Creator. Otherwise, we must leave our minds and go without minds, we must deny our mental faculties. As we have been created, we must believe. And Allah Almighty created this world to be a station for us. We may put our feet on it and go on.

The whole universe is swimming in the endless Power Oceans of *Someone*. Even if you do not accept to say "God" or "Allah," you must know, you must accept, this fact. To believe is one thing but to accept is something else.

We must accept that the whole universe is swimming in an endless Power Ocean of Someone, because those Power Oceans must belong to Someone, since you can't find the smallest part of a place in which there is no power. To the extent that matter is smaller, there is immense power concentrated in it, huge power stations in the smallest particle of matter.

Now, there must be endless knowledge for that Someone. If He doesn't have endless knowledge, nothing can appear in existence. We have a saying in Arabic, *"Fa fi kulli shayin lahu ayat* – in everything in existence there are signs of Allah." Even if you look at the smallest particle of the universe (the atom, as we know), it has a very amazing structure in itself; you can fill a library with that atomic knowledge. That is the universe which we see. It is impossible for even the smallest particle of the universe to appear in existence without carrying endless knowledge or pointing to its Creator's endless knowledge.

Then, that universe which appears in existence also points to Someone's endless art. Without knowledge of endless art, He can never bring into existence even the smallest particle of this universe. Yes; you look at this building and you say that the architect who built such a building is a powerful and a great one. And the entire universe indicates that that Someone must have the most perfect art. If you do not accept this, you must give up your mind or your mental faculties. You *must* give them up; only then you can deny this. Otherwise, you must accept it.

Then, also, we must accept that for that One, for that Someone, there must be an endless will. If no will, if this vast universe exists without a will, how can there come from Power Oceans such a hashma (greatness), in such a charming universe? Without will, how is it going to appear from endless Power Oceans? Therefore, for that Someone, there must be endless Will Oceans, and reason, logic, says that must be so.

And we must accept, if we are people with minds, that for that Someone there must also be vision. Who says that the one who made this instrument [tape recorder] was a blind man? A blind man can do this? Never! And the vision of that Someone must be endless because it is impossible for a blind Someone to make such a charming universe. Hasha, never! And He is someone who sees the inside of atoms and the outside of atoms, as He looks at the inside and at the outside of everything. Otherwise, it is impossible.

Then, we must accept that that Someone must be someone who hears; without ears He is able to hear. From every part of creation, from every place in the universe, He must hear, because everyone or everything in existence is calling to Him and asking from Him. If He does not hear, He can't give all things what they are in need of to exist, and He must have endless hearing so that He may meet everyone's needs.

That One, that Someone, *must be*. And that Someone cannot be two or three because if there were two or three or more, one would order and one would cancel [his orders]. Therefore, firstly, philosophers, by the way of their minds, are looking and saying, concerning that Someone in the universe, that the most perfect coordination exists in everything. Such great order exists among all things that this universe would not be perfect if even one atom were to be out of existence. And they are giving a name to that Someone.

We are now using the way of minds to find an Owner of this universe, because we are not its owners. No one can say that this universe belongs to me, let alone univers*es*. Even on this earth, we are not saying that we are the owners of it because someone may take it away from us and it will be gone. Who can claim that this universe is mine? But, we must ask, *To whom does it belong?*

That is a question for everyone who has a brain in his head, not straw. Therefore, we are asking for that Someone. There must be an Owner, and we are using the way of minds now to find Him.

Mind has realized that there must be an Owner with these attributes: He must have endless Power Oceans, He must have endless Knowledge Oceans, He must have endless vision, He must have endless hearing, He must have endless art, He must have endless will. You may use any name for that Someone, but we are saying that He is Allah Almighty, that Someone – God Almighty, our Lord, the Lord of the universes, the Lord of the sons of Adam, the Lord of every human being, past, present and coming in the future. ▲

3: about god almighty

God Almighty, the Exalted – you can't imagine Him; He is not to be imagined. Your imagination is within limits; then how can you imagine what is unlimited? But foolish people are saying, "Show us! Show us so we will believe."

One grand-*wali*, saint, said, "If I show you Him, can you recognize Him?" I am showing you a photograph. If the name is not written, even in a newspaper, you will not know who it is. Then how can you recognize something that is never going to be within your imagination? Yes – God Almighty, who we call "Allah" (the one true God)… ▲

4: the importance of prophets

What are the duties of the Prophet (s) or of prophets, peace be upon them all? Why did they come? This point is coming now. What is their job, what is their importance, what is their duty, what are their works?

From the beginning, Adam (a) was created in Paradise, and Eve, also, but they landed on this earth. They were rebellious against their Lord, both of them, but they asked forgiveness from Him.

Adam (a) landed in Ceylon, on a mountain. He stood on his feet, first on one foot and then on the other, asking forgiveness, and he wept for three hundred years. And, according to traditions, his tears ran into the earth, and good-smelling trees and herbs grew from them.

Adam and Eve asked forgiveness, and Allah Almighty accepted their repentance and forgave them. Then He made a way for Adam and Eve to return to Paradise. And Allah Almighty gave Adam prophethood for his sons; and from Adam up to the last prophet, Muhammad (s), all the prophets came to announce to people that Allah Almighty is calling them to forgiveness, calling them to Mercy Oceans, calling them to Paradise, to be there forever – calling and inviting people to His Divine Presence for eternal life.

Now the importance of prophets is clear: their importance is to encourage people to believe. To encourage people to believe – that is important, because people have been invited to a place which they do not see or hear or know. Prophets help them to hear about Paradise, to hear about the Divine Presence, help them to know about some worlds that are unseen.

If there were no prophets, no one could know about the unseen worlds and no one could know that there is eternal life after death. But Allah Almighty sends messengers to people from among mankind, not from among angels. And the first prophet was also the first man, coming directly from Paradise, and he knew perfectly, clearly, where he had been before and where he had landed.

I mean to say, the prophets were in perfect relationship with the heavens, with the spiritual world, so that each prophet saw Paradise and Hell, and then they told their people about Paradise and Hell and about eternal life. They looked, saw, knew and gave knowledge to people so that they might believe. Each prophet was invited to the heavens, and the last, the Seal of the Prophets (s), had a perfect journey to the heavens during the night of the Mi'raj,[1] the night of the Ascension. He had a perfect inspection of the heavens, entering Paradise and looking at Hell, also; and when he put his foot into Hell, its fires cooled down and were extinguished.

It would be easy for our Lord Almighty to show everyone Paradise and Hell, and then everyone would know and accept. But we have been ordered to be His servants, and, in the spiritual world that belongs to the heavens, on the Day of Promises[2] we also looked at Paradise and Hell, and we listened to our Lord's addressing us.

Although everything was all right in the spiritual life, Allah Almighty is trying His servants to see if they are keeping their promises. Therefore, He sends our souls from the heavens and puts them into physical bodies, and then asks us to keep our promises. But now we are saying that we cannot remember anything about the Day of Promises in the spiritual world. Most people are denying it, saying, "No, we do not remember such a thing."

---

[1] The holy Prophet's ascension to the seven heavens, during which he was shown Paradise and Hells, and admitted him to the ultimate station of nearness to his Lord among all created beings, following his miraculous journey by night from Mecca to Jerusalem, where he led all the earlier prophets in prayer.
[2] Holy Quran, 7:172.

But Allah Almighty, from His endless mercy, sends messengers to people, to His servants, to make them remember, and from the first to the last, 124,000 prophets just came and made us to remember. But people are trying to deny this, saying, "We do not accept such a thing."

Yet each day they sleep. They are denying the soul and spiritual workings in their bodies but each day they go to sleep. They lose themselves; to some extent they lose their senses, and, at the time of sleep, their souls leave their bodies and are free.

When our souls are free, we feel rest because our souls are returning to the Ocean from which they came. And Allah Almighty has promised souls such a chance each day, giving sleep and making them free from our bodies. Everyone's soul leaves his body. There is only some headquarters in our bodies which does not leave, but most of it goes; only some areas remaining in relationship, in contact.

Therefore, we dream. And I am asking that person who denies everything [spiritual], "When you dream, with which eyes are you looking, and, while your eyes are shut, by what means are you seeing in your dreams? Tell me!"

If you are denying spiritual workings in your body, tell me how you dream. In your dream you walk, you fly, you go from one place to another; you see, you take pleasure, you are punished. How can it be, while you are sleeping there? How can you see, how can you hear, how can you move? And you see yourself moving, looking, lying, kissing, doing everything, and yet you are alone there. What is that?

You must believe; everyone must believe. Therefore, all the prophets just came to help us believe, and we must believe and we must also try to help other people believe. The main source of evil comes from disbelief. Therefore, during the times of the prophets, when people believed, peace came into their hearts, mercy came through their hearts.

If there is no belief, no mercy lives in hearts; if no belief, no justice can you find in hearts. Therefore, Allah Almighty sent all the prophets and gave them miraculous and extraordinary powers.

All miracles were for what? To make people believe, because if a person comes and says, "I am a prophet. Listen to me," we must ask, "What is your evidence, what is your proof that you are a prophet, coming from your Lord? Perhaps you are coming from Satan, calling people to Satan. Where is your evidence?" And all the prophets brought miracles just to make people agree and be in satisfaction with them. If at first they looked at the prophets and said, "You can't do this," after seeing their miracles, they would say, "You are all right."

The Last Prophet also brought so many miracles, thousands. Leave aside all of them. He also brought from his Lord the Holy Quran, the Glorious Quran, and it is forever evidence, proof, for him. But we will speak about another point:

During the time of Prophet Muhammad (s), when his nation stood against him, Heraclius Caesar, the emperor of the Eastern Roman Empire, was in Damascus. Old Damascus was surrounded by walls, and everyone who went in or out was inspected, particularly those strangers who went in or came out.

Abu Sufyan was the Prophet's relative. At first he was against the Prophet and then later he came into Islam, first fighting against the Prophet but finally surrendering and saying, "You are right, we are wrong."

Once he went from Mecca to Damascus for trading in their manner. He and his party entered Damascus and guards detained them. "From where are you coming and to where are you going?"

They said, "We are Arabs from Mecca, come for trading." That news quickly went to Caesar, to Heraclius. He ordered that they be arrested and brought to his presence.

He was sitting on his golden throne, putting his generals on this side and bishops on that side. Then those people, Abu Sufyan and his friends, were brought there. And Heraclius asked, "Who is that prophet's relative, the closest one to him?"

Abu Sufyan came to the front, saying, "I am one of his relatives."

"Look," Heraclius said, "I am going to ask you about that one" (he meant "that important one"). "I am asking you about that most important one who now lives in your country and who is your relative – about him. You must reply to me correctly. And you, his friends, if he is lying, you must tell me."

Afterwards, when he became a Muslim, Abu Sufyan said, "I was too afraid to say anything that was not true, with those people around me saying, 'Lies!' and then I would have been thrown out of that palace in front of Caesar. Therefore, due to that fear, I tried to answer everything correctly." Only, when Heraclius asked so many questions and, as a summary, asked one further question, saying, "Up to this day, what did Muhammad do of badness, of evil?" Abu Sufyan said, "Nothing. But I don't know what he may have done from the time I left him up to today"; only this he inserted amidst everything else.

And Heraclius laughed, saying, "Does he call people to anything except goodness?"

Abu Sufyan said, "No, never. He asks his followers to take care of orphans, to look after widows, to keep respect for parents, to give all people their rights, to protect slaves and weak people, to uphold justice, and to show mercy to everyone. He calls us to the One God and tells us to do every good action."

And the emperor said, "That is right; that is the way of all the prophets. All those earlier prophets did just the same as he is doing now, nothing else. Then how are you denying him, how are you not accepting him? If I could be there, I would wash his feet and serve him like a servant. He must be even more than you are now saying about him because you are not a believer in him now. You must know," he said to the generals, to the bishops, "that that Prophet's nation will come and conquer the soil on which my feet now stand." And Heraclius died with his faith in the Prophet, keeping it here [in his heart], not declaring it with his tongue. But it is enough. Allah looks here.

That is history, not a story – history! You must know! For what are we asking miracles? If a person calls us to goodness, to mercy, to justice, to eternal life, for what more are we asking? Is that not enough for us to believe in that person and to follow him? But people are foolish, asking for miracles – and then, after miracles, fighting, also.

And in our time, people are claiming that they are intelligent, all of them. But they are not looking at the Prophet's ways. All the prophets are calling all people to the Divine Presence, and calling them to uphold justice, to give respect to everyone, to be righteous, to be trustworthy and to be beloved by everyone. But people are running away, asking for their egos' enjoyment.

Everyone – everyone! - - is running after his own benefit; everyone is asking for himself only to be in enjoyment and pleasure but never thinking of others. Therefore, each day crises are mounting, suffering is increasing, darkness is coming down, and people are enemies and are preparing themselves to eat each other, to destroy each other. Yet all the prophets are calling us to believe in our Lord, and to be just and merciful and respectful believers. ▲

5: the value of man

We are listening to what is coming from our spiritual 'Central Headquarters.' Allah Almighty gives us ears for listening, gives us eyes for looking, gives us hearts for understanding. But we are using our ears in the wrong way, our eyes in the wrong way, our hearts in the wrong direction. Therefore, we are looking but not seeing, we are hearing but not understanding, we are knowing but not feeling.

Without feeling, knowledge is nothing. Knowledge, when it moves feelings, *that* is useful knowledge. And I am asking my Grandshaykh to give us from the knowledge of *awliya* (saints), to move our hearts towards our Lord's direction.

While I was praying, some inspirations were coming. Those are important inspirations about the value of man. This point just came; we shall see what comes now to complete it. Grandshaykh is 'translating' to me from the Prophet's heart (s), and I am translating to you from our Grandshaykh's heart, may Allah bless him.

No other religion gives such value to mankind as Islam gives it. And among *tariqats*, none gives that value to mankind that the Most Distinguished Naqshbandi Order gives. And among grandshaykhs, such value as our Grandshaykh gives to the sons of Adam, to mankind, I have never heard.

The most important thing for everyone belonging to mankind is know what is the value of himself and of everyone who is created as a human being, as one of the sons of Adam – that is the most important knowledge that must be learned by everyone. If everyone knows the value of himself and of everyone else, this world is going to be like a paradise.

But now they are losing that value and the whole world is going to be like a hell. Throughout the East and the West, no value for mankind. In the East [the Communist bloc], no value for the individual; in the West, they are also considering the individual as a material being, looking upon him as a robot. In the Western countries, which we call 'free countries,' everyone can find everything that he is in need of for himself, like a robot, and Western countries' systems are stealing the hearts of people and leaving them without hearts.

Throughout the East and West, the value of people has been lost, finished: that is the source of suffering and troubles and problems. While the East has stolen the individual – no more value for the individual person – the West has taken his heart and left him like a robot, both of them finishing the value of mankind.

And between the East and the West, some countries are going after the East, camping in the Eastern camp, and some of them are camping in the Western camp. And the Muslim world is also divided into two camps, East and West. There is now no camp for Muslims to be under, to take a shelter for themselves – no. In the Muslim world they have also lost the value of man, of mankind.

Allah Almighty sent the Seal of the Prophets, the most valuable one, the most important and beloved one, Muhammad (s), to teach mankind forever who they are and what their value is. And Allah Almighty sent one verse in the Holy Quran declaring the value of mankind, and that verse never came from the heavens except to beloved Muhammad (s). You may read or recite it among other verses, not paying too much attention to it, and our scholars have also given some meanings of that verse. It is just part of a verse, not even a complete verse; it is only three or four or five words,

"Wa laqad karramna bani Adam."[3] But Allah Almighty is giving perfect value to the sons of Adam through part of a verse, *"Wa laqad karramna bani Adam."*

If all *awliya* (I am not speaking of scholars; scholars' knowledge stops here – I am speaking of *awliya*'s knowledge) were to give the knowledge that they have concerning that one verse, it would not be sufficient to give the true value which Allah Almighty is declaring by the word *"karramna"* ["We honored"]. For forty years I heard about that word from my Grandshaykh, and with that ocean still in his heart he went away [from this world].

You must know about your Lord and about His prophets, and also about the *sultan* of the Prophets, Muhammad (s). Other prophets' knowledges and all *awliya*'s and all angels' knowledges are like a little drop on a needle when a needle is taken from an ocean, but a limited ocean, while the Prophet's knowledge is like a little drop in an *endless* ocean. And the Prophet (s) gives such value to the sons of Adam as no one can give except Allah Almighty. And Allah Almighty gives such value to the sons of Adam that no one can know the amount of that value.

We may say something about the value of the sons of Adam. The value of one human being is out of this world. If all computers were made to work to give a value, to give a figure or number for the whole universe, one human being is more valuable than that. If there comes another universe like this one, also without man, one man is more valuable. If there come ten universes, still he is more valuable; if one thousand, he is more valuable, also. If you bring millions, billions, that one person is more valuable.

This is a piece of knowledge from *awliya*'s knowledge, not *we* that know that. Therefore, the one who is asking for the pleasure of his Lord, as much as he may give value to His servants, to the sons of Adam, he gives pleasure to his Lord.

---

[3]"And We have certainly honored the sons of Adam." (17:70)

May Allah Almighty give us understanding. We are lacking that. No understanding; in the twentieth century, no-understanding people are living. They are claiming they understand everything, but *not* the value of man. You may understand everything *except* the value of man.

If you understood, you would put on everyone's head a crown, coming from the heavens. *Awliya* are looking and they are seeing that on everyone's head there is a crown, a heavenly crown; but a blind man does not see, will never see. Make a light in your heart, and little by little it is going to appear that everyone is wearing a heavenly crown. And as much as you give value to the sons of Adam, you will acquire more value and advance in the Divine Presence.

Now we come to the opposite of this. Who is the most guilty person, guilty of the biggest sin? What is the biggest sin in the Divine Presence? The biggest sin is not to give value to other people. You understand? The one who does not give a person value, he is the biggest sinner.

We are giving value to people, firstly, if they are rich; secondly, if they are powerful; thirdly, if they are young; fourthly, if they are beautiful or handsome or healthy. "A bright one," we are saying. We are not giving value among the sons of Adam to an ugly one, an old one, a not-bright one, a black one, a yellow one, a red one, a poor one, a weak one; a sick one, also – throwing them away, not giving them value. That is a big sin for everyone, to look at people's outward forms or figures.

In our time, we are giving value according to people's forms. Allah Almighty, the Guardian, is powerful enough, and artful enough, also, to give everyone the most beautiful forms, but He is examining, trying, His servants, to see whether they are looking at the meaning of the sons of Adam or not. But our hearts' eyes are veiled. Therefore, we are not looking at the meaning that the sons of Adam have been given by their Lord. We are only looking at their outward appearance, as Satan looked at Adam from the outside and would not make sajdah [prostration] to him.[4] Had he looked at the meaning of Adam, at the reality of the meaning that he bore, Satan would have been the first to make sajdah. But he looked from the outside view and said, "You created Adam from clay. How can I make sajdah to him?"

This is foolishness, and that foolishness is going on most among people in the twentieth century. They are looking at forms, like Satan, who looked at Adam as created from clay – "How could I respect *him*?" – not looking at the meaning of Adam which made him respected by all the universe, by all the angels, all the angels making *sajdah* to him.

And now Satan has established his sovereignty upon the whole world, making people to look at each other by their forms, their figures. That is a big sin, or the biggest sin, and all must be punished; *must be punished.* And it is from the divine punishment that the East is the greatest enemy to the West and the West is the greatest enemy to the East.

Here we are speaking about *awliya*'s knowledge, which they are granting us. *Awliya* are trying to take away enmity from among people, to make people look at each other and see others as crowned, divinely-crowned, fully-crowned people, and to give their respect to everyone. Therefore, Grandshaykh said, "The meaning of *tariqat* for me is to give respect to everyone."

Keep this, and you are going to be respected among creatures on earth and in the heavens. ▲

---

[4] Quran 7:11-12, 15:28-33, 17:61, 38:71-76.

6: believing in yourself and knowing your rank

All absolute perfections, absolute attributes, belong to our Lord Almighty, and, as He has granted us from His endless favors, we are proud to be His humble servants.

Allah Almighty created the sons of Adam in numbers, and they have been honored by their Creator, Allah Almighty, as no one else has been honored. Allah Almighty created all the universes and everything in the universes, and everything in the universes He put into man.

Man contains or includes everything that is in the universe of *jamadat*, non-living things; *nabatat*, plants; *haywanat*, animals; and then of angels. And there is a secret, *sirr*, which Allah Almighty made especially, only, for the sons of Adam. Even though the angels asked for it from their Lord, Allah Almighty said, "That secret thing from My Divine Presence has been given to Perfect Man and to *Insan al-Qadim*, the Original Man.

That is the secret which mankind has been given by their Creator, Allah Almighty, putting them in the most honored station in the Divine Presence. Allah Almighty gave from His divine lights to mankind. That is the honor and that is the secret reason why Allah Almighty loves the sons of Adam.

You may respect everyone. Don't look at people's temporal garments or ranks, no. Without looking at their outward appearance, you may give them every respect and every rank, which are acceptable in the Divine Presence. And as much as you express and give respect, Allah Almighty is pleased. He is not angry when we give more respect to each one of His servants, no, but rather Allah Almighty is angry with anyone who puts down or demeans His servants. Allah Almighty never agrees to have His servants demeaned.

Wa laqad karramna bani Adam: this informs us that Allah Almighty respects the sons of Adam, and no matter how much we may respect and give honor to others, it is impossible to reach the point of Allah Almighty's respect for His servants.

The word takrim – *karramna, karamah,* to dignify – refers to something that Allah Almighty granted from pre-eternity. He is not a Creator who gives or grants and then takes back; when He gives or grants something, He never takes it back. His grants are from pre-eternity up to post-eternity. No one can take away the grants of Allah Almighty to the sons of Adam, not even Satan. If there were as many Satans as the number of atoms, they could not take away from the sons of Adam anything of the karamah, the honor, the dignity, which Allah Almighty has granted them.

Therefore, Allah Almighty has sufficient trust in Himself that He says to Satan, "Go after them. If you can take from them what I granted to them, do. Use your infantry and cavalry soldiers on My servants. Go! I am looking to see if you can take something from them."[5]

Allah Almighty is sufficiently powerful for Satan and his armies. Only one *wali*, saint, is sufficient. Even if there were to be millions of Satans, one is enough for them all. But we are sinners because we are listening, we are following him; when Satan invites us, we are running after him, quickly running like rabbits – yes! And when we fall down, we cry – and Satan laughs.

Yet, even though we are sinners, no matter how sinful we may be, Allah Almighty is going to be angry with His servant if he says that his sins are greater than his Lord's mercy. *Hasha,* never! *Astaghfirullah!*[6] We are

---

[5] Quran 7:15-17, 15:42, 16:99-100, 17:63-65, 38:80-81.
[6] I seek Allah's forgiveness.

sinners because so many times we are followers of Satan, but even though we are followers, we must keep the endless hope in our Lord that all our sins are going to be nothing, *"Habaan manthura.*"[7] It is a good tiding.

Now, Satan works days and nights, never getting tired. Always, wherever the *ummah*, the nation of Muhammad (s), is, he runs after it. We can't catch that Satan even once – always running, hard worker! Hard worker, but without payment. If they were to make a strike, Satan and his soldiers, it would be better. But they never strike.

Yes, Satan works hard! From the day that Allah Almighty said to him, "Get out!" throwing him out, rejecting him, up to this day, he is hard-working. What does he hope for that he works so hard?

He works hard at making people lazy! Therefore, the number of unemployed people is always increasing, Satan saying, "Oh, no need to work. Everything is all right. Don't work!" *He* works but he doesn't let people work, saying, "You are the sons of Adam, respectable people! You must sit and everything must be made ready for you."

Satan works hard, and on the Day of Resurrection he will bring so many dirty deeds. And he is making us, the sons of Adam, his workers, and, as we are workers for Satan, we will come on the Day of Resurrection with such a huge number of dirty deeds.

Do you suppose that Allah Almighty is going to keep all those dirty deeds of Satan and his workers? Never! As he threw out all of Satan's worshipping because he rejected His command once, so, on the Day of Resurrection, Allah Almighty is going to order all the dirty deeds that Satan did in this life, and his workers' deeds, to be thrown into Hell. Dirty things you put in a dirty place; useless things you put into the dustbin. When the whole crowd of dirty deeds appears, Allah Almighty will order them to be

---

[7]"Floating particles of dust." (25:23)

thrown into Hell and will say to Satan, "Look at your work and your workers' works. Look! I am making them *habaan manthura*. Look at them!"

Therefore, we are saying to the sons of Adam that Allah Almighty granted and gave them from pre-eternity something of which He is the protector. *Inna nahnu nazzalna adh-dhikra wa inna lahu la-hafidhun.*[8] He is the Protector; He does not give that to us now before we are prepared to take care of it. It is like when parents make ready jewelry for their daughter's marriage, not giving it to her when she is a child but keeping it for her for when she grows up, or like someone giving a little toy to a child and saying, "Give me this diamond necklace," taking it and giving that in exchange.

Therefore, Allah Almighty is saying, "We are keeping it; *We* are its protector. I am looking after My servants whom I have respected. *I* have honored them. They may be Arabs, may be British, may be Turks, may be Germans, may be Americans, may be Russians, may be Greeks, may be any kind; may be black, may be white, may be yellow: I am the Lord of all of them and I have granted them something. I am not looking at their shapes, at their colors. *My* color I have put on them. Whoever is not happy with My color may look for another creator to give him another color."

You must be proud and happy; yes. Allah Almighty gives, *sibghat-Allah.*[9] And He looks at your original *jowhar*, essence, that is a secret, like a diamond. Therefore, Allah looks at the hearts that He gave us.

And each one – *each one* – is singular in the universe, no second one like him; each person is unique in himself. Allah Almighty just created everyone to be a witness to His uniqueness. Therefore, you must believe in yourself first. You can't reach real belief, real faith, without believing in yourself.

---

[8] "Indeed, We have revealed the Message, and indeed, We will be its Guardian." (15:9)

[9] "Allah's hue [or coloring]." (2:138)

We do not believe in ourselves yet. When you believe in yourself, then you will reach real faith in the Divine Presence. If all the universes without men were put in the balance on one side of the scale and one man on the other, that one man would be more valuable than all the universes without men. But we do not believe that our ranks in the Divine Presence are more valuable than all the universes and every creature included in those universes.

You must believe this. *Then* you may be a respectful servant to your Lord Almighty. "O my Lord, You have honored me in such a way that my mind can never grasp. It is out of my imagination, as well. You are giving me such a greatness, such an honor, as no one can expect and no one can imagine."

You must believe in yourself! When you believe in yourself, then you will see everyone else in the same rank. Then you will give your respect to everyone, and your respect for all people passes through respect for the Creator. You are not respecting this *person*; you are respecting the Creator who created him; and he, the other person, when he respects you, is respecting the One who created you, thereby giving respect to your Creator.

Therefore, *alhamdulillah* – all respects, all praises, all thanks, all greatness and glory be to Allah Almighty! If you respect someone, it means that you are glorifying your Lord Almighty. And when you give respect, you receive respect, also; you give respect to the servants of your Lord and at the same time you receive respect from them and from your Lord Almighty. Your Lord Almighty gives respect to you, and respect comes to you from all creatures. Wild animals – deer and camels and flies, birds, lions, wolves – came to the Prophet (s) and made *sajdah*, giving respect to him, and trees came and made *sajdah* to him because he is the Original Man, he is the Perfect Man. And Allah Almighty is saying, "Look! He is the best example for you. If you follow his way, you will reach that station."

Every creature must respect that person who has respect for his Lord and has respect for each one of His servants. We must give our respect to everyone. Then Allah Almighty will respect us. ▲

7: honoring god's gifts to his servants

What is honor for a person, and how must a person who has been honored try to keep that honor? All praises and endless honors be to our Lord Almighty; innahu hamidun majid.[10] Endless honors, endless Honor Oceans, endless Praise Oceans, absolute praises and absolute honors are for Allah Almighty alone.

Those honors are from Him to Himself; no one gives *Him* honor. Rather, everyone has been given honors by his Lord Almighty. If *He* does not give, no one can gain any honor or become praiseworthy.

The one who belongs to an honorable person is going to be honored; the one who originally has honor may give honor. Therefore, it is Allah Almighty who gives honor and makes His servants praiseworthy, looking at their capacities and according to their intentions, and as He looks at their hearts, He gives them honor. We have been honored by our Lord Almighty, and that is an endless grant from Him to us.

That is something concerning mankind. We are now among such unknown realities as Allah Almighty gives to us. As we said, mankind is still unknown. As long as we are occupied with everything except our inner selves, it is impossible for us to discover ourselves. This eye is open for outward-looking, this ear is open for outward-hearing; our hands, our feet, everything that we have in our physical bodies, is occupied with everything around ourselves, completely occupied. And there is one organ in our

---

[10]Indeed, He is the Praised, the Glorious.

bodies which is the most important; that is the heart. And we are occupying it, also, with this life's thoughts, so that we are completely occupied. *How can we be free to look after ourselves with even the capital of our body occupied by the enemy?*

Therefore, we are trying now, first to know and to give an understanding about ourselves. We must know about ourselves so that we may know about the Creator Almighty. If you do not go deeply into yourself, you can't get to know about your Creator and about His divine position.

Yes, we, mankind, have been honored by our Lord Almighty – when, no one knows except One; the Creator knows when He honored us, the sons of Adam. We are not such creatures who are beings in existence only for a short time. It is an ignorant person who says that the history of the sons of Adam is a short one, that their existence is only within a brief period.

We must know, firstly, that our period is with Allah Almighty. We were in our Lord's Power Oceans with Him. Only our appearance in our physical bodies is just for a short period, but our realities are connected to the reality of the Creator.

The one who has reality, his reality is eternal. We have realities or we are realities; the sons of Adam are not just an appearance, a form – no. Each one has a reality and that reality never changes. Allah Almighty never changes, and, because all realities belong to Him, they also never change.

We have been given realities from the endless Reality Oceans of our Lord Almighty; that is the honor that we have been given. But yet we are occupied by something that is going to be in ruins, our physical bodies, and to pass away. Allah Almighty says that *ghutha as-sail,* the white of foam, goes, but the real benefit which the river gives remains.

Therefore, we are like such bits of foam, appearing and then finishing, going away. But that reality which we have been given – that is forever, for eternity, for post-eternity. From pre-eternity to post-eternity we have been given that; without our asking, Allah Almighty gave us that as a grant.

No one has been honored with such an honor as the sons of Adam. We should be the most satisfied and happy ones among all creatures. But on the contrary, the most complaining ones among all creatures are the sons of Adam. The sons of Adam are those people who do not give true value to the honor that they have been given.

Now, we know that it is the highest degree and honor for ourselves to belong to our Lord Almighty, to be His servants, His slaves. (Maybe "slave" is a little too strong. Our egos are not accepting it, although they *are* slaves, so we are saying, "To be servants to our Lord – *that* is honor for us.") Therefore, *"Nurun 'ala nur"*;[11] Allah Almighty gave us from His divine lights and honored us. But He wants to give us still more than this.

We are now in this life for a new grant from our Lord Almighty, a light. He is going to give us even more honor than the first grant; He wants to give that to everyone. "I gave you an honor without anyone asking from Me, but now I will give to the one who asks the second *nur*."

Therefore, all the prophets came to give a reminder to the sons of Adam: "O sons of Adam, you have been granted an endless honor from pre-eternity, but your Lord wants to give you more. That one was without your asking, and now your Lord wants to give you, for the post-eternal life, even more than the first one. *But you must ask!*"

Therefore, it is a good tiding for the sons of Adam that finally their *nur*, the light which Allah Almighty gave them without anyone asking from Him, is never going to be destroyed. Instead, Allah Almighty wants the sons of Adam to ask for more than what He gave us, another grant, so that it is going to be *nurun 'ala nur*, light upon light. The one who asks now is going to be given as much as he was given previously. Yet those who are not asking any more, forgetting everything and denying everything from post-

---

[11]"Light upon light." (24:35)

eternity up to this day, will not lose the first grant of Allah Almighty to themselves.

When Allah Almighty gives something, He does not take it back. In the *Shari'ah*, if a person gives a gift to someone and wants to take it back, it can be done, but it is *makhruh*, a disliked thing.[12] How can Allah Almighty do disliked things? *Astaghfirullah; hasha,* never! Therefore, when Allah gives, He gives forever. He gave to us and He will never take it back. And He is obliging His servants to ask more and more, and He is angry with them if they do not ask. *We must ask!*

Therefore, during the period that we have been given in this life, Allah Almighty gives to us according to our intentions, not according to our actions. If we could be in this life forever, we would intend to be His obedient servants. Then, when He tests us and sees that our intentions are meant forever, He gives us our rewards, giving those divine lights endlessly.

That is the second honor. The first we have already been given, but Allah Almighty wants to complete it. Therefore, on the Day of Resurrection, people will run and ask for a completion from their Lord: *"Rabbana, atmim lana nurana*[13] – O our Lord, please complete our light."

You have been given something like a candle and you are in need of a match to light the wick. *We must try; we must try for this.* That is a perfection for the sons of Adam; we may reach that perfection during the short period of our life in this world. Therefore Allah Almighty sent all the prophets and the Seal of the Prophets, peace be upon them all, to make everything clear to the sons of Adam. And now it is clear, according to our capacity; we may understand how those lights and those honors are going to be for us.

And we have also been honored to be of the nation of the Last Prophet, the greatest one, peace be upon him; by that we have also been

---

[12]That is, since in the Islamic *Shari'ah* or Sacred Law, it is disliked to take back something that one has given away, how can it be imagined that the Divine Giver of that *Shari'ah* or Law could take back the gifts which He has freely granted to His servants?

[13]"'Our Lord, perfect our light for us." (66:8)

honored. Then, we have been honored by being in connection with or belonging to one of the chains of *awliya*; by that we have been honored, also. And we are asking our Lord Almighty to complete that honor and to make us suitable, worthy, of that honor and to make us keepers of that honor.

You know, those people who have been given even one star, even one stripe – they are so careful to keep that. Why not ourselves? Why are *we* not taking more care? We must take more care of those honors that we have been granted; we must be so careful about that. And, O honored brothers and sisters, *mumins* and *muminahs*,[14] for every action, we are either granted more honors or we are losing those honors.

Therefore, we must be very careful about every action. It may be a reason for a new honor or it may make that honor decrease. That is important. The Prophet (s) says, *"Ihfadh-Illah"* – you must keep to your Lord, you must guard the honor that your Lord granted you. Then Allah Almighty will protect you, protecting that honor with you. ▲

---

[14]Male and female believers.

8: a guide who knows the true value of man

We are asking from awliya, saints, that spiritual power which passes from heart to heart. Grandshaykh says that spiritual power or divine help comes to an assembly according to their asking; according to our inner desires comes divine help. Therefore, as much as we are ready to take more, they give more.

When a person comes with a coffee cup,[15] he will be given as much as it holds; if coming with a teacup, he will be given as much as it can hold. If a man comes with a soup cup, he will be given more; if a jug, putting in still more. As much as you are asking for, They may give, never finishing. And no one asks for a liter of oil but brings only a coffee cup. Even if he pays money, you cannot put one liter into a coffee cup; it is full, stopping. You say, "Give a bigger cup and I may put it all in." Therefore, there is too much that They may give us, but, like this, it finishes, stopping. And I am asking more of *awliya*'s knowledge.

Our hearts, when the light of faith enters into them, are going to be wider, wider, wider; even if you put all the oceans into them, they may hold them. But our present faith is *taqlid*, imitation, while the other kind of faith is real.

This is imitation, like a figure without a soul, but the first has a soul, also. But that real faith has not yet entered into our hearts. When it enters, the whole world is going to be changed, our view is going to be changed.

---

[15]Referring to a small demitasse cup for Turkish coffee.

Understand? Totally changed; everything is going to be changed. When real faith comes into our hearts and lights them, it will be like a person who was blind, but when his eyes are opened, he sees something other than what he was in before. Therefore, don't suppose that now we are in real faith. No, not yet.

Grandshaykh was in the First World War from the beginning up to the end. He made *jihad*,[16] the lesser *jihad* and the greater *jihad*. And he said to me, "O Nazim Effendi, if I were to tell you about all that the people and I suffered during the First War, in which I saw so many terrible events and sufferings, this whole place would be filled with books, you could write so many books about it. But everything passes. The events of yesterday are buried, finished. Today new ones will come. If they were to stay with you, all of them not passing, no one could bear this life's heavy burdens. But that has passed away. This is our Lord's will.

"In our division there was an Armenian sergeant.[17] He asked one of the soldiers, while I was looking on, 'What is your name?'

"'My name is 'Ali.'

"'Yes. You are Muslim?'

"'*Alhamdulillah*, I am Muslim.'

"But if you say that you are Muslim, I may also say that *I* am Muslim; what I believe is enough to say that I am Muslim. I also believe in One God Almighty and in the angels and the holy books and the prophets and the Last Day and *Qadar*,[18] the Divine Decree,' that Armenian sergeant said. 'I say what you say. But – is that enough to be a Muslim?'

---

[16]*Jihad* means "struggle". The "lesser *jihad*" refers to striving on the battlefield, while the "greater *jihad*" denotes the ceaseless struggle waged within one's being against four enemies: the lower self *(nafs)* and its desires *(hawa)*, Satan, and this world's attractions *(dunya)*.

[17]Shaykh Nazim adds parenthetically, "They [Armenians] lived as neighbors in Muslim towns and villages."

[18]The sixth article of Islamic faith: the belief that all things, both the good and evil, proceed

"'No.'

"'Then what is the sign? If it is only saying as you say, *I* do that, and if you are talking about *namaz*, prayers, I do them, also.'

"'Look," [Grandshaykh said,] "you are asking for a sign. I am saying to you that it is not enough only to say with your tongue, 'I am a believer, I am a Muslim.' You may even recite the Holy Quran. But the sign of a Muslim and a real believer is that he has a light from his Lord Almighty. When he looks down, he can see up to the end of this world; when he looks up he can see to the end of the universe. If he looks at the East, he can see up to the end of the farthest East; if he looks at the West, he sees up to the end of the Western regions. If he looks towards *qiblah*, he sees the Kaba.'"

Then that sergeant fell upon the hands of Grandshaykh and kissed them.

Grandshaykh was saying that the real sign of belief is that a person has the light of faith in his heart, which comes from Allah Almighty. Nothing can keep back that light. Understand? What can keep back *nur-Allah*, Allah Almighty's light? Distance never prevents that person from seeing; darkness never hides anything in it. Therefore, when real faith comes into our hearts, they are going to be lighted. Everything in the universe is going to be in front of us; nothing can be hidden from us. That is the degree of real faith.

Therefore, we are always asking for some lights so that we may keep our services with firmness in front of our Lord Almighty. The value of a person is according to the lights in his heart, and when lights come into your heart, they make it wider, wider than the whole universe. You may find your Lord in your heart. Universes cannot contain their Lord but the hearts of believers may contain their Lord Almighty.

We must know ourselves, because we do not know what we are and what is the true value of ourselves.

---

from Allah Almighty's Will and decree.

In the palace of the Ottoman emperors there is a diamond; perhaps it is the most famous diamond in the world, the biggest one. There is a tale about how that biggest, most famous diamond came into the palace.

One day, a person in Istanbul prayed *Fajr*, the dawn prayer, in the mosque and returned. He glanced at a rubbish heap and saw there something like a stone, a strange thing. He took it out from amongst the rubbish, looking at it from all sides. Then, as he was passing through a market, among shops, he saw a person who made wooden spoons and showed him the stone. "What is this? Would you take it, would you buy it?"

The spoonmaker looked at it. "Hey, I may give you a spoon for it," he said. "Take this spoon and give it to me."

The man was very pleased with a spoon – a big spoon, a nice spoon, and useful, because dervish people used to keep a dagger at one side and a spoon on the other. When they were called to eat, they used it.

What was that stone? Allah knows, but he, that person, did not know. He took the man's spoon and went away.

Then that spoonmaker looked at the stone. "What if I were to take it to a jeweler or a goldsmith?" he thought. And he took it to one and said, "See what this is. How much is it worth?"

The jeweler took it. He understood what it was and said, "I don't mind if it costs me a bagful of silver."

That was as much as the value of the spoonmaker's whole shop; all his spoons would not bring one bag of silver. He was also so pleased and happy, and he went away.

Then the jeweler was the master of this jewel. He worked on it, cutting it like rays of the sun, and kept it for the grand vizier, the prime-minister of the Ottoman Empire. He sent to him, saying, "I have such a jewel. It is suitable for the grand vizier." And the grand vizier paid a large amount of gold, thousands of pieces, for it. Then he presented it to the *sultan*; it went up to the *sultan* himself.

I mean to say that all things are well known by a knowledgeable person; otherwise, they are all going to be the same as stones. The value of human beings is well known, completely known, by Allah Almighty, who created them and gave them their values. Then, the most knowledgeable person concerning the value of man is the Seal of the Prophets, beloved Muhammad (s), and the other prophets take their knowledge concerning the value of the sons of Adam from him. And then, the true followers of the prophets and of the Seal of the Prophets, peace be upon them all – *awliya* - know the value of mankind, and they take human beings and arrange them from every side. Then their values, their true forms, appear, and they take them to the Divine Presence. But without a prophet or their inheritors, people are like discarded stones. Even if they are diamonds, without being cut and made suitable, they are not going to be put on a crown.

Therefore, the most important work of prophets and of their successors, *awliya*, is to make everyone's value clear by arranging each one according to his promises on the Day of Promises. If anyone is asking to be in the Divine Presence, in the first rank, he must follow the prophets or those who follow them, *awliya*. Those who do not follow, no value for them; they still remain like stones. Then finally they must be treated to some training after they leave this life and in *Barzakh*[19] and in the next life in order to allow their values to appear, but they are not going to be in the first rank of those who will be with the prophets and *awliya*.

No value for a person who stays by himself and never follows the prophets and their inheritors! Even in this life, if a person does not follow a college or university course, he never gains any value in his community, people saying, "A simple or ordinary-standard person." But the one who follows a course in a university or college or academy, and it is proved by a certificate or diploma, he has value. As much as you may know by yourself, if you do not follow one of them, no one gives you value. You can't be a

---

[19]The stage of existence between death and the Day of Resurrection.

doctor, you can't be an engineer, you can't be a lawyer, because you aren't following any school.

Therefore, in the spiritual life, whoever is asking for improvement, as long as he is by himself, he may acquire something, but it is of no value. You *must* follow a prophet. Therefore, philosophers, who are asking to reach a point by themselves without following any one of the prophets, have no value. We *must* follow.

As much as you are able to follow one of them, you may reach your real value, and that value will appear among creatures on earth and in the heavens. No one can reach that, particularly heavenly stations, without following someone who belongs to the heavens.

All the prophets belong to the heavens; if a person has no relationship to the heavens, he is not going to be a prophet. The one who has no relationship to the heavens is also not going to be a *wali*, a saint; it is impossible. There must be a relationship between that person and the heavens, and you must follow such a person who has a relationship between himself and heavenly beings. Otherwise, the one who is walking on earth is not going to be a guide to you.[20]

You may find everything on earth, but without a guide you can't find the way to the heavens; it is so difficult and so far and so full of danger. Therefore, there must be a guide for you. Even for a rocket which is sent into space, it is so difficult and so dangerous to be in it or to have the control of it; you can't send a rocket into space just through *anyone*. He must be a person specially trained for that purpose, knowing best how he can send it. To send a person to the heavens[21] – it is more difficult than sending a rocket into space. Not everyone can do that. The one who can do that is one who has been sent to the heavens by the Prophet (s); he knows the way

---

[20]That is, a person tied to worldly desires and not strongly connected to the spiritual world.

[21]Meaning to reach the station of *wilayah* or sainthood in the Divine Presence.

and he knows how he can send others. He comes through the Prophet (s) up to his own grandshaykh, never making a mistake.

Don't tell me, "Why are you not sending us now?" Go and tell that engineer or scientist who is preparing that rocket, "Send it into space now." Will he listen to you? *He is working on it.*

A person is going to be ready to send up to the heavens, Grandshaykh said to me, if forty scholars who know the *Shari'ah* excellently are with him for forty days and they give a report, saying, "This person is all right from every direction. We forty scholars have been looking at him day and night for forty days. In every action and behavior that person is perfect. According to our knowledge, there is nothing wrong with him." If they give such a report, then it is all right to send him.

We are trying now, but then our egos are coming, destroying this path and damaging us. Every bad action damages our inner structure. We are trying to build it, but it is so difficult. But, as we are beginners, it doesn't matter. We are practicing, we are building, we are learning, we are preparing ourselves. It is enough to be here humbly and listening; that gives us divine help and makes us to be ready. Even at the last moment we must be complete, *insha'Allah*; we are going to be complete and go to the heavens, and we will see doors opening to us.

So many people, when they are going from earth to the heavens, are finding doors closed to them because they are not ready. Then they are sent away to make them ready to go up. But those who are coming and listening and accepting and believing, they must be prepared, even at the last moment before leaving this life, to reach their heavenly stations in the Divine Presence. ▲

9: OUR PRIMARY ENEMY

We are listening. If we are good listeners, Allah may give to us from His divine wisdoms. The one who keeps wisdom well may be given it. If not keeping it, no one will give him anything.

The father and mother of the sons of Adam were created in Paradise. Then they were sent to earth and their descendants grew up on this earth. Their father and mother knew what Paradise was: they had been there, they had lived there; they had seen Paradise and knew what it was. And they told their descendants about Paradise, and also about how they came, or how they had been sent, on earth.

Allah Almighty created Adam (a) to be a His deputy. He gave Adam the most honored station among creatures; no one else can be at the station of Adam and his sons. And the one who was created to be Allah's deputy, the highest rank among creatures, all creatures accepted him as His deputy. All of them said that if our Lord makes him His deputy, we all agree with our Lord's Will.

It is written and stated, coming to us through the Prophet's traditions, that when Allah Almighty created Adam and he was lying there, before the divine soul had entered into him, *Shaytan* was the teacher of the angels.[22] We have a saying, "Those who have not been given from Allah Almighty's favors are jealous of others who have been given."

---

[22]As mentioned in 18:50, Iblis or Shaytan (Satan) was a jinn. Because he possessed great knowledge, Allah Almighty had placed him among the angels as their instructor.

Shaytan came with a group of angels, and he saw that the body of Adam was lying at the entrance of Paradise but there was no soul in him – from clay. He went around and inspected every part of him, looking and saying, "This is a new creature, and it is an empty one, not solid," and then he entered from the mouth of that form of Adam. He meant, "I can enter into these creatures and I can take my control." And because our mouths are opening for eating, drinking, breathing, Satan can come in and go around everywhere, in our veins.

Because every creature that has been created is going to be more perfect, evolution going up, *Shaytan* knew that that creature was going to be more perfect (he has so much knowledge, big head!). Then he stood and looked, addressing the angels:

"O angels, what about this one? This is a new one, and there is going to be something important for him. Look at me, O my Lord's angels! If your Lord is going to give that one more honors than yourselves, putting him in a station above your stations, what are you going to do?"

They said, "We are obedient servants."

"Will you accept that new one to be higher than you?"

"As our Lord wants it to be," they said, "we agree with our Lord's Will. As He likes, we like."

"Hm'm," said Iblis, *Shaytan*, within himself. Among all creatures, only *Shaytan* said this, and Allah Almighty was looking and listening to what he said within himself, not with his tongue. "If Allah Almighty gives that new one a rank higher than my rank, I am not going to accept it. I am not going to agree for that one to be more than me, to be over me," he said. "Then, if Allah Almighty has made him over me, I am going to destroy him!"

You understand? Satan was saying, "From both sides, I don't like this new one. If I am over him, I am going to destroy him. And if he is over me, I am not going to obey Allah Almighty and to accept him over me."

And then *that* happened. Allah Almighty gave to Adam from His divine attributes and asked all the angels to make *sajdah*, prostration, to Adam, and all the angels made *sajdah*. But one, *Shaytan*, never made *sajdah*.

Therefore, from the beginning, we have an enemy. That is a rule: the imperfect one is going to be enemy to the perfect one. That must be known; that takes place among people always. Mankind got their first lesson, not from their grandfather Adam, but they got a lesson from the *enemy* of their father and mother.

Therefore, the first in rebellion against Allah Almighty among all creatures was *Shaytan*. And when he rebelled against his Lord, everything was taken away from him. His name had been 'Azazil; it was an honorable name, and he had been among the angels in such a station as no one can be in. He had been honored by his Lord Almighty, but when he went against his Lord's order and rebelled, his name was changed to *Shaytan* and he was thrown out. And what Allah Almighty had given him of a luminous and goodly form was taken away from him, also, so that he is now such an ugly person.

If anyone looks at Satan and sees him in his real form, for forty days he will be sick at his stomach; yes, such an ugly, such a dirty one! Rebellion caused him to be in a very ugly and very hated form, and he continued in his sin, in his guilt, not repenting.

One day Moses (a) was going to Mount Sinai and he met Satan on his way, saying to him, "O Moses, you are going to your Lord, to converse with Him. Ask if there can be *taubah*, repentance or forgiveness, for me, because I am fed up. If there is forgiveness, I will ask for forgiveness. Ask from your Lord!"

Moses said, "Yes, I will," and he went up to Mount Sinai. But then, listening to Allah Almighty's divine speech, he forgot.

Then Allah Almighty made him to remember. "O Moses, why are you not bringing that request of *Shaytan*'s?"

"O my Lord, I just forgot!"

"If it is from forgetting, it doesn't matter; that is forgiven. But if you are saying, 'That Iblis – for what shall I bring his request?' that is dangerous. If you are looking at it with the idea of putting him down, I do not agree to that."

You must see how Allah Almighty looks out for His creatures. Satan is also one of His creatures, and Allah Almighty never likes His servants to be in *kufr*, disbelief, and to be rebellious. And Moses, trembling, said, "O my Lord, I only forgot."

"What did he say to you, what was his request?"

Moses said, "You know well, O my Lord. He was asking if he has forgiveness, if there can be repentance for him."

"Yes," Allah Almighty said. "If he is asking for repentance, forgiveness – yes, I forgive him. But there is a condition. If he does what I ask, I will forgive him. I will give him back all the ranks that I took away from him and I will give him new ones, also, more than those."

"What is that condition?"

"Tell him to go quickly to Adam's grave and make *sajdah*," Allah Almighty said. *Ma yubaddalu-l-qaulu ladayya*[23] – My word no one can change. That is My order, that is My Will. He must make *sajdah* to Adam; then I will forgive him. I am his Lord; I can order, no one else! Who is he that he does not obey My order? He puts himself above My Will? Tell him to quickly run and make *sajdah* at the grave of Adam. Then I shall forgive him."

Yes; you must know who Allah is. If He orders thirty days of fasting, you must fast. He ordered some nations before the nation of beloved Muhammad (s) difficult fasting, ordering them to do no work while they were fasting and no movement, no action; they had to stop everything, ordering them to break their fast only twice in fifteen days. To some of

---

[23] 50:29.

them He ordered three days' fasting; to some He ordered fasting with only drops of water to break their fast. Some of them were forbidden to swallow their saliva, even. Yes, He is our Lord; He can order!

When Adam (a) rebelled against his Lord and ate from that Tree, for thirty days he did not eat anything, until the traces were completely gone. Our grandfather Adam fasted for thirty days to make his body free from that prohibited Tree, to make it clean – thirty days. And it was right for his sons, also, a fast of thirty days. When your Lord orders, don't be afraid that you are going to die – no! When you have the intention, even if Allah Almighty orders you to break your fast only once in thirty days, it is all right. You must say, "We are ready, O our Lord. As *You* order."

But from His endless mercy, He gives us a fast from the time of dawn up to sunset, only a few hours. Then we eat as much as we left in the daytime, eating twice as much – yes! But we must know that He is our Lord and that He can command, and we must be obedient servants.

To whom are you going to be obedient servants – to people like yourselves, coming before him if he is a rich man, if he is a powerful man? Who is Iblis, *Shaytan*, Satan, to refuse the command of the Lord of the universes? How *could* he refuse his Creator's command?

But he was drunk. Satan was drunk with pride because Allah Almighty had given him a chance to worship, and he was one of the greatest worshippers. Allah Almighty had also given him knowledge that no one among the angels had been given, and because of his worshipping and because of his knowledge, he became too proud, thinking, "How well I am making *sajdah* to Allah!"

The one who is commanding you, the one who is ordering you – *that one is drunk!* Therefore, every proud person is drunk; yes.

And Satan was still drunk when Moses came back. He was waiting, waiting. And he said, "What about me?"

"Yes," Moses said, "He is going to forgive you. But there is one condition."

"What is that?"

"Your Lord says to you, 'My word is not going to be changed, My order *must* be obeyed.' You must go to the grave of our grandfather Adam and make *sajdah* there. Then He may forgive you."

Then that drunk Iblis jumped to his feet, saying, "If He is not going to forgive me without making *sajdah*, I will never make *sajdah*! I refused when he was alive. Then how am I going to make *sajdah* to a person's dirty corpse?" – saying that and running away.

Therefore, on the Day of Resurrection, Allah Almighty will order him to Hell. And once every 120,000 years Allah Almighty will order Malik,[24] the Keeper of Hell, to bring Satan to the door of Paradise. When the angel brings Satan to the entrance of Paradise, he will order Adam to come to the entrance and will say to Satan, "Allah Almighty orders you to make *sajdah* and enter."

But Satan will say, "I will never change, I will never make *sajdah*! I will go back." He agrees to be in Hell forever but not to make *sajdah* to Adam. Make *sajdah* and enter! "No," he says, so many times not entering when he sees Adam there.

Therefore, the one who is stubborn will never enter Paradise until he is cleansed, here or there, because Paradise is for clean people, pure people. No dirty people may enter Paradise. And therefore Allah Almighty has ordered purification for every nation so that its people may enter. If a person is pure here, he will be in paradise here, also. But the one who is not pure is not in paradise. Instead, hell comes upon him.

---

[24]The great archangel who is in charge of Hell.

We must know our first and most dangerous enemy: this is the summary for our Association[25] today. We must know who caused Adam and Eve to come on earth, and we must know that every trouble which exists among the sons of Adam is because of the enmity of Satan for them. *He* makes people to be enemies; *he* is the enemy of the sons of Adam and he gives that enmity to everyone.

By what thing does he give it? He gives enmity to people by means of this temporary life's pleasures, cheating people with *dunya*, with this life. Satan says to everyone that this belongs to you, while *dunya* does not belong to anyone except Allah, and Satan is just cheating people. And for the cause of this world, nations are fighting, people are quarreling, and troubles and sufferings are going on.

We must know our most dangerous enemy, Grandshaykh, may Allah bless him, was saying, and we must leave off enmity for each other. *Nafs, hawa, Shaytan* and *dunya*[26] – these are the four enemies of the sons of Adam, and three of them are marching along under the command of *Shaytan*. Whoever takes more than these four enemies is rebellious against his Lord, because Allah Almighty is saying to people, "Your most dangerous enemy is *Shaytan*, and next, your ego, *nafs*. And *Shaytan* and ego are cheating you by means of this world's, this life's, pleasures. *Be careful! Warning!*"

On a door I saw a picture of a dog's head and "Warning – Dog!" was written under it. If an illiterate person looks at the dog's head, he takes precautions. Allah Almighty is saying this, also, but the sons of Adam are never taking precautions against Satan.

That is a surprising thing. Allah Almighty is saying, *"Be careful! Warning!"* through 124,000 prophets, and at the last, the Seal of the Prophets (s) is saying, "Take your precautions, O my Lord's servants! There

---

[25] A shaykh's discourse *[sohbet]* .

[26] Ego or the lower self, its desires, Satan and attachment to the world.

is a dog, a terrible dog, after you. Be careful!" But we are saying, "No; it is our friend, a friend of mine."

The one who knows his enemy takes his precautions and he is going to be protected, here and in the Hereafter. If not taking precautions.... Yesterday I saw a picture in a newspaper: a person wearing red clothes was sitting in a hospital cell of death, with bars. What was written under it? "Bitten by a rabid dog"; it had bitten him and death was approaching.

Satan is more dangerous than that rabid dog. *Guard yourself!* ▲

10: the capacity to act like pharaoh

During the Ascension, the Night Journey, Allah Almighty said to beloved Muhammad (s), "O Muhammad, if I were to give everyone the same chance or the same occasions or the same opportunity that I gave to Pharaoh, all of you would be like Pharaoh.

"If I were to put anyone on the throne of Egypt and all the people came and bowed down to him, no one would *not* be a Pharaoh; everyone *must be* a Pharaoh. But I am keeping them back. Therefore, no one is going to be like Pharaoh."

Allah Almighty means to say that if a person finds suitable conditions for his ego, his ego is going to make him like Pharaoh. You have seeds. If you put them on the floor, on stone, they will never open, or perhaps they may open as an onion sprouts in the kitchen but never gives a head, while if you put it in a field, it will give the head of an onion. All people are getting their egos to sprout, but after a little bit, finished. But if they find a field like Pharaoh's field (and there was a very suitable field for Pharaoh's ego in Egypt), then they shout and say, "I am your Lord!"[27]

We are not finding that field. Therefore we must thank Allah Almighty that He does not give us that chance. And you can see also that anyone who is over another person makes himself like Pharaoh on that person and wants to destroy him. People are always proclaiming everywhere that there are two kinds of people, one oppressed and the other oppressors; one down below, one on top.

---

[27]79:23-24.

That is a dangerous ego. Such a person is more terrible and dangerous than any wild beast, and all troubles arise from that point, because there is no more spiritual training. If we have spiritual training, our ego will never raise its head and say, "I am your Lord!" But if there is no spiritual training or practices, then, if your ego finds one person whom it can dominate, it says, "I am your Lord. You must obey *Me*. You must be My obedient servant, you must be My slave!"

Therefore Islam fought against slavery, trying to bring people out of slavery – yes, both inwardly and outwardly, that slavery which everyone knows and the other slavery from the hands of our egos, to bring people into freedom. But in our time, people are understanding freedom in another way and they are becoming more enslaved. Now, therefore, everyone, particularly in Western countries, is proclaiming that 'freedom,' this country's 'freedom'.

In these times, people have been given unlimited freedom so that their egos are making them unlimitedly enslaved. The more you give that 'freedom,' you make people more enslaved.

This is an important secret that psychiatrists must know. For most people who are suffering and going to psychiatrists, the reason is only because they have been given unlimited freedom. *That* makes people ill and suffering. ▲

11: GUARÐING YOUR heART

May Allah Almighty give us from His divine wisdoms, because we may have knowledge, but if no wisdoms, knowledge is going to do nothing. We are in need of wisdom, and a little wisdom is more important than all this world's knowledge. Knowledge cannot push or pull you, but wisdom can pull you or push you. In wisdom there is power. Therefore, knowledge without wisdom never gives benefit.

If knowledge could give benefit to anyone, it would have given benefit to *Shaytan*. He is the first in knowledge, knowing the *Injil*,[28] the Torah, the Psalms, the Holy Quran. No one among scholars can compete with him; he comes first, he knows so much! But without wisdom; he had so much knowledge, without wisdom, and then he fell. Therefore, it is not important to learn so much, to know so much, but it is important to ask for some wisdoms from Allah Almighty. Even one wisdom is going to be enough for you forever, to take you to happiness and peace here and in the Hereafter, to our Lord's pleasure.

Allah Almighty sent 6,666 verses in the Holy Quran. Each verse is like an endless ocean, and the oceans are full of precious pearls. But if pearls could be had easily, they would be cheap. Why are pearls precious, valuable? Because pearls are found in the deepest places in the seas, and dangerous places, also. Allah Almighty always makes something valuable and precious protected, so that it is not easily reached. A rose without thorns and a treasure without dragons – no!

---

[28]The divine scripture revealed to the prophet Jesus (a).

Everything that you can get easily is cheap. You can buy tomatoes, potatoes, onions, everywhere, but rubies, diamonds, pearls you cannot find everywhere, although you can find so many of glass. Therefore, from oceans you can take fishes, you can take shells; the sea throws shells on the beach but it never throws pearls. And each verse of the Holy Quran is like endless oceans. The one who makes himself to dive in may take.

How would a person dive into the sea with clothes? No one dives into the deep sea wearing clothes; people like to take off as much as they can for diving. And for "Verse Oceans," for the Oceans of the Holy Quran, you must take off everything and then you can dive into them.

What are you going to take off? Not things like these clothes. You must take from your heart everything belonging to this world; you must take away from your heart *dunya,* this world's pleasures. And you must know what *dunya* is.

Everything that engages you or occupies you from your Lord and you have enjoyment with it, is *dunya;* everything that occupies a servant from his Lord – that is *dunya.* This is the most important point for everyone, for every believer, whether his faith is Jewish or Christian or Muslim. *When Allah Almighty looks at his heart, by whom is his heart occupied?*

Allah Almighty does not look at our titles that we put here – no. He looks at our hearts and sees by whom they are occupied. Is that heart just engaged by Himself alone or by *dunya*?

You must know that Allah Almighty gives permission for all of your body that it may work, may be engaged by this life, *excepting* your heart. You may be occupied in your body; it doesn't matter, because we are living in this life and we have some responsibilities. Allah Almighty gives permission for our organs to go, to come, to look, to do, but He says, "Only your heart – don't let it be engaged by *dunya.*"

Keep your heart for your Lord only and He is going to be pleased with you. And when He is pleased with you, He is going to make you pleased with Him. That is *sa'adat al-kubra*, the highest happiness. You will have been given endless happiness when Allah Almighty makes you pleased.

We are asking His pleasure with us, we are trying to make Him pleased with us. *Anything other than that* does not give our Lord pleasure with us. Complete pleasure from Allah Almighty with His servants is when His servants give their hearts to Him Almighty.

But it is not easy. It is the most difficult of commands and the most important of worships. And every worship and prayer that we are doing with our bodies, bodily worship, is only for that purpose: to transfer from our bodies into our hearts, because worship is giving our respects to our Lord.

We are giving our respects with our organs, and that is within limits. But for the one who gives his respects with his heart, it is going to be unlimited. And we have been ordered to worship our Lord unlimitedly. You can't do that with your body but you can do it with your heart.

That is a wisdom to know and to work on. And it is enough for us, rather than learning thousands and thousands of books to make stores of knowledge. Then you aren't able to carry it; it is too heavy a burden. But it is brief wisdom that makes us move towards our Lord. He is inviting us, and we must go to Him.

Allah Almighty chooses among His servants for giving His divine wisdoms. When He looks at His servant's heart and sees Himself, He gives to that person from His divine wisdoms. But if anyone keeps his heart for *dunya*, for his *nafs*, he may be given so much knowledge but without benefit. Therefore the Prophet asked from his Lord Almighty *'ilman nafi'an*, knowledge that gives benefit – and that is *hikmah*, that is wisdom.

It is not going to be easy, but we must work on it. Firstly, you must cut your ego's desires and you must put a limit on your ego, on its desires. If you leave your ego, your *nafs*, free, you won't be able to find any limit to its desires, so that it will always occupy you and make you its slave, with no time for your Lord's service, for your Lord's worship. Therefore, we must put a limit on our *nafs* and its desires. And we are living in a time and in a place where everything is urging our egos to ask for more and more, unlimited desires.

Firstly, we must stop that. You must say, "That is your limit" – for eating, for drinking, for dressing, for working, because all the holy books came by divine order to put limits for the sons of Adam, and this is well-known as *halal* and *haram*, permissible and prohibited.

Allah Almighty puts limits. Don't exceed them! Those are the limits, and if you do not put up that barrier, you *must* exceed them. And the whole of the *Shari'ah* is for all people, for every son of Adam. *Everyone* has responsibilities for keeping that *Shari'ah*, that holy Law.

Allah Almighty knows our egos and their desires; He knows perfectly. If not putting a limit, it is dangerous and terrible. The first step is to know those limits. Don't leave your ego to ask everything from you without limits!

Now we are in the holy month of fasting. That fasting is teaching us how we may be able to put a limit on our egos' desires. Therefore, it is the most important worship. Without that worship, it is impossible to stand in front of your ego and to address it, to order it, "Do this, leave that." If you can't do that, you are weak and your ego is riding on you and leading you anywhere it wants, and it is dangerous and terrible. Therefore, fasting is the main door of every worship because it is useless to do worship while you are unable to stand in front of your ego and command it.

And when we move towards Allah Almighty, when servants ask for their Lord and go towards His Divine Presence, He also makes His divine Will to approach His servants. When you take one step, He orders your goal to come ten steps nearer.

Sometimes our goal comes so near. We may reach it if we can move one more step, but our ego, our *nafs*, cuts the way. When that happens, we find ourselves far away. We do not take care about small things, but they give us so much harm, making us as we were at the first step, falling down.

Therefore, every believer, every Muslim, must know that when he moves towards his Lord, there are four enemies around him, to make him turn from his way. If you want to take one step, one hundred Satans come to prevent you from taking that step. Then one thousand attack you, to bring you back.

You can't do it without your Lord's power. Therefore we are saying, *"La hawla wa la quwwata illa bil-Lah al-'Ali al-'Adhim."*[29] We are saying, "O our Lord, we can't turn from the bad way to Your good path without Your power, without Your Will. O our Lord, give us from Your divine power, to make our feet firm on Your path."

These days and nights of Ramadan come once each year and they are soon going to be ended. They are the days of *ghanimah*,[30] days of treasures, precious things, and also the days most open for divine Mercy Oceans. And our Lord is waiting for us to ask for more and more of His divine mercies and powers, and more and more divine support for ourselves.

You must ask, particularly during the last third of Holy Ramadan, in which one night is going to be the Night of Power, Laylat al-Qadr[31] – particularly to search for *that* night. To find that manifestation during that holy Night – that is our goal throughout our lives, and the one to whom it is given to find that Night, Allah Almighty takes him under His divine protection.

The one who finds the Night of Power is granted by his Lord endless Mercy Oceans and endless favors, and he is protected. If prophets are innocent,[32] the one who has found the Night of Power has the attribute of

---

[29]"There is no might nor power except with Allah, the Most High, the Almighty," an often-repeated phrase by which Muslims often repeat to express their total reliance upon Allah.

[30]Booty, gain, profit, benefit.

[31]The night during which the holy Prophet (s) received the first revelation of the Quran in the cave of Hira' near Mecca. It is commemorated annually with nightlong worship. According to *ahadith*, it may fall on one of the odd-numbered nights during the last ten days of Ramadan

[32]According to Islamic belief, prophets are free of any defects of character and innocent of

being protected. And for the one who is protected by divine favors, it is impossible for Satan to come and take him out of our Lord's protection.

We must try. We are such weak people in our faith for finding that Night, but we are asking our Lord to give us from that Night's *barakah*, its blessings, and that *barakah* may also give us protection forever. ▲

---

any major sins.

12: thank god and intend the best

Allah Almighty likes His servants to be always be pleased. That is important; you must be pleased with your Lord. Therefore He begins His Holy book, the Quran, by saying, *"Al-hamdu lil-Lahi Rabbi-l-'Aalamin."*[33] Yes, you must understand what He means.

Awliya, saints, say that it means, "O My servants, all of you, say, *'Alhamdulillah* – all praise is for Allah.'" He is asking us to be pleased with Him. That is important. Be pleased with your Lord. If you are pleased with Him, He is going to make you pleased with Him, pleased with everything. Say, "O my Lord, I am pleased with You."

This order covers our lives, from beginning to end. When you are able to understand yourself, you are ordered to be pleased with your Lord. When you reach fifteen years, the age of maturity,[34] you must say that you are at the age which is like a new rose; you must look at yourself and you must say *"Alhamdulillah."* From that age up to the end, you must say, "Thanks to my Lord. All praise and thanks to my Lord Almighty." That is the Holy Quran's teaching to us.

"Wa akhiru d'awahum an il-hamdu lil-Lahi Rabbi-l-'Aalamin."[35] The first and last word of servants to their Lord is to say, *"Al-hamdu lil-Lahi Rabbi-l-'Aalamin* – endless thanks and most respectful praises be only to our Lord, Almighty Allah." That is the divine teaching. Allah Almighty is teaching

---

[33]"The praise is for Allah, the Lord of the worlds." (1:1)

[34] Referring to puberty, the time of reaching consciousness and the flowering of the body, mind and heart.

[35]"And the last of their call will be, 'The praise is for Allah, Lord of the worlds.'" (10:10)

people through His prophets and through the Seal of the Prophets (s) and through his inheritors, *awliya*, to say *"Alhamdulillah.* Thanks be to our Lord, endless thanks!"

He is going to be pleased when His servants say *"Alhamdulillah."* If you live your life from the beginning up to the end and say *"Alhamdulillah, alhamdulillah, alhamdulillah, alhamdulillah, alhamdulillah, alhamdulillah, alhamdulillah...* "and nothing else, you are going to reach your Lord. You are going to be a neighbor to the Prophet, beloved Muhammad (s), and you are going to be a neighbor to Allah Almighty Himself.

On the Day of Resurrection, all people will come to *Mahshar*, the place of judgment. It is going to be on the plain of Damascus, the Prophet said. All people, from East and West, from North and South, will come, some of them walking, some of them riding.

Who will walk on the Day of Resurrection? Those who did not know how to ride on their egos, they will walk, and they will carry their egos on their shoulders, also. But for those who rode on their egos, Allah Almighty will send Buraq,[36] the holy horse from Paradise, and they will ride, coming to the plain of Judgment Day.

All those people will fill up that plain, so many people, from the beginning up to the end, are going to be present there. There will be so many people that one thousand people will try to put their feet on a space one-foot square. But those people who have come to that plain on their Buraqs, their heavenly mounts, will have private stations of their own.

Then, before beginning judgment, Allah Almighty will order an angel to call out to all the people, saying, "Those who always said *'Alhamdulillah'* – who, at every occasion, for every condition they were in, said, *'Alhamdulillah*, thanks, endless thanks and most respectful praises to our Lord' – those people stand up!"

---

[36]Buraq is the heavenly mount on which the holy Prophet (s) rode during his Night Journey and Ascension.

They will stand up among all the people, and angels will come to them, one taking them from this side, one from that side, and they will go from *Mahshar*. And Allah Almighty will order, "Take them to My Paradise. No judgment, no accounting for them. They were pleased with Me at all times and I am pleased with them. No need for judgment here. They may enter My Paradise, they may enjoy themselves, because they were pleased with Me."

We are trying be pleased with our Lord, but as much as our egos are with us, it is difficult to be pleased with Him because we are mostly trying to make our egos pleased with us. *Wrong way, wrong method!* Your ego, your *nafs*, is not going to be pleased with you, ever. No matter how much you may give it, doing everything for it, your *nafs* is not going to be satisfied and to say "Thank you" to you.

You know this? Does it say "Thank you" to you? It *never* says "Thank you," a very proud creature! It never says "Thank you" to Allah Almighty; then how is it going to say "Thank you" to you? Yes; as much as our ego is with us and we are listening to it, it is so difficult to say to Allah Almighty, "Thanks to my Lord." Therefore, it is a great fight, a great war, between you and your *nafs*. When you win that war, then your *nafs* is going to say to you, "O my master, thank you," and, "As you like."

This fasting is a most important worship. It produces respect, teaching your *nafs*, so that when you are fasting and hungry, and then you break your fast, it will feel like saying *"Alhamdulillah,"* teaching you how you may be pleased with your Lord.

Now your ego, your *nafs*, is crying, "Too hungry! Too thirsty!" Then you are saying, "No! Wait until the time comes." And it is saying, "It's all right! Doesn't matter about the time," and you are saying, "Two minutes more."

"Leave two minutes out of this! Give me something to drink, to eat!" And you are saying, "No. You must wait two minutes more, one minute more. *Now!*[37] And your *nafs* learns to say "Thanks," firstly to you, and then to say to its Lord, "Thanks, endless thanks to my Lord, Allah Almighty."

May Allah Almighty help us with our egos! But you can't receive divine help without intention. When you intend, divine help comes to you and supports you. If you do not have that intention, you cannot receive divine help and support.

We are living in a very difficult time, and if you look around yourself, you may decide that it is impossible to be a Muslim or to keep the divine orders in a Western country, in a circle that surrounds you with doubts. Everyone is trying to catch you out and you are weak. But still you are intending and saying, "O my Lord, I am a weak servant to You and I am surrounded by devils. And everything is catching me from one side, to take me from *iman* to *kufr*, from belief to unbelief, from Islam to non-Muslim circles, from obedience to rebellion against You, from honor to dishonor, from light to darkness, from goodness to badness. And I am weak, perhaps the weakest one, and I am asking Your divine protection and divine help, divine support."

Then you may find yourself protected – fasting, praying, keeping yourself far away from devils. Rather, devils will run away from you and you will become like Sayyidina 'Umar. *Shaytan* said, "If I see 'Umar coming from this way, I turn to *that* way in order not to come face to face with him." Yes; as much as we feel our weakness, there comes more help, more support.

Now a sister has brought a baby in a basket. If she comes with three little children, her eyes are going to be on the weakest one, to give more support to him. Then, as much as you say, "O our Lord, I am the weakest one among those people," more divine support will come to you. But if you say, "I am a doctor," "I am a *disciple*," "I am a shaykh," "I am a scholar," "I

---

[37] That is, when the fast is broken at sunset.

am a worshipper," you will be left to yourself, you will be left in the hands of your ego.

When you say, "I am sufficient for myself. I have enough knowledge, I have enough prayers," you are left in the hands of your *nafs*. Therefore, throughout all his life, the Prophet (s) called to his Lord, Allah Almighty, saying, "O my Lord, please don't leave me in the hands of my ego." He was the Prophet, he was divinely protected, but he meant to teach us. The one who is left in the hands of his ego has lost his honor here and in the Hereafter, and he is disgraced and shamed.

We must ask our Lord so that He may keep and protect and support us in the face of our egos, because our ego is the wildest creature that has been created. It has been given to the sons of Adam because the ranks of the sons of Adam are the highest among creatures, and, as you know, kings or heroes ride on gigantic horses. (But someone like me rides on a donkey. If I ride such a horse, it will throw me.)

The most respected creatures among all creatures are the sons of Adam, and therefore Allah Almighty gives them such a horse as our ego, so powerful, for riding on and going into the Divine Presence. But we must very careful, because *nafs* is going to cheat us and ride on us, quickly making us its horse. You *must* ask for divine support.

That is the characteristic that Allah Almighty likes most to see among His servants: to say, "I am Your weak servant, O my Lord. I can't do anything. I am only a helpless and powerless servant." And Allah Almighty is going to be pleased with that servant, quickly sending His divine power, divine support, to keep him.

This fasting is teaching us these good manners and giving us divine support when we are intending that. Therefore, in Islam, intention is the most important thing, and for every action, for every worship, intention is *fard*, obligatory, the most important order from Allah Almighty.

Therefore, a person may have lived as an unbeliever for ninety years and his death is approaching. Then he intends to be a believer, to be a humble servant to his Lord, but there is no more movement, no more activity with him; he can't even move his hands or feet, nothing. He only makes the intention in his heart that if he were to be healthy, he would be his Lord's obedient, humble servant. Even if he is not able to say with his tongue, "I accept You, O my Lord, as my Lord," when Allah Almighty looks at his heart and sees that he is coming from unbelief to belief, without any action but *intending*, He sends His mercy angels to take his soul, with mercy, to Mercy Oceans.

Therefore, intention is the most important order of our Lord, and by means of intention we are going to be on the path of the prophets and *awliya*. May Allah Almighty give us inspirations and correct our intentions from badness to goodness, from unbelief to belief, changing our intentions to the best. ▲

13: limiting the desires of the nafs

Everything happens as a result of our deeds. Good deeds bring good things, bad deeds bring bad things. You must believe in this; it must be well known. Nothing [evil] comes upon a person who intends goodness and whose deeds are good. Goodness brings goodness, badness brings badness.

Therefore, in America, in Asia, in the Middle East, in England, in the East, in the West, every trouble is to be found. People's deeds are causing that; they are always playing with fire. Some individuals are influencing or instigating others, and people are following them, not asking who that person is and what his intentions may be. *All* are running after him.

Here, also. Yesterday I was coming [through a demonstration in the London streets]. For one hour, these people's "Hur-r-rah! Hur-r-rah!! Hip hip hurrah!!!" did not finish. People were running like a river. For what is this? What is the meaning?

In England, welfare is at the highest point. In what other country are there as many people on welfare as in England? But we are not saying "Thanks" to Allah – we are asking for more. You may be able to eat everything you like, drink everything, wear everything; your cars, your houses, your hospitals, everything is there. *For what is this asking for more, asking for more?*

Never satisfied; that is our ego's characteristic. We know that. However much you may give it, ego does not see what you gave it but asks for *that*, also. "Now I am finished with this. *That*, also, I am asking for." You can't find any limit to stop it.

Therefore, religions are making a limit for our endless desires. But now, without religion, people are atheists, saying, "No God." Therefore they must be punished. That punishment has not come yet, but a big punishment is arriving now. Allah Almighty never jokes; no, no joking for Allah. *We must fear Him*! ▲

14: keeping allah's presence

We mumins, believers, must know about this world and about Akhirah, the Hereafter. If we do not understand what is the value of dunya, we will never be safe from dunya's fitnah, this world's mischief, and dunya's fitnah is the worst fitnah for believers, particularly in such a time where people are worshipping dunya, not worshipping anything else. Therefore, the one who knows what dunya is may be protected by his Lord Almighty.

We must know that this life is a temporary life. All of us know this, but heedlessness is making us like drunk people. We are going; whether we want to stay or not, we are passing from this life to *Akhirah* – believers and non-believers, also. No one can stay here, even if he says, "I don't believe in *Akhirah* and I'm not going." *Everyone* must go. We believe that this life is for a temporary period for all people, but that after this life will come a permanent, eternal life for everyone, for both believers and unbelievers.

Now, we know that we are going, passing on. Everything around us is going to cheat us, but the *mumin's* face must be in front of Allah Almighty's Divine Face. You must ask for your Lord, not for *dunya*. That is the main goal of the *mumin*: to reach his Lord's satisfaction and pleasure.

Therefore, you must be careful, because *dunya* is a temporary place. At any time, the Angel of Death, 'Izrail (a), may come and say, "Give back the *amanah*, the trust, that Allah Almighty gave to you." And when he comes to take your soul to your Lord, Allah Almighty will ask, "How did you find My servant? Was his face turned to Me or to *dunya*? Where was his heart – with Me or with *dunya*?"

O people, O believers, we must understand about this life. We have been ordered to be with our Lord, Allah Almighty, and He is with us. At the first level, Allah Almighty says, *"Wa inna 'alaikum la-hafidhin, kiraman katibin.*[38] O people, you have two angels, two honorable angels, with you. Therefore, you must know that you are not alone. Anywhere you may be, those two honorable angels are with you."

That is the first stage for the *mumin*, for the believer. But concerning the highest degree, Allah Almighty says, *"Wa Hua ma'akum aina ma kuntum.*[39] O My servants, you must know that, more than angels, *I* am with you." And we must keep that.

O servants of our Lord, He is with us at every time, everywhere. You must keep His being with you. He knows where you are looking, He knows to what you are listening, He knows what you are thinking about. Keep your heart, especially during Ramadan, and then Allah Almighty will keep your heart the whole year. ▲

---

[38] "And indeed, over you are guardians, noble scribes [writing down your deeds]." (82:10-11)

[39] "And He is with you wherever you are." (57:4)

15: about eating and drinking

When you eat or drink anything, as much as you are with your Lord, it is going to be very light for your body. But if you eat heedlessly, *ghafilan-Illah*, without reflection, thinking about making your ego pleased, then it all comes on you as a burden.

Therefore, you may eat and drink any *halal*, permitted, thing, but on the level of *nafs* you must be very careful. When you have had enough of food and drink, you must stop. If not stopping, it may hurt you, may disturb you, may destroy your body. ▲

16: CONFLICT BETWEEN THE EGO AND THE SOUL

At the time when Sayyidina 'Ali and Sayyidina Mu'awiyah were fighting to arrive at a decision concerning the caliphate, one *sahabi*, Companion of the Prophet, at the time of prayers, went to pray with Sayyidina 'Ali. At the time of eating, he went to Mu'awiyah. And at the time of fighting, when it was too hard, he sat on the hill.

Both sides were very angry with him, asking, "Why? What is this? At the time of prayers you come to pray with Sayyidina 'Ali, at the time of meals you go to Mu'awiyah, and when they fight you go up on the hill!"

Then he said, "The *imam* is Sayyidina 'Ali. He has the imamate and praying behind him is more acceptable than behind anyone else. And Mu'awiyah's meals are the best." "What about for fighting?" "At the time of fighting, there is safety on the hill. I go there to be safe."

When fighting is taking place between your soul and your ego, you go on the hill. Stay there until they finish and come down. You understand? It means that when your soul and ego are fighting too much, sleep.

An-naum adh-dhalim 'ibadah.'[40] When an oppressor sleeps, people may rest from him and it is *'ibadah*, worship, for him. Let him sleep; don't awaken him. When he comes, he comes with *dhulm*, cruelty. ▲

---

[40]"The sleep of the oppressor is worship."

17: the most crucial attribute of a servant

Knowledge is one thing and to live is something else. Allah Almighty sent His prophets to teach people how they must live – how they must live *as His servants*. The real purpose was not just to give them holy books for reciting. And when *Umm ul-Muminin*[41] Sayyidatina A'isha, may Allah bless her, was asked about the Prophet's attributes, she replied, *"Khulquhu-l-Quran* – his attributes were just like the Quran."

You can't find the attributes of the Prophet, beloved Muhammad (s), deviating from the Holy Quran. Whatever the Holy Quran says, you can find his attributes agreeing with it. Therefore Allah Almighty orders His servants, believers, to take His beloved Muhammad (s) as their example.

You must use the Prophet's attributes as examples for yourself, and you must know that he is the most perfect example for the sons of Adam. You may look at the Prophet (s) from every direction and you will find him perfect from every direction. If we can be correct from only *one* direction (not from *every* direction; that is too remote for us), it may be enough for us. If we can follow our Prophet, beloved Muhammad (s), even in one *sunnah*,[42] it will be safety and pleasure and happiness and success for us forever. Therefore, as much as we are trying to learn, that is good, but we must also try to *do* as much as we are able, and if we can keep even one per cent out of one hundred, it is a good thing for us.

---

[41] The Mother of the Believers, the Prophet's wife 'A'ishah.

[42] Practice, actions, dealings, what he recommended or approved of in others.

What was our Prophet's main attribute? His main attribute, according to all the books of our knowledge, was that he was in perfect agreement with his Lord Almighty in everything, agreeing with his Lord on behalf of himself and everyone else.

He was the perfect one in *ma'rifat*, knowledge of his Lord; in knowledge of Allah, no one can reach the point that our Prophet, beloved Muhammad (s), reached. He has an ocean of divine knowledge, and if we could take all the divine knowledge that all creatures have been given, including the knowledge of other prophets, of *awliya*, of angels, it is only a little drop in that ocean. They have only a little drop, and that little drop, compared to other creatures, is itself oceans. But perfect knowledge among all creatures is for beloved Muhammad (s), and therefore he was the first among all creatures to be in agreement with his Lord in everything.

As much as we can approach that point, we will reach perfect servanthood. But it is difficult. It is not an easy way, it is steep. Whoever is asking for high positions must be tired. Whoever wants easy things, easy is cheap; easy products are cheap products. But difficult products are expensive, precious.

Therefore, that is our Prophet's main attribute: to be in agreement with his Lord for every action, seeing it as perfect. And once you step on that path, everything is going to be easy for you. Therefore, your level is always going to be above the level of rebellious people.

People are of two groups, one group seeing, the other group blind people. Those to whom Allah Almighty gives from His divine lights may look and see *Lawhi-l-Mahfudh*,[43] the Preserved Tablet. Those who may see that are always going to be in agreement with every action of their Lord Almighty, no objection. But those who do not see are always fighting with their Lord.

---

[43]The heavenly record of God's decrees for all eternity

Abdul-Qadir Jilani (q), a king-sized *wali*, said, "The one who makes objections against the divine orders being carried out, falls into *shirk* (associating partners with Allah). He is going to be like a partner to Allah Almighty because he says, 'This is not right, I object to this point, I give veto.'" Abdul-Qadir Jilani means that when someone says, "What is this? This is wrong," he is like a partner in Allah's sovereignty, going against Him. *Who is he to say this?*

Why was Satan thrown out? That is the reason: objecting to Allah's Will, so that everyone who goes against and objects to our Lord's Will is the same; at that moment he is the same as Iblis, as Satan. Therefore, we must say, "Astaghfirullah, astaghfirullah – may Allah forgive us! We repent and turn back to you, O Lord. How could I do this?"

And Abdul-Qadir Jilani said, Maut at-tauhid, maut ad-din, maut al-iman.[44] If someone opposes the judgments or decrees of Allah – if, when Allah Almighty's Will is working, he tries to keep it back – that is dangerous for a believer, because it will bring about the death of faith, the death of upholding the unity of Allah Almighty.

We are Ahl at-Tauhid, people of the Unity of Allah. When you say "No!" or "Why?" you become divided, without unity, because will and orders come only from One. Therefore, among the six pillars of faith in Islam,[45] the sixth, concerning qadar, is so important. It indicates unity and servanthood: that we are servants and we are in agreement with our Lord's Will.

But, as we said, at our level, the common level, we are quarreling, we are fighting, we are not real Muslims. A real Muslim is the one who

---

[44]"The death of *tawhid* [belief in the Oneness of Allah and the interconnectedness of all things under one divine Will] is the death of the religion, the death of faith."

[45]The six basic beliefs or "pillars" of Islam are (1) belief in the One God, (2) in His angels, (3) His divinely-revealed scriptures, (4) His messengers and prophets, (5) the Day of Judgment and Heaven and Hell, and (6) that all things, both good and evil, proceed from the divine Will. *"Qadar"* means the amount, measure or extent of what has been decreed by Allah.

surrenders to his Lord's Will; no more objections from him to his Lord. As his Lord says, he says, "As you like, O my Lord."

Therefore, it is the highest degree and the main attribute of our Prophet (s) to agree with his Lord in everything. His heart was always in agreement with Allah Almighty, and his body also did as his Lord willed. Everything which the Prophet manifested was according to his Lord's Will. Therefore, in Islam we must practice, firstly, to be in a state of islam,[46] and that means to submit, not only to be obedient to orders. And we are trying to be obedient to orders, but, among orders, the most important one is to agree with our Lord's Will.

One day Satan came to the Prophet (s) and the Prophet asked him, "Who among my ummah will save himself from you?"

And Satan replied, "The one who is in agreement with his Lord. If his Lord puts him in any situation and he says, 'I agree with my Lord,' no way for me on that member of the ummah."

If anyone agrees and is satisfied with his situation, Satan says, "No way for me on that person." It means that that person's attribute is in keeping with his Lord's Will. "If Allah says this, if our Lord's Will orders this, I also agree with it."

It may be against our egos because our egos are always making objections, but our souls are never going to object to anything. Our souls are swimming in our Lord's Mercy Oceans, and they see everything as a manifestation of our Lord's Mercy Oceans – everything. They see the whole universe as swimming in Mercy Oceans.

Therefore, souls are perfect; they are pleased with their Lord. Only our egos are displeased, our egos are making objections. And the one who is on friendly terms with his ego goes far from his Lord Almighty; he is not going to make his Lord pleased with him. He is only trying to make his ego

---

[46]That is, in a state of total surrender and submission to Allah.

pleased, and you are never going to make it pleased with you. You can't find any limit for making your ego pleased with you; it always has objections. But if you keep with your soul, you are in comfort, you are in peace and in pleasure.

Therefore, the Prophet (s) informed us that there would be a group of people among his ummah such that, even if there is every fitnah, every trouble, among the ummah, those troubles would never reach them. They are always above troubles.

Who are they? They are those people who are always in agreement with their Lord. They always see themselves as swimming in Mercy Oceans. And if someone looks at himself and sees himself in Mercy Oceans, for what is he going to make objections and fall into troubles and miseries and sufferings?

Everyone is trying to keep orders, but the first order that makes us Muslim is agreement with our Lord; we must be in agreement with Him. And our agreement already took place on the Day of Promises; we already made it but now we are losing it. We gave our agreement that You are our Lord and we are Your servants, and for everything, we agree that it will be as You like. No one said, "I am going to act as I like"; each one gave his promise to his Lord that I am going to be as You like, not as I like. And happiness and peace are for those who are in agreement with their Lord for everything, here and in the Hereafter.

We are practicing, and Allah Almighty is trying His servants. Everything in our lives is a trial from Allah Almighty; by every means He tries us. By every means, Allah Almighty looks to see if we are in agreement or we are canceling that agreement.

If you keep your agreement, He is going to keep His agreement. If you keep your promise, He is going to keep what He promised you – here, in the mosque, in your home, with your brothers, with your wife, with your children, with your relatives, with your business, with your animals. You are being tried in your cat, in your dog – yes!

You must always be awake. Maybe Allah Almighty is trying you by something and asking you to be in agreement with Him. Anything may happen in this life, to you or to others. You may say, "As my Lord likes, I agree with my Lord."

At night, when you get into bed to sleep, you must ask forgiveness from your Lord Almighty, saying, "O my Lord, today I was such a guilty servant – so many objections to Your Will. I am asking forgiveness and I am trying to be as You like, O my Lord. Keep me on my way, as You like." And whoever keeps that adab, good manners, with his Lord is going to be among His awliya. That is the way of awliya, because they are wearing the main attribute of beloved Muhammad (s). That is the secret of all wilayah, sainthood. ▲

18: previous meetings in the spiritual world

In the spiritual world, we were all together, so that we are sitting here now. If we had not been together in that spiritual world, we couldn't be all together here. He comes from Nigeria, she comes from Scotland. And you? German, Swedish, Irani, American – you can't be in the same place if your souls did not meet in the spiritual world. *That* brings us here to meet each other.

Therefore, there is familiarity in our meeting, not wildness, so that I am looking at Catherine as if I had seen her before, so many years ago. She is not a strange person to me because my soul met with her soul and she looked at me, like this, and I looked at her. I looked at Edward and he looked at me. May Allah Almighty make us be in happiness, here and in the Hereafter. ▲

19: everything passes away quickly

Night has gone and day has come. Yes, the night is buried; now the day comes. And when the night comes again, every event in this day, also, will be buried, gone.

Everything is going, passing away. You can't imagine how speedily everything is going. And we think that we are stopping, as when I am in a plane and cannot see that it is going. But sometimes (I always sit by the window, to look down) I am seeing another flight under our flight. From that I can see that we are like that flight, also flying; otherwise I would understand that we are standing still, not moving. And then the time is over, quickly going on to its destination.

All the people in this world are passengers, sitting on our planet. When I think about that, sometimes I tremble. Going in space... Who is the captain of it? Who is the director, the pilot – who? Without a captain? Never! A big planet, with all its passengers, and the passengers fighting with each other, throwing this, that – all of them.

In space, how are we going? To where? If it goes out of orbit, finished; the people, all of them, will be thrown off, like this, like that. *Ya Latif!*[47] And we are sitting on fire; there is fire inside the earth. But people are not afraid because they are non-thinking people, drunk people now. *La hawla wa la quwwata illa bil-Lah al-'Ali al-'Adhim!* There is no power or might save with Allah the Most High. ▲

---

[47]*Al-Latif* is one of Allah's Holy Names, meaning "The Kind". *"Ya Latif"* means "O Most Kind One."

20: the need for certainty

It is impossible for a person to leave evil and to take the right path unless his Lord helps him. Therefore, we must ask help, divine help, for everything.

You can't take yourself away from evil if you do not ask for your Lord's help, and you can't put your footsteps on the right path without asking help from your Lord. Therefore, when you are in need of leaving evil, you must ask divine help by saying A'udhu bil-Lahi min ash-Shaytani-r-Rajim."[48] That makes a protection, a fortress, for you.

Any time you feel that Satan is approaching you, you must say, "O my Lord, Satan wants to make me his servant, to make me his follower. O my Lord, keep me from Him" – that sort of a meaning. Even if we say it only with our tongues, it gives benefit. If you say it with your heart, it is so strong.

And when you are asking to put your feet on the right path, you must say, "Bismillahi-r-Rahmani-r-Rahim."[49] In our time, if a person is asking to walk on the right path, one hundred satans are rushing at him to catch his feet so that he cannot move them forward, and when you say "Bismillahi-r-Rahmani-r-Rahim," it takes them away and gives you power to walk on that straight path.

Yes, that is true; "Bismillahi-r-Rahmani-r-Rahim" is so powerful. That is the key to every miraculous power. As much as you may be certain of

---

[48]"I seek refuge with God from Satan the Rejected."

[49]"In the name of God, the Compassionate, the Merciful."

that, even if you put your foot on water, you may walk on it. It is only certainty which can achieve that.

Everyone knows something, but only a few people have certainty. Knowledge may be for everyone, but certainty is not.

Hasan al-Basri, may Allah bless him, was a famous imam. During his time there was Habib al-'Ajami, who was not an Arab; he was from Persia or from Bukhara. He did not recited the Quran as Arabs recite. He was an illiterate person, also.

Once Imam Hasan al-Basri came and saw Habib al-'Ajami praying Maghrib prayer. When Hasan al-Basri heard that that shaykh was unable to say "al-hamdu"[50] but pronounced it "el-hemdü," he thought, "His recitation is not correct," and did not pray behind him; he prayed alone.

Then hatif ar-Rabbani, Allah Almighty's divine voice, came (Allah Almighty sometimes 'phones' some of His beloved servants and they listen to what He says). "Except for that prayer which you did not pray behind Habib, I was going to accept all your prayers," Allah Almighty said through ilham, inspiration, and Hasan al-Basri was listening. "But you left that prayer. You are still looking at the words, not looking at the heart of the imam, with whom is his heart. And I am looking at the one who is imam but I am not looking at his recitation; I am looking at his heart. If his heart is with Me, that imam is all right. If his heart is not with Me but he is occupied with making his voice and his recitation beautiful, engaged with that and permitting his heart not to be with Me, angels are taking that prayer to Me. But the one whose heart is with Me when he prays, I am accepting his prayers directly without any intermediary."

Therefore, all prayers are of two kinds. One is the kind of the person who goes to pray and when he says "Allahu Akbar,"[51] he puts everything aside and is with his Lord, and Allah Almighty takes his prayers directly to

---

[50]Words of the first *surah* (chapter) of the Quran, *Surah al-Fatiha*.
[51]The *takbir*, "Allah is Most Great."

His Divine Presence. But for the one who says "Allahu Akbar," and throughout his prayer he is traveling, selling and buying, going and coming, sleeping and awaking, eating and drinking, running after this and that, angels are taking his prayer to Allah.

But Allah Almighty directly takes the prayers of those who are with Him. "O Hasan al-Basri, I would have accepted all of your prayers for the sake of the prayer that you left because of the way it was recited." And Imam Hasan al-Basri wept so much.

•••••••••

Once Hasan al-Basri was sitting near the Tigris River in Baghdad, waiting for the boat to come in and to cross over to the other side. Then Habib al-'Ajami came, saying, "O *ustad*, my master, what are you waiting here for?"

Hasan al-Basri said, "I am waiting for the ferry boat, to cross from one side to the other."

"You are the *imam* and you are sitting here, waiting for that raft? Come and say '*Bismillah*' and walk." And Habib went and, saying '*Bismillahi-r-Rahmani-r-Rahim*,'' walked on the Tigris and passed over.

And Hasan al-Basri cried, "This *'ajam*, this foreigner, an illiterate person, is crossing the Tigris, and *I* am sitting here!"

Yes. Hasan 'knew' what the power of '*Bismillahi-r-Rahmani-r-Rahim*'' is, but that foreign person had *certainty*. Hasan didn't have enough certainty to say '*Bismillahi-r-Rahmani-r-Rahim*'' and step on the water.

Therefore, we are in need of more certainty rather than more knowledge. That is important. But in our time people are always running after learning so much. What is the benefit? You may learn so much and you will forget so much. But certainty never leaves you. Certainty is the seed of knowledge. You may plant it and it grows.

———

Once when Habib al-'Ajami was sitting in front of his *khanaqah*, his *takiyah*,[52] Hasan al-Basri came running. "O Habib, hide me," Hasan said, "because Hajjaj, the caliph's governor, is sending his soldiers to catch me. Hide me!"

"Go inside and hide yourself," Habib said.

Hasan went in and, finding a place, hid himself. Then afterwards, soldiers came running, asking Habib, "Have you seen Hasan al-Basri?"

"Yes. I saw him inside. He is inside."

They went in and looked around, looking everywhere, and he was looking around in fear. Then the soldiers went out, saying to Habib, "Now, aren't you ashamed, telling a lie? Where is he? Hajjaj will deal with the one who cooperates with Hasan al-Basri, and that will be appropriate for you. You said that he was inside, not ashamed of lying!"

"Inside. I am not lying. He is inside."

Once again going, coming. Then, very angry, the soldiers went away.

Then Hasan al-Basri came out. "O shaykh, what is this? I came to you, asking you to keep me, and you told the soldiers 'Inside'."

"Ya Hasan, ya imam, najaut min sidqi-l-kalam[53] – you were saved by my truth. I told the truth and Allah protected you because I spoke truthfully. I said, 'O my Lord, this Hasan al-Basri, Your servant, came to me and said, "Hide me, keep me!" I can't protect him. I entrust him to You, giving him to You as my trust. *You* protect him.' I only said that and recited *Ayat al-Kursi.'*[54] *Therefore* the soldiers had run around, looking at everything and doing like this on his head, even, but never understanding that he was there.

———

[52]A dervish monastery.

[53]"O Hasan, O *imam*, you were saved by the truthfulness of my speech."

[54]The Verse of the Throne (2:255).

Yes. If Allah Almighty protects His servant, it is all right. *Awliya* are deputies of our Lord Almighty. If a person runs to a *wali* and asks for protection, he may protect him, here and in the Hereafter. Those are miracles for *awliya* – miracles for *anbiya*, prophets, and miracles for *awliya*.

We are in need of some certainty. Once again, Hasan al-Basri came to visit that shaykh, Habib al-'Ajami. When Hasan arrived, Habib al-'Ajami, may Allah bless him, brought two loaves of bread, putting them in front of him as a courtesy to his guest.

Just as Hasan was beginning to eat, someone came hungry and asked for something for the sake of Allah. Then that shaykh, Habib al-'Ajami, came and took both the loaves from Hasan al-Basri and gave them to that person.

Then the *imam*, Hasan al-Basri, said, "O shaykh, you are a good person, but if you had some more knowledge of the *Shari'ah*, it would be better for you. You should know a little bit about the *Shari'ah*; you are in need of that." He meant to say, "One loaf for me and one for that person, not taking the two and giving them away."

The shaykh did not say anything. Then, after a bit, someone came to the door. The shaykh ordered, "See who is there."

A *disciple* went and looked, saying, "A person has brought a tray full of food."

"Bring the tray here," the shaykh said. "Now *imam*, eat! You know so much," he said to Hasan al-Basri, "but you have little certainty. You must try to have more certainty."

Because he had certainty, that shaykh knew that if he gave this for the sake of Allah, more than this must certainly come. "You were angry with me when I took the two loaves, giving them to that person. Look! If I had not given both of them, this would not have come. I am certain that when I give, Allah Almighty will return it at least tenfold."

Yes. Therefore certainty gives more benefit to everyone, and we are in need of that. If there is no certainty, knowledge can never give benefit but is only like an ornament to enable people to say, "We are doctors, we are scholars."

What is certainty? Someone was saying, "If I put my hand in the mouth of a dragon and my heart is all right, it is never going to be afraid that that dragon will bite my hand – no. I know with certainty that only if my Lord gives the order it will bite. Therefore, without doubt, if I were to put my hand there, I would not be afraid."

Imam Shaarani, one of the people of *tawwakul* (those who trust in their Lord completely) once said, "Once I was traveling and it was near *Maghrib* time. I saw a dome and walked towards it. When I entered it, I saw that there was a tomb in it under the dome, in ruins.

"After a short while, peasants came running, saying, 'O shaykh, you must not stay here but must come with us. Our village is nearby. This is a terrible place, particularly at nighttime. So many snakes, big snakes, come out, and if anyone sleeps here, in the morning we find only his bones, nothing else. They eat him; only bones are left. Therefore we are warning you not to sleep here.'"

Then Imam Shaarani, may Allah bless him, said to the peasants, "O my brothers, when you tell me that, I can't move; I can't take even one step out of this place. Because when you warned me about those big snakes, my ego was too afraid of them, and I am so ashamed in front of my Lord because my *nafs* was too frightened of snakes, not fearing Allah Almighty but fearing snakes. Therefore I am not going with you; I can never accept your invitation. I must sleep here this night; it is better for such a *nafs* that I be eaten by snakes. Therefore, it is impossible that I should leave this place."

Eh! The peasants said, "You know best, shaykh. You are the shaykh; *we* don't know. We are inviting you, and we are also warning you about the snakes."

"Yes. Thank you very much. You go and I will be here this night. If, without saying anything about snakes, you had come and invited me officially, saying, 'Come with us,' it would have been all right; I might have come. But since you are saying, 'There are snakes, there is a danger, this is a terrible place,' I can't move even one step from here. Go away!"

They went, and in the morning they hurried back with shovels to bury that shaykh's bones. And they saw that the shaykh was sitting and making *dhikr*,[55] and the snakes were like this, like wooden beams, beside him. When he lay down, they went around him; in that sandy place they made tracks, traveling around and hissing. And he was at rest. Yes; if you know your Lord and trust in Him, He protects you. If you are familiar with your Lord, everything is going to be familiar with you.

That is certainty – *important*! And we must try to improve in certainty, not trying to keep so many verses of the Quran, so many *hadiths*. But if we can acquire the secret power in them, that will be certainty for us.

Whoever has it may give it. The one who has something may give it; if he doesn't, how can he give? You ask for bread from a person, for example. If he has it, he will give it to you. If not, he will never give it.

Certainty is with the prophets. Their certainty brought the angel Gabriel to them from the heavens, and the *awliya*, also certainty is with them. You may take certainty from those people. All *awliya* have certainty; you can't find a *wali* without certainty.

Therefore we are asking our Lord to let us find one of them so that we may acquire certainty; *they* give certainty. There are some lamps of only five watts and some of one thousand, of ten thousand. As much as a person needs, they give; as much as you are asking, they give certainty. We are in need of that. May Allah bless you and forgive you, and grant us certainty from His beloved people. ▲

----

[55]Repetition of phrases of glorification , Quranic verses, or Allah's Holy Names.

21: seeking forgiveness for others

*One morning Shaykh Nazim spoke about the carefree attitude of members
of a rock music group, who rehearsed next to a mosque in London
where Shaykh Nazim often gives lectures.*

Very happy people! They are happy, we are happy, alhamdulillah. They
are not asking to be like us, we are not asking to be like them. Everyone is
happy.

Every group must be happy. If not happy, its people will change to
another group. This is important. Allah Almighty says, Kullu hizbin bima
ladayhim farihun,[56] "every party is happy with what it finds." Every group is
sitting at a feast; from that feast they are taking their pleasure. If not taking
pleasure from this group, they will get up from there and go to another one.
If not taking it there, then their pleasure is going to be with a third camp.

I mean to say that everyone belongs to a group – by his thoughts, by
his actions, by his behavior, by his attributes, by his customs, by his beliefs.
Even within religions there are so many groups. In London, some Muslims
go to Central Mosque, some go to Peckham Mosque, some go to
Shacklewell Lane Mosque, some go to the West Indian Mosque. Now
Turks are three or four parties, also, each of them going with someone.
And they are pleased. If not pleased, they would not go there.

---

[56]23:53.

That is a rule in the world. Allah Almighty has put that rule and He is saying, "Everyone is happy with the group that he finds in front of him, like a table put there for certain people." One person may say, "Yes, this is best for me," and sits at it. Someone else just comes and looks. Sometimes a person comes and sits, sits, sits, and then goes out. It means that he does not agree with our Association, does not agree with what pleases us, and is asking for something else.

Therefore, now, the people next door are pleased. They have so many people gathering; they are happy. We are also gathering and happy, alhamdulillah.

Allah Almighty gathers some people for evil. Some others He gathers together for good. They are carrying something, some load. If they do not do that, if they leave, others must take that place. Perhaps it may come to us to play a trumpet. If those people are no longer alive, it is impossible for us to be free: those trumpets must be played. If there is no one else, perhaps the turn may come to us.

Therefore, we are thanking Allah Almighty that there are some servants to play the trumpet so that we are free for Your service, O our Lord. And we are saying, "Those people are tiring themselves by doing such a thing. O our Lord, forgive them and take from them their burdens."

They are not praying for us, but pray-ers must pray for them. Understand? They are not thinking of praying for themselves or for anyone else, but pray-ers, believers, must be more generous than those people who are carrying around evil and representing evil and working through evil, and we are thankful to our Lord that we are free, away from evil. They can't think of praying for themselves or for others, but you must think about them, those people, because they are under a heavy burden, and say, "O my Lord, forgive them."

That is a high degree of faith. It is the level of the prophets, particularly the level of the Seal of the Prophets, peace be upon them all.

He asked forgiveness for those people who had been used for evil, because our Prophet had knowledge of divine wisdom.

If he had not known divine wisdoms, he would not have been the Last Prophet. More than any other one of the prophets, he knew the divine wisdom concerning the sons of Adam, concerning the believers and concerning the others, unbelievers. And he knew about Satan, about nafs and about this dunya; and for everyone he knew well concerning the Last Day and after the Last Day, concerning eternal life, and he was the person who knew most about the divine wisdoms concerning Paradise and Hell. Therefore, he always asked forgiveness for his nation, for his ummah.

And all the people living now and earlier, up to the end of this world, are from his nation, because when Jesus Christ (a) comes again,[57] he is not going to be a prophet and there is not going to be a nation for him, but he is going to be from the nation of Muhammad (s). And the Prophet is asking forgiveness for everyone in the Divine Presence. Allah Almighty has given him a promise, saying, "On the Last Day I will say to you, O Muhammad, that as you like, I will do. As you like, I will give to you. As you like, I will forgive. As you like, I will give – for you!"

No one can reach that point, that station. It is the highest station, maqam al-mahmud, the most respected station in the Divine Presence, the most praiseworthy station, which has been given to only one among all the sons of Adam, among all the prophets, among all the saints. And Allah Almighty will say to him, "Ask and I shall give, as you like." Then the Prophet will ask, and Allah will say, "Ask more!" He will ask more, and Allah Almighty will say, "I am giving. Ask more, ask more, ask more!"

And the Prophet will be ashamed and will stop. Then our Lord Almighty will say, "Now look at what I will give to My servants!"

---

[57]This refers to the return of Jesus (a) to the earth in the end-time of this world, as is mentioned in numerous *hadiths*.

When He opens a Mercy Ocean and divine rewards appear for the servants, the Prophet (s) will be ashamed to look at those divine rewards that he asked for the second time. He will look at what Allah is giving to His servants and to the nation of Muhammad (s). As much as he asked, it will be only a little drop from an ocean on the point of a needle, and that is from endless Oceans.

Man is going to suffer throughout his life; but however much he may suffer during his life, when he leaves this life, in his grave, in Barzakh, and on the Day of Resurrection, he must keep his hope in his Lord, Allah Almighty, at the highest level, because He says, "Sabaqat rabmati 'ala ghadabi – My forgiveness surpasses My anger."[58] Therefore, however much the sons of Adam may suffer, finally they will reach their Lord's endless Mercy Oceans. ▲

---

[58]This is a *hadith qudsi* -- that is, a saying of the Prophet (s) concerning the person or attributes of Allah Almighty which was transmitted to his heart by divine inspiration.

22: no one lives life precisely as they like

No one lives his life as he likes, but the one who lives his life as *He* likes is successful and happy. We must live as He likes, not as *we* like. We can't do that; no one can live as he likes, not even the President of the United States, not even Her Majesty, the Queen of England, not even the King of Saudi Arabia. Everyone must live as his Lord likes and as He makes an orbit for him to go on. You can't take yourself out of that orbit. It is impossible. ▲

23: being flexible in our habits

You may not always find everything that you want to eat. Therefore, you must eat anything that is put in front of you; you must try to learn to eat any kind of food. Don't say, "We are not accustomed to this!" *Alhamdulillah*, Western people are easy; anything that you put for eating they will eat, but our people are foolish, not eating everything.

For dressing, also, and sleeping, houses, cars. Don't say, "I must get a Rolls Royce." Any kind of a car is all right; you may take a bus, also, not always a minicab or a taxi. You have to accustom yourself to every kind of condition, to hard conditions; you must try, little by little, because you can't find everything at all times, since every sort of condition may occur to man. Sometimes rich people may become poor, sometimes powerful people may become weak, sometimes you may be in a tight place, and so on. You must consider every possibility.

On one of my pilgrimages with our sisters from Cyprus, I went to Mecca and arrived at the *mutawwaf's* house.[59] Then I attended to one lady. "O-ooh!" she said. "I can't stay in this place."

I said, "For what are you asking – a palace? No; this is the best place for us. As far as our money allows, it is all right, and it is near the *Holy Kaba*. If you are asking to live in a hotel, all the money that you have brought is not enough for even one night. What are you saying? You must stay here."

---

[59] A caretaker of pilgrims during the *Hajj* or pilgrimage, who provides them with lodging, food and other necessities. Here Shaykh Nazim is talking about a situation which he encountered as a *Hajj* guide to Cypriot pilgrims.

Only one mat – yes; she was accustomed to being in her house where everything was all right.

Sometimes you must sleep on the ground. So many things are happening in the world – people fleeing, leaving everything. Therefore, now our mosque is like a palace. Perhaps next year there will be a more suitable place. We shall see.

Yes. Whoever agrees with his Lord is going to be happy; whoever goes against the plans of our Lord suffers. It is easy: the one who goes with Him is happy, the one who goes against Him gets into the wrong lane of traffic. You must keep the way. *Don't be against your Lord.*

But we are *always* against Him. Allah Almighty says, "My word must prevail." We are saying, "No! *Our* word must prevail," and it is impossible for our words to prevail. And sometimes I am thinking about that and saying, "*Alhamdulillah* that my word didn't prevail and that my Lord's word did. I am happy."

You may understand afterwards, not at the same time. Afterwards, you may know that His word is the best for you, that His choosing is the best for you, not *your* choosing. You can't choose anything [correctly] for yourself. Each time you choose the *worst* thing; each time He chooses for you the *best* thing.

That is the summary of the whole *Shari'ah*. If we may think about that point, we will be happy people, never suffering. Sufferings always come when we try to be against our Lord's choice. You understand? *Don't be against Him!* Look – one day you wear a red dress, one day a blue one, one day a white one, very happy with that. Yes, as He chooses for us, that is the best. ▲

24: Divine wisdom
and Building Goodness

Mankind, the sons of Adam, are acting by divine wisdoms. Nothing is without wisdoms. In every action there must be so many wisdoms. You can't find anything in the universe that is useless, not even one particle. Sometimes in the sunshine there are coming specks of dust. You can't say, "What are these for? If they hadn't been created, what difference would it have made?"

That is a foolish thought. In the universe there is a balance. If that dust particle were absent, that balance would change, would be upset. It must be.

Even now, scientists are looking at that wisdom, and they are saying that if even any kind of insect disappears, becomes extinct, the balance will be upset. It means that the balance is going against creatures, because if those become extinct, after a time that extinction must come to every creature. In the view of scientists, it is going to take perhaps billions or trillions of years, but it gives a sign that if any species becomes extinct, the turn must come to everyone.

Every atom, was created for a purpose, for a divine wisdom. Who is the Creator of even that speck of dust? There is a Creator; our Lord created even that speck of dust. Therefore it is also important. If there were no importance for that speck of dust, it would not have been created.

You must look at everything in existence as having divine wisdoms for being in existence. And Grandshaykh, may Allah bless him, was saying that each indivisible element of an atom is madhhar ism min asma-Allahi 'Azza wa Jall, a manifestation of one of the Holy Names of our Lord Almighty.

We know that the Holy Names of Allah Almighty are ninety-nine, but there are still more. There are three thousand Names of Allah Almighty: twelve hundred for the angels to know; one thousand for the prophets; three hundred in the Taurat, three hundred in the Injil, three hundred in the Zabur,[60] and ninety nine in the Holy Quran, altogether making 2,999. And there is one Ismu-l-Lahi-l-A'dham, the Greatest Name.

And Allah Almighty made the three thousand Names into three names and presented them to Muhammad (s) and his nation. That is Bismillahi-r-Rahmani-r-Rahim.[61] If a person says Bismillahi-r-Rahmani-r-Rahim, he is actually saying three thousand Holy Names of our Lord, including the greatest one.

The keys of miracles are with Bismillahi-r-Rahmani-r-Rahim; whoever keeps to Bismillahi-r-Rahmani-r-Rahim has miracles. If you say, "Why don't we?" We are still too weak people to carry miracles; we have them, but it is forbidden to do that at our level because we are not powerful enough.

And all the prophets were given miracles by Bismillahi-r-Rahmani-r-Rahim. Abraham (a) got out of the fire of Nimrod by Bismillahi-r-Rahmani-r-Rahim. Moses (a) went through the Red Sea by Bismillahi-r-Rahmani-r-Rahim. Solomon (a) commanded all the sons of Adam and jinn by Bismillahi-r-Rahmani-r-Rahim. And Jesus Christ went to the heavens by Bismillahi-r-Rahmani-r-Rahim.

Allah Almighty is eternal, His existence is endless. And His territory is also endless – endless territory, endless sovereignty. Endless existence with endless attributes, and endless Names, also, for our Lord Almighty. And everything that belongs to our Lord Almighty extends eternally, endlessly. Therefore, if you could divide all the universes into atoms and all the atoms

---

[60]*Taurat, Injil* and *Zabur*: the original scriptures revealed to the prophets Moses, Jesus and David (a).

[61]This is actually *bi-ism Allah* [in or by the name of Allah], *ar-Rahman* [an attribute or Name of Allah conveying beneficence, compassion and mercy], *ar-Rahim* [an attribute or Name conveying endless compassion, benevolence and mercy] -- three Names joined in one endlessly repeated phrase.

into particles, also, of which a huge number will come up, you can say that Allah Almighty has as many Names as that number, and everything which comes into existence also manifests more Names of Allah Almighty, because everything is a manifestation of the Holy Names of Allah Almighty.

Therefore, we are beginning today by saying that everything is created with divine wisdoms. You can't say, "This – for what was it created? There is no need for this to be in existence." That is foolishness, that is a kind of kufr, unbelief. Everything is created for a purpose, and everything has a private, special station and a private situation in existence, so that no one else can be in that station or in that situation under those conditions.

That is prophets' and awliya's knowledge. They are looking at every creature with such a vision. But we – we are not even accepting everyone who is alive among the sons of Adam; we are looking at so many people as useless. "Why did You create those people," we are saying, "those atoms, those other things?" We are objecting about why there are so many millions of people, saying, "We must plan, population control." We are saying, "For what is this? Too many people are coming, useless people!"

They are useful and the coming people may be useless. Look how egotistical people are! They are going with Satan; Satan is teaching them to do this. Pharoah killed the Children of Israel, and Nimrod also killed every child in his time. Now new Pharoahs and Nimrods are planning that – yes, the same action, because Allah Almighty looks at intentions.

Why no rights for them? Do they eat from their portions, or does Allah send provision for them? Why are they not controlling wastefulness, ingratitude for Allah's favors? Why are they not controlling people's throwing away so much food – why not, instead of controlling people so that they will not have children?

Don't be a partner to your Lord! He knows well. If He creates, He also creates His creatures' portions. No one is created without a portion, but the sons of Adam have too much concern about their portions. No other creatures worry about their portions.

Once Abu Yazid al-Bistami, may Allah bless him, a grand-*wali*, was traveling (*awliya* are always traveling, and the prophets traveled, also). He came to a city and prayed in the mosque. After praying, the *imam* looked at him, and seeing that he was a stranger, asked from where he had come.

"I come from the earth," Abu Yazid said.

"All of us are from the earth," said the *imam*.

"Why are you asking, if you know [the answer to] what you are asking?" said Abu Yazid. "I come from the East, from eastern lands."

"What is your job? What do you do?"

"Nothing."

"If you do nothing, how do you live? No job, no trading, no farms — *nothing*? How do you live?"

"And how are you an *imam*?" Abu Yazid asked. "I prayed behind you, thinking that you were a *mumin*, a believer, but you are not a believer. Let me repeat my prayer and then I shall give you an answer. *Don't you know who gives creatures' portions?* How can you be an *imam*?"

Yes, we are like such an *imam*. And Abu Yazid was angry with that *imam*, saying, "Why are you not asking cats how they are living? 'Any trade for you, any farms for you, any houses for you?' Why are you not asking the dogs in London, also, how they live? One million dogs are also living — joyfully living, with pleasure, with respect, living. Why are you not asking?" (I am acting as 'translator' for Abu Yazid al-Bistami, may Allah sanctify his secret.) "Catch *them* and ask! Why are you asking me from what *I* am living?"

Yes; now dogs are living. No one is asking, "You have a pension, something from the government, every week, every weekend, money?" No one is asking that, but they were asking about Abu Yazid, "From what are you living?" and all people are imagining that Allah Almighty created man without portions!

We are believers. We believe that even if the whole world is filled with the sons of Adam, Allah Almighty can still give their portions. But we are sinners. We are wasting His favors, and then we are seeing that the future is going to be dark and that people are suffering.

We must believe in our Lord, that He gives everything to His creatures. But we are saying, "Now, for what are there so many people on earth? Must be planned!"

We do not believe in God Almighty! People are going to plan everything. But Allah Almighty is letting them do everything. Then He will bring such a plan that six out of seven will go, will die, and one [out of seven] will remain.[62] Allah Almighty is saying, "I am going to make a plan for you now, O people, so that if there are seven million, only one million will remain; if three-and-a-half million people, only half-a-million will remain, three million going. *I* am planning for you."

Now it is coming, to make this earth empty, uncrowded. We will walk, walk, walk, and we will see only one other person in half-an-hour. We are not keeping *adab*, correct manners, with Allah Almighty! Therefore, this is the time of *jababirah*, tyrants, little and big ones.

Everything in the universe, everything in existence, has a private station and a private, special importance and situation for itself. No one can substitute for it. You are keeping your station only for yourself, and you, and you – *everyone!* This is related to *adab m'a Allah*, good manners towards our Lord Almighty, so that we may keep respect for everyone. And then we are going to take care of everyone, to help everyone to be in his station, to support him, and we must know that if he goes, the balance is going to change.

If we know that everything is by divine wisdoms and that for everything in existence there is an important situation, we will take wisdoms

---

[62] A reference to World War III.

from everything. *'Fa fi kulli shayin lahu ayat'*[63]; in everything you can find a miracle of your Lord – in *everything*.

Then we come to actions. No one can act, can move, without there being a divine purpose and wisdom in it; everything, every action, must carry with it a divine purpose. And now we come to an important point, also: that among people on the earth, some of them are going to be *muslih*,[64] good-builders, and some others *mufsid*,[65] evil-builders. Evil-builder and good-builder; good-builders, good works (I am a builder of words; yes).

Allah Almighty likes pleasure-builders – a new word – who make people pleased and in pleasure. Those are beloved people in the Divine Presence. The other party of the sons of Adam are evil-builders, harming people, making people cry, making people suffer, making people fall into troubles. They are like wolves; their guide, their example, is Satan. But for those who are good-builders, their examples are all the prophets.

All the prophets came to teach people how they may build goodness, how they may order their lives by being good- builders, and to warn others, "Don't be evil-builders, because you will make a cell around yourself. Evil is going to surround you. *'Wa la yahiqu-l-makru-s-saiy'u illa bi-ahlihi'*"[66] – that sort of a meaning. "O evil-builders, you must fear evil because every time you build something evil, you are surrounding yourself with evil and you can't find any way to escape. *Be careful!*" That is a warning from all the prophets to people.

Once Abu Jahl[67] dug a well in front of his house. He was the worst enemy of Muhammad (s) and he used every means of evil to harm the Prophet.

---

[63]"And in everything there are signs [of Allah]."

[64]One who corrects, restores, does good, sets things right.

[65]A mischief-maker, evildoer, corrupter.

[66]"But the evil plot does not encompass except its [own] people." (35:43)

[67]A leader of idol-worshippers, who was bitterly hostile to the Prophet (s) and to Islam.

He knew well that the Prophet (s) was a person of high character, most high; when he heard that someone was ill, he would go and ask how he was. Then *Shaytan* instructed Abu Jahl that you must disappear for a few days so that Muhammad may ask, "Where is Abu Jahl?" and you will tell your slaves to say, "Abu Jahl is ill now."

"When he knows that you are ill, he will come to see how you are, perhaps because he wants you to be a *mumin*, a believer;" because when a person is ill, his heart becomes soft, not hard like rock.

"You will make a hole, a well, and cover it. When Muhammad comes, he will go down; finished, disappeared. 'I don't know [what happened to him],' you may say. 'Perhaps, like Jesus Christ, he went away.'"[68] This, Satan was teaching him. For evil-builders, their teacher is Satan. *Don't be a student of Satan!*

Abu Jahl dug with two or three other people, and they covered the hole. Then Abu Jahl lay like this and looked out; he put his bed at the window and secretly looked to see if the Prophet was coming.

When the Prophet (s) heard that Abu Jahl was ill, he said, "I must go and talk to him. Perhaps now his heart is going to be soft and he will believe in his Lord Almighty."

Abu Jahl was secretly watching, looking keenly. And the Prophet (s) came. Just as he was about to put his foot on that covered hole, Gabriel (a) came down, saying, "Don't put your foot on it! Your Lord gives you greetings and orders you to turn back." And the Prophet turned back.

When he did that, Abu Jahl, quickly forgetting everything, shouted, "Why did he turn back?" and, jumping from his bed, he ran and... went down. We have a saying, "If you dig a well for your brother, dig to your own height so that you can climb up and get out. Don't dig too deep."

---

[68] A parody of the Islamic belief that Jesus (a) was not crucified but was taken up to Heaven.

And he was in it, shouting, "O people, come! I am here!" And people, his servants, were running about, like this, like that.

"Where is he? Where is his voice coming from?" A voice shouting; from where shouting? And then they saw – *oh!!!*

He was calling, "I am here! Come here, take my hand!" He stretched out his hand to them, and the people, his servants, also, gave their hands to him, but without reaching.

"Bring a rope," he said. They brought a rope, sending it down to him, but still not reaching. Then, "Bring another one, longer! What is this short one? A long one!"

Then they brought a long one and still it did not reach. "What has happened? Why did you dig such a well? I ordered you to dig to two heights of a person! What did you dig such a deep well for? Bring another rope!"

They brought another rope. "A long one!" A long one. "Tie them all together!" – ropes going from here to the City. Asking for ropes from next-door neighbors; neighbors' ropes coming but still not enough, not reaching. And Abu Jahl saw that it was impossible. If all the ropes on earth were to come, they would never reach him.

Then he called his servants, saying, "Go after Muhammad. Tell him that I am going to believe in him!"

They ran after the Prophet (ṣ) and said, "Abu Jahl has fallen into a well and we can't get him out. Please come and look after him."

The Prophet came running and said, "O Abu Jahl, if I take you out, are you going to believe?"

"Yes, yes!" he said. "Quickly take me out!"

"I am going to rescue him," the Prophet said. He reached down his hand, taking him out.

"I never saw a magician like you," Abu Jahl said. But still he did not believe.

We are telling this tale to show that whoever does evil, evil surrounds him. That noble verse of the Holy Quran shows that the one who does evil is surrounded by evil, and then he is going to be caught in it, as amongst silken threads. You know the silk worm? It makes that thread and its prey gets entangled inside it – finished, never escaping.

Therefore, among people, from the beginning up to the end, some are always good-builders, pleasure-builders, and the others are evil-builders. Allah Almighty orders us, "O people, use your minds and be good-builders, not evil-builders." That is the summary of prophet- hood, the summary of the divine message to the sons of Adam: *Be good-builders. Don't be evil-builders.*

At every step you must know if that step is for building a goodness or for building an evil; you must think about that. Therefore, the Prophet (s) said that one moment's thought, reflection, is more valuable perhaps than sixty years of praying. Therefore, O believers, O brothers, for every action you must be present with your action. Don't be heedless! When you are heedless, you are doing badness, you are working for evil, you are working for devils, you are supporting Satan and his sovereignty.

Keep this: in every breath and in every step, be good-builders. ▲

25: Ridding our hearts of bad intentions

We are valuable. The sons of Adam, all of them, are so valuable; each one is more valuable than the whole universe, not including man. And there is something that makes us more valuable, but something else which makes us be of no value. Which thing makes us be of no value, taking away from our value?

Now I am 'translating' from our Headquarters, from the 'Main Central,' the spiritual Central of Grandshaykh. We must know this so that we may live it: Whoever harms others loses his value. If, by your speaking or by your hand, you harm anyone, even one person, you are going to lose your value.

Satan was a worshipper. No one worshipped like him in his time and he was the most learned one among the angels, but he harmed one individual among all the rest and he fell.

He harmed Adam (a), not respecting him. The whole universe gave respect to Adam. Only Satan did not give his respect and harmed Adam, and therefore he fell. No value for him from that time on.

Anyone who harms a person, either by looking or by speaking or by his hand, is on the same level as Satan and loses his value. This is an important point that we must know – and must practice, also. It is not enough only to know it; more important is practicing. Don't give trouble to anyone, don't harm anyone.

When you are a Muslim, you are a valuable servant, you are a beloved one in the Divine Presence. And Allah Almighty is trying His servants; no one is going to remain without being tried. Everyone will be tested throughout his life; each day you may be tested by your Lord, and He is looking at your attributes with His servants.

Whoever gives harm to others, Allah Almighty leaves him, and heavenly beings, angels, also leave him. And if Allah Almighty leaves a person, every suffering and trouble falls on him, rains on him; he will never be in peace or happiness in his life. And Allah Almighty, our Lord, wants us to be in a happy and peaceful life, but we are changing a peaceful life into an unpeaceful one, full of suffering and troubles. We are doing that.

If we listen to our grandfather Adam, the first man, he advised his sons and ordered them to advise their sons, all the prophets repeating Adam's advice to their nations, and his advice is reaching to our time as well. He advised his sons, "O my sons, look and learn from my example. Every good thing and every happiness was mine, but I lost it all because I abandoned my Lord's pleasure. I made Him angry with me, and I lost all happiness and took on all the sufferings of this life. You must take an example from me. Don't make your Lord angry with you!"

Therefore, all the prophets advised their nations, "Don't do any deed that makes your Lord angry with you. It costs too much, is too expensive. Allah Almighty wants a peaceful and happy life for you. Keep it. But if you make your Lord angry with you, you will lose everything."

But now in our time we are not asking about our Lord's pleasure or anger; no. We are saying, "I don't care if He is pleased with me or angry," because most people are not accepting that there is a God in existence, looking at them; they are denying the existence of a God and Creator. That makes Allah Almighty angry with them. Of all sins, that is the greatest one.

That will bring a huge, very terrible, terrible punishment. It is coming on men now because they are saying, "No God"; that is carrying a terrible punishment for all nations. Only those whom Allah Almighty shelters under His divine shelter may be in safety, and the others are going to be punished.

Because Allah Almighty sent His Last Prophet (s) to be a mercy for all nations, when they are rejecting him, Allah Almighty is causing people to be in two camps and to be in enmity among themselves, so that one side will fight the other, the second will fight the first, and through one to another, through that to others, He will give His punishment.

Now the whole world is working only toward that point; people are making everything ready for that punishment. Allah Almighty will give punishment to the East by the West and to the West by the East. No one can escape; no way for people except to go under the divine shelter. But those who are saying, "No God," will not be sheltered; their Lord is angry with them. Only those who are pleased with their Lord and their Lord with them will be sheltered.

Therefore, my Grandshaykh said, this terrible punishment soon to come on earth is approaching. Awliya are looking. As we know that rain is coming, they see that the divine punishment is soon coming, covering the whole earth. And Grandshaykh told about who would be under the divine shelter:

Whoever accepts his Lord, saying that there is a Lord, the Lord of the universes, in existence, and I accept Him and am His servant – whoever says this must be sheltered. Whoever says, "O my Lord, forgive me, and I am Your servant," must be sheltered.

And secondly, the one who never has the intention of harming others, even more than actually harming them – not harming anyone and never holding in his heart any bad intention towards any person. If a person keeps a bad intention in his heart towards anyone, that bad intention will 'shoot' him as a bullet would; if anyone wants evil for others, that bullet will come around and shoot him, even if he is able to take shelter under seven undergrounds.

Therefore, whoever is bold for badness, intending evil for anyone, even that intention will take him out of this life; because this is going to be the greatest war and the last war on earth, taking away so many people that you can't imagine it, a result of the divine anger because so many people and nations are thinking badness and evil for each other, individually and as a nation. Therefore, that divine punishment will take most people away. Only those will remain who never intend to harm anyone. Allah will protect them and the divine anger will be far from them.

Don't approach the area of your Lord's anger! No one will be able to protect you, no one will be able to save you. You may be the president, you may be the richest one, you may be the most learned person; no need; useless. If you do not change your heart to think good, to have good intentions for everyone, no one can save you from punishment. Like Nimrod;[69] when Allah sent against him an army from among His armies, a mosquito army, he escaped, but a crippled, missing-legged mosquito ran after him and got inside, going from there to his brain and eating it. No one can escape. Yes, Allah Almighty is making people to be afraid!

Therefore, we are asking forgiveness from our Lord because we are doing too much harm, and it is no good. We are believers. We must think goodness, we must have good intentions. That makes our Lord pleased with us. ▲

---

[69]According to Islamic tradition, Nimrod, the infamous tyrant-king mentioned in 2:258, met his end, after exalting himself as a god, when a mosquito got inside his skull and tormented him to death.

26: About Envy

Give happiness to people and you will be happy. If anyone wants to be happy by himself only, he can't; he will never be happy. But if he is going to share happiness with all, he will be happy.

This is the cause of our trouble and suffering: everyone wants everything only for himself, not for others. If power, he wants it only for himself; if wealth, he wants it only for himself; if knowledge, he wants it only for himself; if beauty, he wants it only for himself; if intelligence, he wants it only for himself, not for any other person. Therefore, there are so many troubles for envious people. That is the worst thing for the sons of Adam, to be envious.

One day Moses (A) was going to Mount Sinai to speak with his Lord, Allah Almighty. A person, a very poor person, said to him, "O Moses, when you go to your Lord and speak with Him, please ask for something for me. I have nothing. Let Him give me something."

Moses said, "Yes, I will." Then he went, and he said, "O my Lord, my neighbor, a very poor person, is asking You to give him something. Anything You may give will be enough for him."

And God Almighty said to Moses, "I accept to give him everything, but tell him that when he is asking anything for himself, he should ask for his next-door neighbor, also. If asking for something, he must say to Me, 'O my Lord, I am asking for an ox for myself and an ox for my next-door neighbor.' Then I will give, too much. This is what I am asking from that person, My servant."

Moses (a) went back, and the man was waiting. "What news, O Moses? What does your Lord say about me?"

And Moses said, "Your Lord says, 'When you are asking something from your Lord, you must ask for your next-door neighbor as you ask for yourself.'"

Then that person was so angry. "If He is not going to give to me without giving to my next-door neighbor, I will not ask for myself, also! I am not in need."

Look! This gives so much awakening to people. Envious people, the worst people they are. He did not agree that there should be anything good for his next-door neighbor; if he had the same thing, *he* would not accept it. Therefore, our ego, our *nafs*, is asking everything only for itself, not for anyone else, asking happiness also for itself, not for anyone else, and if anyone does not ask for others, God Almighty does not give. You *must* ask. Therefore we are asking for ourselves and for everyone else, for the whole *ummah*.

Insha'allah, you will be a father sometime. You may have ten children, or twelve or fifteen. Very good. As a father, would you agree that everything should be for you when you sit down to eat – everything for you, and not to give anything to your children?

No, you would make a division. First you would give to your twelve sons and twenty daughters. Then, even if nothing remained for you, you would be pleased, also. You are going to envy your sons? Is anyone going to be envious of his or her children? Never!

Therefore, all the prophets looked upon their nations as their sons, their children. "The Children of Israel," they are saying – yes? Israel was Yaqub, (a), Jacob. Jacob looked upon all of them as his children, not envying them. But Joseph's brothers became envious;[70] among the twelve

---

[70]The story of Joseph and his brothers is told in the twelfth *surah* of the Quran, *Surah Yusuf.*

children of Israel, envy made them enemies. Look! Even between brothers, between brothers and sisters, envy destroys them. What came upon them and upon their father and upon their brother, so many sufferings – what was the reason? The reason was envy.

If a person is clean from envy, he is at the top level of humanity. His claiming humanity will never be correct until he leaves envy finally, completely; if no envy, he has perfect human nature. If anyone feels envy within himself, he must try to leave that bad characteristic; *he must try, he must train himself.*

How can we be successful? As we said now, if a person is a father, he has no envy for his children, but brothers become envious of each other. Therefore, don't be like brothers to each other. Rather, you must be like a father to his children. That is *makarim akhlaq*, the best good character.

And Allah your Lord looks at your heart. If finding envy, He says, "Go away. Dirty person – don't come to Me! Be clean and come. Am I not giving you what you ask?

"Ask from Me," He says. "I will give to you. If I give to another person, does it finish what is with Me? My treasures are never-ending. Ask! I shall give to you. Why are you envious of My servants?"

And now everyone has envy. Therefore, troubles, sufferings, fighting, wars, battles – evil, the kingdom of devils, from East to West, from North to South. Darkness is coming on the earth, such darkness that, when it is complete, it will be like the darkness of the time when the Children of Israel worshipped the Golden Calf after Moses (a) went to meet his Lord on Mount Sinai.

You know? Before Moses returned – because he stayed on Mount Sinai for forty days – they made a golden calf. Then their Lord was angry with them and ordered them to kill themselves.[71] All those who had never worshipped the golden calf were to kill the others; but those who were to be killed were their relatives – maybe their sons, maybe their fathers, maybe their brothers, maybe their mothers. Therefore, when Allah Almighty ordered that killing, a dark cloud came down; the whole of that area was like nighttime. No one knew who was killing or who was killed; both sides did not know.

That darkness came down and they were killing, up to sunset. Then Moses and Aaron tried to save them, saying, "O our Lord, the Children of Israel are going to be finished. Forgiveness! Your mercy, Your mercy!" And that dark cloud went away.

That was the time when seventy thousand of the Children of Israel who worshipped the Golden Calf were killed, finished. Now I am fearing a darkness coming on earth, covering from East to West. You are asking about a third world war. That war is coming now. That dark cloud is coming down, covering the whole world so that people do not know what they are doing. They are going to kill each other. That is the Third World War. It is written in holy books.

Of envious people, no one can stay; they will kill each other, envious people. Only those people who do not keep envy in their hearts will be in safety, and the others will go. Therefore Allah Almighty is saying, "O My servant, ask from Me. I will give to you. As I gave to that one, ask from Me and I will give to you, also. Why are you envious of him? *Ask from Me!*" But envious people are saying, "Neither for me nor for him!"

---

[71] 2:54, 7:148, 20:88.

That is the worst thing; that is the suffering of the sons of Adam in our time. Therefore, in the Holy *Injil*, the Holy Torah, the Holy Quran, the Holy Psalms *[Zabur]*, in every holy book, Allah Almighty, the Lord of the sons of Adam, is saying to His servants, "No envy, no envy! But ask everything from Me. *I* will give to you." ▲

27: keeping to our lord

The Last Prophet, Sayyidina Muhammad (s) came and gave us the last Message from his Lord Almighty, and after him no one else is coming to be a prophet. Prophethood is now complete. And Allah Almighty has also completed our religion, which is going to be for each one of the sons of Adam.

Even if time goes on – if the Day of Resurrection is far away, not coming quickly – even if it comes after 100,000 years, it doesn't matter. If the Day of Resurrection comes after millions or billions of years, no need for a new prophet. The Last Prophet, the Seal of the Prophets, beloved Muhammad (s), is the perfect one. From the beginning up to the end, even from pre-eternity up to post-eternity, he is the most perfect one among all the prophets and among all creatures.

Then that Last Prophet is addressing each one of the sons of Adam, and at every time he is showing what is the safe way to reach the right path, to reach peace, to reach satisfaction, to reach our Lord's pleasure.

He spoke thousands, perhaps millions, of *hadiths*, and all the *hadiths* of our Prophet have come to our time through the reports of trustworthy people. He is such a prophet that no other person's life is as clear as his life. It is even *impossible* for the life of any other individual from among mankind to be as clear as our Prophet's life.

He was given his name, and his greatness, also, as a good tidings for all nations, beginning with Adam up to the end. Therefore, if all the prophets, all 124,000, could have been present during his time, they would have come under the flag of Muhammad (s); no other flag for them. And on the Day of Resurrection, all people will run after his flag. We can be sufficiently proud to be of his nation; if anyone wants to be proud, he can be proud through saying, "I am from the nation of the Last Prophet, beloved Muhammad (s)."

The Prophet's traditions have come from his time up to today. The first thing that the Prophet, Sayyidina Muhammad (s), called people to do was to proclaim the truth, the eternal truth – to say *"La ilaha illa-Llah."*[72] That is the eternal truth forever, and the whole of mankind has been ordered by its Lord to proclaim that there is no deity except God Almighty.

That is the truth. Then the one who proclaims that truth must be a true person; if he is not true, he can't proclaim that truth. Truth begins by saying *"La ilaha illa-Llah"* – there is no deity but God, but Allah Almighty. That is the sign that Muhammad's *ummah* is a true one, because a person with no *iman*, no faith, will lie. *Iman* is always going to be with the truth; if we are true, that is *iman*. And we are proclaiming that eternal truth.

Therefore the Prophet (s) taught his Companions to be true ones, and everything that they heard and listened to and kept in their hearts has come to our day as traditions. And Allah Almighty is the builder of Islam on the strongest base; nothing can shake it, that structure sheltering all nations. If they are asking for a shelter here and in the Hereafter, they must come under the shelter of Islam, the structure which Allah Almighty has built for us. The ones who are running away, no one, no power, can shelter them.

O people, O believers, we are approaching the Last day, the Day of Resurrection, Judgment Day; it is approaching for us. Don't say, "There are so many thousands of years still," not paying attention to these words. You must know that at any time you may be invited to the Divine Presence. He may send His messenger to you, saying, "Give back your *amana*, your trust. The One who gave it to you is asking you to return His *amana*" – yes, at any time. Don't say, "That is only for old people. We are young people, we are

---

[72] "There is no deity except Allah."

happy now." No; at *any* time. In our day, death comes to young people more than to old people.

Therefore, we must take care for the Last Day. And before the Last Day, there are the days of suffering, the days when the signs of *Qiyamah*, the Last Day, appear. And we are living in those times.

O believers, we are in need, we are most in need now, to take a shelter. I read that people are making underground cities to build shelters from the evil that will come on them from the skies. Allah Almighty mentions, *"Yufina bi-nadhri wa yakhafuna yawman kana sharruhu mustatira,"*[73] indicating that what will come upon them from the sky will be *sharr*, evil — bombs of death, raining on them. Allah Almighty is showing and informing us.

We are in need of a shelter. But nothing in this world can be a shelter for those who do not take shelter with their Lord Almighty. It is enough for the one who believes in his Lord Almighty to take His shelter. Allah Almighty ordered His beloved Muhammad (s) to say to his people, to his *ummah* (nation), *"Ihfadh-Illah, yafadhkum,"*[74] three words only, indicating to everyone, to believers, how they may take shelter with Allah Almighty. *"Ihfadh-Illah* – O believers, keep to your Lord." And when you keep to your Lord Almighty, Allah Almighty is going to keep you.

How can we keep to our Lord? You must keep to your Lord Almighty for everything. For every order that you know, you must keep the commands that He laid down, saying, "Don't transgress this." Keep to Him, and then He will keep *you*.

When a government puts traffic lights on the roads, you are keeping *that*. We must be at least as respectful to our Lord, Allah Almighty, as we are to those governments. How can we say we are respectful servants and

---

[73]"They [the righteous] fulfill [their] vows and fear a day whose evil will be widespread." (76:7)
[74]"Keep to your Lord; then He will keep you."

obedient servants to Allah Almighty when we do not at least keep what He has forbidden?

Keep to Him in relation to every forbidden thing. When you keep that, divine protection will come upon you. If East and West send their bombs on you, you may be protected. The Prophet says, from Allah Almighty, "Keep to your Lord, through His commands. Then He is going to keep you." ▲

28: avoiding the forbidden

Every religion came to teach people how they may respect their Lord, and Sayyidina Muhammad (s) also came as the last prophet to teach all people how they may respect their Lord. And every teaching in Islam is for that purpose: to encourage people to keep respect for their Lord.

Worshipping is easy, but to keep orders when Allah Almighty prohibits us from something – *that* is important. We may pray, we may fast, we may do *Hajj*, we may give our charities, but to keep ourselves away from *harams*, prohibited things, when we are facing them – that is difficult. This holy month of Ramadan is going to teach us how we may keep ourselves when *harams* (forbidden things) face us or come at us.

You must know that even if you are able to worship your Lord Almighty with the power of 124,000 prophets, and if worshipping is put on one side of the scale on Judgment Day – if, out of respect for your Lord, you leave only one thing that is *haram*, that is more important than all worshipping. Who is able to worship as the prophets did? We can't do that. But you must think about this point.

Islam came to guide people to obedient to their Lord, obedient servants, and you must try to be for Him only, not for anyone else. And the first of those claiming to be partner to our Lord Almighty is our ego, our *nafs*, which says, "O my friend, you must obey *Me* only, not anyone else."

Our *nafs* (ego) is attracted to do *haram* things. It wants to do every action which is prohibited to you and it forces you. And you are saying, "As you like," not fighting it; you are surrendering. You are afraid of your ego, not afraid of Allah.

And Allah Almighty is looking: "At what is My servant looking?" Do you know that He is with your looking, or not? *You must know!* Allah Almighty is with us at every time, everywhere. Therefore, to turn your eyes even once away from prohibited things is more important than to bring to His Divine Presence the worshipping of all people.

The Prophet (s) says, *"Tarku dharratin min maharim-Illah afdhalu 'ind-Allah min 'ibadatin thakalain."*[75] The Prophet is not speaking on behalf of himself; he is speaking from Allah Almighty's *wahy,* revelation, heavenly speech. And he says that if a person leaves only a very, very small forbidden thing, it is more beloved, more acceptable, in the Divine Presence than the worshipping of all mankind and jinn, and add to that all the angels' worshipping.

That is Islam, that is faith, that is *iman.* We must keep it; we must try. This holy month is going to teach us how we can stop ourselves in the face of *harams.* In this country you are doing *mujahadah,* fighting with your *nafs.* But don't think that after Ramadan everything will be finished. We must take much power after Ramadan, and we must practice for that.

Now we are living in a time when Islam is only by name. "Islam" is written on our identity card; otherwise, we are keeping Islam only by form. But we are in need to keep Islam in our hearts. Hearts are the *sultan,* the ruler, of our organs. When our heart, our *sultan,* is with our Lord Almighty, every organ must obey our heart. If you are with your Lord, every part must keep its way, must be obedient to your heart. Therefore, there must be an *'alam-ilahi,* a divine flag, in our hearts, so that when *Shaytan* looks at it he runs away.

You must keep your heart, because it is only for your Lord Almighty. You must keep it for your Lord alone. ▲

---

[75]Literally, "To leave off the smallest part of what Allah has prohibited is better in the sight of Allah than the worshipping of the two species [mankind and jinn]."

29: killing is prohibited

You must not kill; you have not come for killing. If you have power to preserve life do so, because you are going to be accountable on the Last Day for anything you have killed, even a small insect. ▲

30: Respecting the personalities of others

Islam came to give people perfection, to prepare them for the Divine Presence. And Allah Almighty is teaching through His prophets and through the Last Prophet, peace be upon them all, that the sons of Adam are in need to acquire good manners from prophets.

There are good manners and, in contrast to them, bad manners. For every bad manner that we take away, a good manner comes in its place. And by himself, it is impossible for a person to acquire good manners because, if he has been living in the hands of his ego, he can't acquire good manners. He must learn good manners from the prophets and from their inheritors, *awliya*.

In Islam you cannot criticize personal features. You can't criticize someone for being a black one, a white one, a red one, a yellow one, a tall one, a small one, a fat one, a thin one; you can't criticize *that*. All the sons of Adam, in the sight of Islam, are respectable personalities; originally everyone has a respectable personality. Islam does not deal with people on the basis of their colors, their nationalities; all these distinctions are nothing in Islam. The Prophet (s) says, *"La fadla li-'arabiyin 'ala 'ajamiyin illa bi-taqwa"*[76] – you cannot give more respect to a person for being an Arab or being a Turk or being English or being Pakistani or being Ceylonese. Then which thing gives us a high position in the sight of Allah Almighty?

---

[76]"There is no superiority of an Arab over a non-Arab except through *taqwa* [mindfulness of Allah]."

He does not look at your eyes' color, at your face's color, but Allah Almighty looks at whether His servant has *taqwa*. *Taqwa* means to be more obedient and respectful to our Lord. *That* person acquires rank in the sight of Allah.

Therefore, the things which give value and honor to the sons of Adam in the Divine Presence are good manners and good character, *akhlaq hamidah*. But then there are some other characteristics which make people go down, such as bad manners. The one who has bad manners loses his value in the Divine Presence, and then he loses his respect among people, also, his reputation coming down.

But we must be careful about one point; we must speak about that. Bad manners make people lose their honor, their respect, among people. Does anyone give respect to a drunk person? No; you give respect to those people who keep respect for their Lord, and the one who has good manners is going to be respected. Therefore, whoever leaves good manners and has bad manners, you are going to be unrespectful of that person.

But you must be careful. When you look at that person, you must put down those bad manners but you must be careful about his personality. Personality is one thing and bad manners is something else.

The personalities of the sons of Adam are originally respectable, but only the bad manners which they have make people run away from them. Like your clothes – if you are wearing clean clothes, you may be honored and accepted amongst the community, but if you fall into a sewage pit and come out dirty, people will run away.

They are not running from that *person* but they are running from those dirty clothes that he is wearing. Or, we may say that people have sympathy for an ill person and look after him, and doctors particularly take so much care; for the worst illnesses they take even more care, yes? We may have tolerance, everyone has tolerance, for ill people and pity them. But we haven't enough tolerance for bad-mannered people. We are quickly angry with them, fighting with them and intending to kill, to destroy them.

It is easy to kill, to destroy. But all the prophets came to cure people of their illnesses, not only the physical body's illnesses but our egos' illnesses. And they have wide hearts, from East to West and more than East and West, so that they may carry their nations.

The prophets are carrying their nations. As far as they are sinners, every sinner has bad manners; and yet the Seal of the Prophets (s) said, *"Ummati, ummati –* O my Lord, I am asking only for my nation, my *ummah."* And he said, *"Shafa'ati li-ahli-l-kabairi min ummati*[77] – I am making intercession for my *ummah*, particularly for those who are great sinners." How much compassion he had in his heart for his nation, knowing that they are ill people and taking care of them, not saying, "May Allah put them in Hell! Let them be in Hell forever." Instead, he said, "I will enter Hell and take people out." And Allah Almighty has given him permission: "Go and take out as many as you can. I will give you as many as you are asking for."

That intercession is for all the people who have that faith, who are saying that there is a God Almighty and that Muhammad is His prophet and who are accepting all the prophets. Some of them are declaring their faith, but some others are not permitted to say it during their lives, up to its end. And even if, at the end of their lives, their tongues are not speaking but their hearts are going to the side of faith, it must be so, and Allah is looking and He forgives them, His mercy coming upon *them*, also.

Don't be worried! Our Lord is merciful, most merciful, and He says, "I am not keeping My mercy for Myself. I am not in need of My Mercy Oceans. O My servants, it is for *you!"* And you must look at the Prophet's attribute of mercy, coming from his Lord's attribute.

Every prophet has that attribute. The Christians say that Jesus Christ, out of his compassion for people, sacrificed himself. (We believe a different way; we do not believe as they believe. Allah Almighty could have sacrificed someone else for the nation of Jesus Christ or for His servants; no need to

---

[77]"My intercession is for the great sinners from among my *ummah."*

make His beloved prophet [Jesus] to be accursed. We do not accept that, nor making him say, "How can you leave me, O my Lord?"[78] No, we do not accept that.) But Christians know that prophets have compassion for all people.

The prophets and their inheritors, *awliya* are carrying in their hearts tolerance and compassion for all people, and they are looking at those people as if they are ill. But it is not an illness that we know. They are ill from their egos.

As believers, we must behave to all people with good manners as much as we are able, and we must have tolerance for bad-mannered people and must look upon them as ill people. *Don't be angry!* But we are becoming angry, and that is also from *our* bad manners.

We must be tolerant people, with every sinner, with every bad-mannered person, because originally they are respectable personalities in the Divine Presence. Therefore we must be patient with them. If your son or daughter is ill, you are patient with him or with her; you do not throw them out, no.

Therefore, the more a person improves in his spiritual life, the more you can find tolerance with him. And the more he is at the first level -which is equal to the zoo, the animal level - the more he is an angry, difficult person, while we see that good-mannered people are easy with everyone.

That is an important point to make to everyone. As much as they may be tolerant, that is the highest degree for the sons of Adam. The one who is in a narrow place[79] is not able to accept anything because his heart is narrowed, and you can't find *iman* or faith in a narrow place, because if faith goes into a heart, it makes it wider.

---

[78]Referring to the words attributed to Jesus in Matt. 27:46 and Mark 15:34, "My God, my God, why have You forsaken me?"

[79]Contracted within himself.

We have been ordered to acquire our Lord's attributes. Look at our Lord, Allah Almighty, God Almighty! We can't look at everyone's actions but Allah Almighty looks and sees everyone's every action. And He is *sabur*, patient, and He gives everything, also, even to the worst person. Allah's attributes are not like our attributes. He does not get angry. He says that He is going to be angry but it is not like our anger, no. His mercy surpasses His anger.

If our Lord's mercy did not surpass His anger, no one could be alive. Quickly one lightning bolt would come and take everything away. But Allah Almighty's mercy is endless mercy and His tolerance is endless tolerance. Look at our Lord's favors, how we are living, while in this country, every day and every night, millions of people are doing *haram*, prohibited, things. For even one of those *haram* things Allah's Throne shakes, yet look at our Lord's mercy, coming down! But *we* look at someone's bad manners and we are on fire with anger.

We must be patient. If you are angry, you must be angry with yourself, with why you are looking at people's bad manners. But if we *do* look at someone's bad manners, we must put the bad manners aside and we must hold his personality in respect.

That personality is respectable. Therefore, a person may be an unbeliever but still his personality is respectable because he is our Lord's, a work of Allah's. Allah Almighty created him. Therefore, we must be respectful of his personality and we may put his bad manners aside. If we are going to do anything for curing, we must do it on those bad manners, but we must keep respect for him, as a physician keeps respect for a sick person but cures his illness. ▲

31: BEARING with people

What is past is dead and buried, finished. If it is buried, the second day there is no need for a new burial. That took place once and has passed away. Make your way clear, not returning a second time to the same spot, making trouble: "Why did he put this? Why did he take that?" You have passed that; finished.

On our way there is always going to be something that we are not accustomed to or we are not going to like, because people are not going to be as we like, since everyone has a private orbit. And we must keep ourselves, not doing harm to anyone nor having harm come to us from anyone. Otherwise, people are always going to suffer.

Look at the skies. Millions, billions of suns, stars, galaxies are going on their orbits, none of them hitting the other, causing an accident. The divine 'traffic' makes a way for them to go. We must look at the divine traffic for everyone in our life, and we must know that everyone is going on his own orbit.

If you keep yourself from doing harm to anyone, no one can harm you. Don't fear others. If you do not do harm to anyone, restraining yourself, no one is permitted to do you harm.

Then, you may ask how people did harm to the prophets. [In reality] they never did harm to the prophets; they harmed *themselves*. Grandshaykh said that a *mumin*, a believer, is like a gigantic mountain. Do winds or storms harm it? Do snow storms demolish it? No. And *mumins* are like oceans. Even if everything from sewers runs into them, they never get dirty.

Therefore, we must bear with people. That is important in our *tariqat;* the most important thing is to bear with people. To pray, to fast, to say *dhikr,* to make *aurad*[80] – that is easy; but to bear with people when you go among them – *that* is difficult.

We must train ourselves to bear with others. Doesn't matter if sometimes we do it and sometimes we can't; this is *training.* We have not reached the level where we have passed through that atmosphere and afterwards nothing will affect our egos. ▲

---

[80]Plural of *wird,* the personal, daily *dhikr* assigned by a shaykh to his *murids.*

32: the elegant manners of a muslim

Allah Almighty says, "You must not forget people's personal ranks among themselves. That gives them honor." And the Prophet says, "You must give your respect to a person who has respect among his community."

If you are in a foreign country and people give respect to someone among themselves, you keep your respect for that person, also. He may be Christian, may be Jewish, may be from another faith. Give him respect because those people are giving respect to their respected one. Don't disrespect him. That is Islamic good manners.

Islam is so polite and elegant, so well-mannered. In London there is Big Ben. A person may stand and look at Big Ben from all directions, and from each of the four directions that you may view Big Ben, you see that it is all correct, not one side correct and another side slanted; from every side, from every direction, you see a correct building.

A Muslim must be, in the sight of people, such that from any direction which a person who possesses a natural, correct mind may look at him – looking without being jealous, without being ill-intentioned, without being his enemy – he must accept him as correct from every direction.

You are not going to be like rocks. A Muslim may be like pure water, in every situation taking its form. No difficulty for a Muslim to live anywhere without giving any harm, any trouble, to anyone. Therefore, his country is from East to West. In every place he may be acceptable.

You must be beloved people among the community. That is *real* Islam.

▲

33: the outward aspects of islam: a means, not an end

When you are occupied with outward forms, you lose the meanings. Therefore, the one who is occupied by looking at outward things, by externals, is going to lose his inner life.

Religion is not only an external structure, outward forms. Now in our time, our scholars are making Islam, making religions, only a form, and speaking on and on about those magnificent forms from the outward aspect. But they can't imagine how magnificent it is inside.

But it is so difficult to enter into it. There are guardians, asking from them an identity card and saying, "To whom do you belong? Which identity card?" If a person shows an identity card saying, "Servant to his Lord," and signed by the Prophet (s) and by his shaykh, he may enter; if he has a real identity card of being *'abd-Allah*, the servant of God Almighty, the doors will open for him to go in. But if his identity card shows, "This is a worker for devils," or "A slave of his ego," or "A slave of this life or of *dunya*," they take him away; he can't enter. Whoever is sometimes for his ego, sometimes for *Shaytan*, sometimes for *dunya*, sometimes for *hawa*, a slave to his desires, never gets in.

And it is so difficult for a person to be successful, to make himself free from the hands of his ego and from the hands of *dunya* or from the hands of *Shaytan*. Therefore, we must consider what is in Islam. We must look at that magnificent structure, the edifice of Islam, to see what is in it and what it is for.

For what is Islam, for what purpose? What is the main goal of Islam, of *iman*, of praying, of fasting? Are they ends in themselves? Yes, we must know.

Worships are not ends. They are not ends but rather they are the means of taking you to your Lord's Divine Presence by making you His obedient servant. To be an obedient servant takes you into His Divine Presence. ▲

34: obedience to our lord almighty

Allah Almighty orders in His Glorious Quran, "Ya ayyuha-l-ladhina aamanu, ati'u-Llaha wa ati'u-r-Rasula wa uli-l-amri minkum."[81]

We must believe in our Lord's holy verses and we must practice them. We promised that on the Day of Promises. That was the day when each one of us, the sons of Adam, from beginning to end, was in the Divine Presence with our souls. We looked at the Divine Appearance, and we listened and we understood. We were present on that day and we knew what we were saying when our Lord asked all the sons of Adam, "Am I not your Lord?"

We listened, heard, understood, and gave our answers: "Yes, You are our Lord, You are our Creator, and we, all of us, are Your servants. And we will be Your servants forever, and You will be our Lord, our Creator, to post-eternity. No one else is going to be Lord, not prophets nor *awliya* nor angels. All of us are our Lord's servants, obedient servants."

We promised Him to be His obedient servants; that was our promise. But we forgot it because it happened in the spiritual world, and then we came to our mother's' womb and then to this world, to this life. If I ask one of you, "Do you remember the time when you came from your mother's womb to this life?" you can't remember. Even if I ask, "Do you remember anything from the time when you were one year old?" no one is able to say, "I remember" – even for the age of two years. He must be a keen, clever person to whom Allah gives more light to remember when he was even

---

[81]"O you who believe, obey Allah and obey His Messenger and those in authority among you." (4:59)

three years old. Or if I ask, "What is the first thing you can remember of your life in this world?" a person would be puzzled about which event he can remember, no certainty for him to say what is the first event that he clearly knew when he was three years old.

We are coming to this life and we are forgetting. What about the fact that our souls were in that Divine Presence – who can remember? Therefore Allah Almighty sent prophets, one after the other. The first man was also the first prophet, Sayyidina Adam, peace be upon him and upon all of them up to the last one, Sayyidina Muhammad (s), the Seal of the Prophets. One hundred and twenty-four thousand prophets came to guide us: "O sons of Adam, you gave your promise to your Lord to be His obedient servants and you must practice that," because we are not angels (if we were angels, no trouble for us to be obedient servants). But Allah Almighty is trying us, testing His servants, to see who is correct, who is right and who is sincere, who is keeping his promises.

Now, the sons of Adam have been given an ego, *nafs*, which no angels nor anyone else has been given. *Nafs* has been given to the sons of Adam because they are deputies of the Lord; they have been created to be deputies for our Creator, Allah Almighty. Therefore we have been created differently from angels. We have been given an ego to be like a horse for us to ride on and to return to our Lord's Divine Presence, because all the sons of Adam are invited by their Lord to come and look and be in His Divine Presence. Therefore, we have been given honor above the honors of all creation, and we are carrying more responsibilities than anyone. Allah Almighty offered our responsibility to the earth and to the heavens, offering it to the gigantic mountains. They said, "O our Lord, forgive us. We can't carry it." But you, sons of Adam, *you* are carrying it; you said that you could carry it.[82]

Therefore, we must think about ourselves. We are living in a time, the twentieth century, when everything is making man *not* to think; that is the

---

[82]Referring to 33:72.

illness of the twentieth century, soon to be the twenty-first century. This illness is that there is no time for the sons of Adam to sit down and think about anything. But we *must* think about ourselves more than we think about this life because we are passing through this life; we are not staying, remaining, for this life. Like a river, coming from one side and going from the other side, man, like rivers, runs away. You must think about yourself; you must keep a time each day, even for a few minutes, to think about yourself and about your future after this life, after death.

It is impossible for different people in different times to agree on one opinion. You must think about that point, also, because from the first prophet, who lived when the sons of Adam were beginning to live on this earth, up to the end, up to the Seal of the Prophets, it is impossible for 124,000 people to agree on the same point, all saying, "O people, take your care. We are warning you. *Caution!* There is death, there is after-death. There is a life after this life. It is going to be eternal."

If they were liars – *hasha*, never! – liars cannot agree, all liars, each time. But they are all agreeing on the same points: *"Amantu bil-Lahi wa malaikatihi wa rusulihi wa Yaumi-l-Akhir.'*[83] Concerning eternal life, all the prophets said the same. How can it be?

Therefore, we must think about this, we must know what this life is. Each day we are seeing people going away, dying. We see some person today; tomorrow we do not see him. We must think about the fact that death is coming for us – a trip, a journey from here. We take them underground.

Therefore, to think is one of the most important worships in Islam because you may correct your steps by thinking. And in our time, devils have established their sovereignty from East to West, and they are not leaving people to think about themselves, making them drunk, saying,

---

[83]"I believe in Allah and His angels and His scriptures and His messengers and the Last Day," the summary of Islamic belief.

"Don't think about anything!" And we *must* think about ourselves, we *must* think about our egos.

All the prophets came from the Divine Presence. They brought us something from the heavens and they said, "We are inviters. We are inviting you to your Lord. O people, take your care! You have been invited to return to your Lord's Divine Presence."

As you were formerly in the Divine Presence, now you are going to return to your Lord's Presence. And you must think, "*How* am I going to return? I gave my promise to my Lord to be an obedient servant to Him, but I was really an obedient servant to my ego, to my *nafs*. How am I going to meet my Lord Almighty if I am the servant of devils or I am the servant of my *nafs* or I am the slave of *dunya*? *How am I going to meet Him?*" You must think about that. ▲

35: being present with your lord

Each day, Allah is sending a new provision for His servants, and something new is also coming for our souls each day. When Grandshaykh finishes, I finish; when there is nothing more with the Prophet (s), then Grandshaykh stops; and if what is with Allah Almighty is finished, then the Prophet stops and Grandshaykh also stops. But Allah Almighty never stops, never ends. Therefore, each day new words are coming. Only we must deserve more, to be worthy of new ones. We must be careful and respectful and believing so that divine favors may come upon us.

Allah Almighty is asking His servants to be good-builders, *muslihin*. He never likes evil-builders, *mufsidin*. That is the first order from God Almighty to His servants. And when Adam (a) was sent down on earth, he was sent as a messenger, as a prophet of his Lord, and his first advice to his sons was, "O my sons, be goodness-builders. You must not be evil-builders. Take your teachings from me. I tasted my Lord's punishment. Don't *you* taste that punishment!"

One hundred and twenty-four thousand prophets, peace be upon them all, just came to repeat the advice of Grandfather Adam (a). That is the main problem for the sons of Adam, and also the source of troubles and sufferings. If anyone builds evil, he must be punished, here or in the Hereafter. All suffering is to cover our badness, our sins.

Anyone who is asking for his Lord's pleasure with him must keep that advice to be goodness-builders as much as he is able. Don't say, "What can I do? I am only one drop."

Yes, that is right, but drops gather in the sky and join each other, and then they become rivers, and rivers become seas and oceans. Therefore you must know that if everyone gives one drop of that goodness-building, goodness rivers are going to run on earth. And also evil; if everyone gives one drop from himself, evil is going to run on earth like rivers. We must think about this.

Yes, Allah Almighty wants to build His sovereignty on earth, divine sovereignty, and He is calling people to help with His divine building so that everyone may take his share in that divine sovereignty. But He is also warning His servants and saying, "O My servants, from the beginning, Satan is your enemy, the first one. The most dangerous and terrible enemy to you is Satan, so you must take your care against that terrible and dangerous enemy. *Beware!* He has so many tricks and traps, thousands, for hunting you."

Satan is a man-hunter, a hunter of the sons of Adam. He does not sleep. Daytimes, nighttimes, he runs after the sons of Adam to hunt them, to take them as slaves of his sovereignty. And there are so many millions of employees of Satan's sovereignty now in our time – among every kind of people, not only among ignorant people. He is not humble enough to hunt ordinary, standard people. No, he runs after very learned people, to catch them – such high-ranking people, such rich people, such important personalities; no need for common people. If he can hunt down one top person, he can bring millions – ten million, one hundred million – into his territory, under his sovereignty, because he employs people.

We must give thought to everything. For every action, you must be present with your Lord Almighty. This action that I am going to do, is it for the advantage of Satan or for the advantage of my Lord? Is it for my Lord or for my enemy? Am I working for my Lord or am I working for my enemy, Satan?

You must think about that. Then Allah Almighty will correct your steps, correct your actions. If a person, before doing anything, is able to think about his action, he is never going to be wrong, to be mistaken. And that is our error: we are doing something but are not thinking.

There are two powers now on earth, the power of Allah Almighty, who is asking His servants to be with Him, and the other, *Shaytan*, who has been given permission [to try to lead mankind astray], and who has so many traps and tricks. *Be careful about everything!*

Now, this is something well-known; anyone may understand it. But we are asking for practice; we are in need of practicing what we know. That is important. You may learn so much, but if not practicing, it means nothing. Therefore, once when the Prophet (s) was asked, "What is the best of works?" he replied, *"Al-'ilmu bil-Lah*, the knowledge of Allah."

This is an ocean; this is the true answer of every religion, it is a true answer of every prophet. No one may be able to suggest, after that reply, any more important or better work. That is an ocean for the sons of Adam to know and to practice: *"Al-'ilmu bil-Lah*, the knowledge of Allah."

What is this? They asked him about works, about deeds, but he replied, "Knowledge. The most important work is the knowledge of Allah." He means to say, "O doers, O workers" – *an important meaning* – "O workers, when you are working, be with your Lord, Allah Almighty." That is the meaning.

For every action that you are doing, for every work that you are working – *every work* – you must know that Allah Almighty is with you. *That is your knowledge.* You must know that I am working with my Lord. I am not alone; I am with my Lord. And I am nothing, only something with my Lord. I am looking with my Lord, I am speaking with my Lord, I am hearing with my Lord, I am thinking with my Lord, I am taking with my Lord, I am doing with my Lord, I am walking with my Lord. *I am with my Lord.*

That is *al-'ilmu bil-Lah*. You must consider, you must reflect, that in every action, you are with your Lord. Then your action is going to be excellent, your action is going to be the best. Yes – in front of your director you are doing everything well; when he looks at you, you are trying to do it the best. And when you see that Allah Almighty is with you, you must do it the best.

You must know that in everything, your Lord, Allah Almighty, is with you; you are not alone. *"Inna Rabbaka la-bil-mirsad"*[84] – Allah Almighty is looking at you. *"Fa-innaka bi-a'yunina"*[85] What does it mean? If at any time He cuts off His watching you, you will be finished, disappear. The whole universe will disappear; if, in the smallest unit of time, Allah Almighty is not watching over it, the whole universe will disappear – yes.

Therefore, this is an important *hadith*. What is the best work? It is to know Allah: that He is with you when you are looking, when you are speaking, when you are listening, when you are thinking your thoughts – throughout your heart, throughout your body, throughout every cell, looking at the cells, making them work.

If you leave off this, another enemy will come upon you. Yes; if you do not take care about your Lord, then punishment will come upon you. Therefore, *muraqabah*, meditation, is necessary.

We are in need, in our time, of a new method of working. We are always looking around, making our hearts to be absent. We must try to be with our Lord; we must practice that. That is the "best work". Therefore, *Shaytan* fights for those people who ponder or meditate upon their Lord in their hearts.

You may practice with your heart, not by looking around at anything you may be able to see – no. When you take back every power that you have sent around yourself, gathering them all into your heart and saying, "*Allah bus* – only Allah and nothing else," at that time you may find the way for the best works.

---

[84]"Indeed, your Lord is in observation." (89:14)

[85]"For indeed, you are in Our eyes [i.e., sight]." (52:48)

You may remember, you may think about this, and it will give you power to be with your Lord Almighty. We must do this; everyone must do this, because it is the way to salvation for the sons of Adam.

I am wondering about this word, "salvation". There is the Salvation Army. Yes, we must be from the salvation army against devils. They are very weak people, a very weak army, in the face of those satanic armies, so weak, the Salvation Army, but we must support the salvation army against *Shaytan* and his armies. As much as we are supporting this salvation army, our Lord will support us.

Don't be worried! It doesn't matter that we are only one or two hundred people or less. When we intend to support goodness on earth, our Supporter is our Lord Almighty. We are not worried about armies; all armies are nothing. If there is no support for them, they can't do anything.

You must remember your Lord's power, your Lord's endless power. Allah Almighty destroyed Nimrod's armies by mosquitoes, and Abraham was only one person. There were no armies with him, and the whole area was under Nimrod's power. Allah Almighty destroyed the sovereignty of Nimrod and He can destroy the sovereignty of Satan now, also. *You must be with your Lord always.* ▲

36: BECOMING the FRIENÐ of GOÐ

We are now going to speak on some wisdoms that have been granted to *awliya*, and, through *awliya*, we know and speak. And we are asking our Lord to make us walk on those paths that wisdoms are showing to us.

Allah Dost. *"Dost"* is Persian; it means "Friend". The Friend is Allah Almighty. If you are asking for a friend, you must take your Lord, Allah Almighty, as a friend.

Allah Almighty sent, from the beginning up to the end, 124,000 prophets. All of them were friends of Allah Almighty. He sent His friends – for what?

The purpose of prophethood: we are speaking now about that wisdom. To make people friends to Allah; all the prophets came to make the sons of Adam friends to their Lord. That is the main purpose, that He might become a friend to us. And the Seal of the Prophets (s) became His friend and also beloved. Even more than friend, our Prophet Muhammad (s) is our Lord's *habib*, beloved one.

When we know this, we must try to be Allah Almighty's friend. That is the most important, the highest honor, for anyone – to be the friend of Allah Almighty. Now, you may say that to be a friend to Allah Almighty would be very easy if you had no ego; if no *nafs*, it would be so easy. But our enemies are cutting the way, so that it is so difficult to be the friend of Allah Almighty.

Therefore, firstly, you are going to be a friend to everyone, beginning with the sons of Adam. Allah Almighty will never accept you as a friend of

His if you are not going to be the friend of His servants. And that is a difficult thing.

It is not easy to be a friend to everyone. Yes, it might be easy to be a friend if you had no ego. But your ego claims, not to be your friend but it claims to be your Lord or your king or your governor or your boss or your patron. It does not accept you as its friend but demands to be over you and you to be a servant to it.

The clearest characteristic of our ego is to be proud. No one may be on the same level with it; no, it does not accept that, saying, "I am the first. No one is going to be first except me." Therefore, we need training so that we may take away that pride from ourselves. If you do not take away pride from yourself, you *can't* be a friend to everyone.

Therefore Allah Almighty orders His servants, when they meet each other, to give salutation, saying, *"As-salamu 'alaikum,"*[86] and the Prophet (s) says, also, that whoever begins the greeting is the better of the two. Why? Because when you say *"As-salamu 'alaikum"* to a person, you are taking away pride from yourself. You are sufficiently humble to greet him, to give him honor, while your ego is asking to have honor for itself only. That is the divine teaching to take away pride from us so that we may look at the person whom we greet as being more than ourselves. And you reply, *"Wa 'alaikum as-salam."* Even if you are a king, even if you are a *sultan*, even if you are a learned person, a shaykh, you are also coming down from your high position and saying *"Wa 'alaikum as-salam."*

Allah is teaching His people to be humble. If you do not know how to be humble, you can't be a worshipper. You must know that you are a servant. Even though you may be a *sultan*, you may be a king, you may be an emperor, you may be a prophet, you may be a *wali*, originally you are a servant.

---

[86]This age-old Islamic greeting, meaning "Peace be upon you," goes back, according to tradition, to Adam's greeting to the angels in Paradise at Allah's command, to which the angels responded, *"Wa 'alaikum as-salam,* upon you be peace."

Don't be cheated by the various ranks that you may be given during this life, or if you are sitting on a throne or a high place; no. Originally we are servants of our Lord Almighty. I heard from our Grandshaykh, just as if I were hearing it now, that on the Day of Promises, when Allah Almighty called all the souls of mankind to a general meeting of the sons of Adam in the Divine Presence and asked, "Am I not your Lord?" Allah Almighty named everyone with seven names. In the Divine Presence everyone has seven names, and the first one is *'abd-Allah – 'abdullah*, the servant of God Almighty. You can't take that away.

You are originally a servant to your Lord; yes. All the prophets came to teach people, to make them remember that they are servants to Allah Almighty. Then Allah Almighty is giving us the honor of being His friends, also; the way is open for all servants to be friends to their Lord. And the most important teaching to take away pride from our egos, to make us humble, is to know that you are a servant. If anyone comes to the Divine Presence with pride, he and Satan are going to be at the same level; no intercession for that person because he is the inheritor of Satan. Satan was thrown out because of his pride, and whoever has pride is at the same level, in the same station, as Satan.

That is the teaching of Islam, and it is the teaching of all the prophets and finally of the Seal of the Prophets, beloved Muhammad (s). Every religion teaches people how they may be humble servants to their Lord Almighty. But in our time there is a wrong understanding among people, particularly among Muslims, and especially those Muslims who are living in Western countries. They are more proud than other Muslims, and pride is forbidden to everyone, particularly to Muslims.

Satan is always running after Muslims, or after believers. He has left the unbelievers and has nothing to do with them because they are already following him as he commands; no worry concerning them for Satan. But he is always running after believers to take them away from faith, from beliefs, from their Lord, and running after worshippers to make them leave worship and be his servants, not our Lord's servants. And when he runs after Muslims and they do not listen to him, then he comes at them from another way.

Look – these are important wisdoms that we must know! He comes from another way. When he comes from the left side, no one gives him any importance or face. Then he comes from the right side, comes and says, "Oh, you are Shaykh ʿUmar, an important person!" "Oh, Kamal! You are a very good Muslim person." "Oh, Fayyiz, you are a shaykh, an important person," coming in this way and saying something good about us that our egos like. If anyone makes a high rank for our egos, they become like this, like a turkey. You know a turkey? Comes like this, sometimes looking at himself, preening; to be proud among the hens, he goes like this.

Satan has a long elephant trunk. If you are *ghafil,* heedless, he puts it into your heart and blows. Then you are going to be bigger than your capacity. Little by little you will fill the whole world, even the whole universe: you are a worshipper, you are an obedient servant, you fast, you pray, you are a Muslim, you are a believer. He comes and says to you, "You are a doctor (we forgot to mention doctors), a Doctor of *Shariʿah,* you are a big *ʿalim,* a learned person," and as we learn more, we grow bigger, becoming like a balloon. And yet our Prophet (s) came, saying, "I sit as slaves sit and I eat as slaves eat," teaching us humbleness.

Every knowledge that we gain must take away something from our ego so that nothing remains with us, so that we become like dust, but instead, we are using our knowledge and our worshipping as the means of being proud. That is an illness of our egos in our time. Satan comes from that side, saying, "You are a learned person, you are a worshipper, you are a good servant," making us proud, while all the prophets came to teach us to be humble. As we are trying to be *something,* they are calling to us, *"Be nothing."* But our egos are never going to be satisfied to be nothing, never. They want to be *something,* and in our time everyone is happy when he is going to be *something.* "Who is that person?" "That is such-and-such. He is important!"

Everyone makes some rank, some status, for himself so that there can be a rank, a position, also for him among people. But the *Shari'ah* came to make us be nothing. If you are *something*, you can't enter the Divine Presence with *something*. Therefore, Allah Almighty call- ed to Moses (a), when he came to Mount Sinai, saying, *"Fakhla' na'laik,*[87] take off your shoes."

You understand? That word is addressed to everyone who takes something with him. "Take it off," Allah Almighty says. "You must be satisfied to be *nothing*." When you come and say, "I am nothing," then He gives to you. If you say, "I am something," He leaves you with yourself to be "something".

We are trying to be nothing, but people are asking to be something – and then, after being something, they are asking to be *the whole thing*. Pride, to be proud – it is a worm, eating up our faith. Some years ago, there was a worm in England eating up trees, gigantic trees coming down – a very small worm. That pride is like such a worm, eating away our faith.

For what are we saying this? If you are going to be Allah Almighty's friend, you must be a friend to everyone, and you can't be a friend to everyone if you are proud. And we want to take that pride from ourselves. Then we can be friends to everyone – to *everyone*.

In England, people are friends to animals more than to people; yes. But they are stepping on the wrong place. First you must be a friend to every person and then, at the second step, it is all right to be a friend to animals. And animals are going to be friends to you by the order of their Lord Almighty.

In the past, Grandshaykh would order his *murids* into *khalwah*, seclusion, and to test whether they were all right or not, he would say to them, "Go out now." When a *disciple* went out, if birds came to him, if hens and turkeys and geese ran after him, he was all right; he was a friend of his

---

[87]20:12.

Lord, and every animal would run after him, looking at him as our Lord's friend. Therefore, the first step which is important is to be a friend to everyone. Then you may be the friend of animals if they understand about you.

Rabi'a al-Adawiyah,[88] the famous lady saint of Islam, was sitting in the desert making *dhikr*, and geese were sitting with her. Once Hasan al-Basri, may Allah bless him, came and saw that geese were sitting around Rabi'ah. When they saw him, they ran away.

"O Rabi'a, why are they running away?" he asked.

"Perhaps they can smell that you eat from their flesh," she said.

That is divine familiarity, friendship. If you are in friendship with Allah Almighty, animals will come to you. But the first step is that you must be a friend of your Lord's servants.

There are two kinds of servants. One of them accepts – accepts that he is a servant. Some others run away, not saying, "We are servants," even though they *are* servants. You must consider both kinds as your Lord's servants, and you must train yourself to be a servant to every servant of your Lord who is doing His service, whether he is worshipping or not.

That is an important point. If we know it, peace and pleasure and mercy will cover the whole world. As long as we do not know this wisdom, fighting will continue, wars will continue, people will destroy each other, and enmity, endless enmity, will exist among people. ▲

---

[88]Rabi'a Basri.

37: helping others

We have four seasons in our lives. First, springtime comes; second, summertime; the third season, autumn; the fourth one, winter. So many people may go during springtime, at the beginning or the middle or the end. Some people come to summertime, also; at the beginning, the middle, or the end of summer, they may go. Some people come to autumn; yes.

Some people go away at the beginning or middle or end of autumn. Then, a very few people come to wintertime. In wintertime, some people are going at the beginning, some people are going in the middle, but most must go at the end of wintertime. This is our life.

Now, for the whole world, also, there is a period with four seasons. Springtime went away. Summertime went away. Autumn time went away. We are now in the final season, the winter season, of the whole world.

Allah Almighty, the Creator, created the universe, and in all the universe He prepared this planet to be for the sons of Adam. No one can look and see any other planet on which there are sons of Adam or any other creatures, no; they are only imagining something. He prepared this planet, *Dunya*, this world, to be the residence, the landing-place, for the sons of Adam, and we believe that Adam and Eve landed on this planet from Heaven. And each one of the People of the Book[89] believes that Adam and Eve came from Heaven and landed on this earth.

---

[89]*Ahl al-Kitab* -- that is, Jews and Christians, whose religions originated in divine revelation.

The first man, Adam; the first prophet, Adam. The last prophet is Muhammad (s), and between the first and the last, Allah Almighty sent 124,000 prophets. It means that when the last one has come, we are now in wintertime. That period is going to be ended because for every beginning there must be an ending.

Allah Almighty made a beginning for the sons of Adam on earth and He is also going to make an end for the sons of Adam on earth. Therefore, we know, according to holy books and in particular the last holy book, the Holy Quran, that we are in the final part of this world's life. And we are, step by step, approaching the last station.

Now, what is important for believers – for anyone who believes in the Last Day, for anyone who believes in the Last Judgment, for anyone who believes that for every action there must be an effect on its doer in the next life and that we are going to see the effects of our actions on Judgment Day? We believe that we will see every action, whether of goodness or of badness, and, whether of goodness or of badness, we will be pleased or we will be sorry about that action. *Who is going to be pleased with his action?*

All the prophets came to teach us what thing makes a person pleased on Judgment Day, so that we may keep that way and that action, and what makes people weep, to ask to return again to this life – what actions make their doers sorry. All the prophets just came to give that knowledge, to teach people concerning that point, not to classify people – those are Christians, those Jews, those Muslims, those another kind; no. Titles are not important but actions are important.

But we are not understanding; even in this time, ignorance is common for people. They think that titles give benefit in the Divine Presence on the Day of Judgment. *No benefit!* Your title can continue only up to the time that your coffin is brought to a holy place – to a mosque, to a church, to a synagogue; up to there your title goes on, but after that it stops. So we must ask for titles which can continue with us up to the Day of Judgment and give us benefit on that Day.

Therefore, don't be cheated by titles. All titles are going to be nothing except that title which your Lord gives you – not from people, not from this world; no. But your Lord's titles are not like a medal, put here or here, on your shoulders or on your chest. He gives you from *His* titles, and they are on your heart and on your face.

Sometimes we shine. Therefore, Christians make pictures of prophets or of saints, and they put lights around their faces, haloes, so that anyone who is not blind may see their light. But a blind person cannot see even the sun in the daytime; he cannot look at a face and see its light.

Therefore, people are of two kinds or groups. One group may see with these eyes, and the others see with their hearts. Therefore, for prophets, who are the best quality among the sons of Adam, most people in their times rejected them, saying, "You are the worst people." Every prophet was attacked by devils, by evil people. Prophets are the best quality; precious diamonds they are, but so many people who looked only with these eyes said such things. But those people who looked at them with their hearts' eyes said, "Oh-h! You are beloved people of our Lord," accepting and believing in them.

Yes, all the sons of Adam are in two groups, in two camps. In one camp are believers, in the other unbelievers. Unbelievers are blind people, never seeing light; for divine lights, they are unable to see. And prophets and saints have lights from Allah Almighty. What do they say to us about what it is important for people to do? Which action gives us benefit on the Day of Judgment? We must know it.

There are so many actions which give us benefit, but some things we may do give benefit to ourselves and some give benefit to others. One of these belongs to you, remains for you, and some actions benefit other people. Now we will look at which of them is more lovely to our Lord: to work for yourself or to work for others.

Yes, it is good to do good actions for yourself, actions whose benefit returns to you, but actions which give benefit to others – those are excellent and more lovely to our Lord. You must know this.

To do charities for others, to think about others, that is excellent. Therefore, all the prophets came to give charities or to teach people to give benefit to others, and they bore every kind of suffering from people but yet they gave. Every saint, every *wali*, thinks of giving benefit to others and forgets himself; their pleasure is in giving benefit to others, not to themselves. They may give to themselves. That is good, but the best and most excellent thing is to give your benefit to others.

Therefore, it is our beloved Prophet's most high attribute, most important and lovely attribute in the Divine Presence, that he never asked anything for himself; he never said, "For me." Each time he would say, *"Ummati, ummati* – for my nation, for my nation, O my Lord," never asking anything for himself but only asking for his nation. That is the highest point that gives honor to Muhammad (s), the Seal of the Prophets, in the Divine Presence. And we must follow his way and must prefer others' benefit over our own.

Don't take everything for yourself instead of giving! Inasmuch as people in our time want everything for themselves, crises are mounting, not decreasing. Everyone wants everything for himself. Even if someone is given the whole world with its treasures, he asks for more, not saying "Enough" – no. For everything that a person may take pleasure from, he says, "That should be for me. That for me, this for me," as a little child, when you take his hand and go into a toy shop, looks and keeps this all for *me*.

We are little boys. We want the whole world to be for ourselves, not for anyone else. That is the reason for the crises and sufferings of people in the twentieth century, nothing else. We have left the teachings of the prophets, the ways of the saints; finished. It is impossible for such people to save themselves from suffering.

However much Allah Almighty pours His favors upon them, they are not satisfied. Yes; we have everything but still we are not satisfied. We must follow the ways of the prophets and particularly the way of the Last Prophet (s). It is enough for all nations to make him their guide only because of one single matter: that he said, "For my nation," and never said, "For myself"; that he always said, "For others, for everyone," but never, "For me."

That is enough for all the world, for anyone who may think about the Last Prophet, the Seal of the Prophets, (s), indicating that he is on the right path, he is on the truth. No need of anything else, to ask for anything more. If a person says such a thing and guides people according to it, for what are we asking anything else? It is enough. He is advising us, "O people, everyone works for others. Then this world will be Paradise" – yes! But everyone is asking only for his own pleasure, and his pleasure and his desires are unlimited; you can't find any limit to stop them.

Therefore Allah Almighty likes the one who works for others, who gives benefit to others, who gives charity to others. Then Allah Almighty says, "The one who works for My servants, for the sake of My servants, I am his Guarantor, and, more than Guarantor, I am also his Supporter." Not good? What are you asking for more than this? *Allah Almighty is going to be your Guarantor and Supporter! Who can bring you down?*

But we do not believe; we only read but we do not believe. Our beliefs are here [on our tongues], not coming here [in our hearts]. *That* is the reason for the illness of the twentieth century's people.

Everyone is making claims. Christians are claiming, "We believe," doing like this to Jesus Christ, to Mary, to the saints, coming like this on their knees. Only here [on the tongue]. Muslims, also; most of them are talking from here, not from *here*. Every kind of people – they are reading, they are saying good words, but from their hearts they are not doing anything; yes.

If they say, "You are wrong, shaykh, you are wrong" – if I am wrong, then where is your Lord's support for the Muslim world, or where is your Lord's support for the Christian world? Half of them are unbelievers! *Where is it? Give me a proof.* "Bring your evidence,"[90] Allah Almighty says. There is evidence? No!

"Wa Allahu fi 'auna-l-'abd ma dama-l-'abdu fi 'auni akhihi"[91] this saying is from the Prophet, the Seal of the Prophets (s). "As much as a servant supports his brother, Allah is going to be his Supporter, his Helper, his Guarantor." But, although this is an Arabic saying, Arabs do not understand it; a Turkish saying, but Turks do not understand; an English saying, but English-speaking people do not understand it. What are we saying? Which language must we speak?

Now there is an answer, but I am listening to it, hearing it, from your hearts; I am not hearing it from your tongues. Your hearts are replying to me, saying, "Speak to us in the language of your heart. If anyone speaks to us in his heart's language, we may understand. We do not understand even Arabic or Turkish or English. We can understand only one language. The one who speaks from his heart we can understand."

Yes, that is true, because what comes from the heart goes into the heart, but when it comes from here [lips], it goes from here, quickly, like the wind. Therefore, 124,000 *sahabah*, followers of the Prophet, peace be them and upon him, did not know any language except Arabic, but, in a quarter of a century, during the passing of only twenty-five years after *Hijrah*, the Prophet's Migration, Islam spread from East to West.

---

[90] 2:111; 21:24; 27:64; 28:75.

[91] "And Allah is in support of the servant as long as the servant is in support of his brother."

Now there are in the Muslim world perhaps fifty million scholars – yes, knowing so many languages. But what are we *doing?* Our beliefs are only remaining *here* [on our tongues]. And Christians, also – perhaps one hundred million scholars, people of religion. What are they doing?

I am asking, I am demanding from all, from every religious person, "What are you doing? Everyone is speaking from here – oh, so much! – but people have so many illnesses in their hearts. The whole world is becoming darker every day. *Where is your power to take away darkness from the earth, to give light to hearts? Where are you? What are you doing?"*

I have rights to ask. I am nothing, I am not claiming to be anything – nothing, no title. But all of them have titles, yes. I haven't any title. I am asking to be a very weak, humble servant, if my Lord accepts me. That is the ultimate, the highest degree for me; the highest, final pleasure for me is to be accepted by my Lord as His very, very humble servant, if He accepts me. Yes, that is honor, that is my aim, nothing related to all the world; finished. I am going; what am I asking from this world? We are in wintertime with Mr. Stanley.

By which language did the *sahabah*, the followers of Muhammad (s), address people, speaking to them, giving faith, beliefs, to those strange people? From East to West, so many nations came into Islam, including us, also, Turks; including non-Arabs – Irani people, Pakistani people, Bukhara people, Afghani people, so many nations with different languages. *How did they explain?*

They spoke from their hearts, that is all. Therefore it is important to return to the language of hearts because everyone understands the heart, but not everyone understands *this* language. Therefore, it is a more important thing for understanding.

We *must* understand when I am telling this *hadith* of the Prophet (s): *"Wa Allah fi 'auna-l-'abd ma dama-l-'abdu fi 'auni akhihi."* Someone may say, "There is an English translation, there is a Turkish translation, a French translation," but anyone may read but may never practice, never understand.

You *must* understand! Don't ask help from him. You give your help *to* him, then take your support from your Lord, the greatest Guarantor, Guarantor and Supporter, more than the United States, more than the British government. How is it that Allah Almighty is saying to you that I am going to be your Guarantor and your Supporter but you are not listening, you are not acting, you are not practicing? What is our Islam, what are our beliefs? You *must* think about that point.

Therefore, the Prophet's main and most lovely attribute was to give everything, every help, every support, to his nation and never, never to think about himself. Why would he think about himself? Allah was the Guarantor for him! Guarantor enough, or not? Yes, because the Prophet stood up amongst a nation of people who worshipped idols, 360 idols. Without anyone being at his side, he stood up amongst those people and said, *"La ilaha illa-Llah,* there is no deity except God."

Who supported him? Now there are more than one billion people saying *"La ilaha illa-Llah."* Did the Prophet give money to bring those people into Islam? Who was his supporter? God Almighty! You must believe; *you must believe in God Almighty.*

When you speak from your heart, you may speak in any language; doesn't matter. The Holy Quran, the Glorious Quran, was written in Arabic in its original words, but you may listen to it from the English translation or from the Turkish one or the French one, if not understanding Arabic. People may not understand Arabic but the Holy Quran, the Glorious Quran, carries them. Their souls understand. Their minds may not, but their souls may understand, may be pleased, filled with enjoyment, when they listen.

Do *you* understand Arabic? No. Then how can you listen? That is something miraculous; the Holy Quran is miraculous. You can't find that with the Old Testament or the New Testament. They may read it in English or in Greek, but those who are listening do not take any pleasure in their hearts because they have lost the originals of the Old and New Testaments, and they have also lost the holy words and the holy language that came through Gabriel (a).[92] But for the Holy Quran, Gabriel took whatever Allah Almighty said in His divine speech and brought it to the Prophet, beloved Muhammad (s), and the Prophet recited it. The original has never changed. *Therefore* it goes into hearts.

The *sahabah*, the noble Companions, the followers of the Prophet (s), knew no language but Arabic. Then they went from *Hijaz* in western Arabia to the East and the West, and they encountered various nations with many languages. The *sahabah* brought Islam to strange peoples without knowing any language of the Far East or the Far West, so many languages – you can imagine. Look at India; only there, there are forty different languages. How did the *sahabah* explain to those people what Islam is, what faith is, what *ikhlas*, sincerity, is? How did they take the message of Islam from East to West? You must think about that!

They spoke by means of their *ikhlas*, their sincerity. Therefore, it went quickly from their hearts to people's hearts so that they became Muslims, Islam covering from East to West. If they had been like ourselves, not knowing English, they would have sat like statues. What would you say to people? And even if you said something, it would go in one ear and out the other, also.

They spoke with their hearts. The *sahabah* would recite the Holy Quran and the people who heard them would say, *"Amantu bil-Lah*, we believe in your God, we believe in your Prophet. We are saying *'La ilaha illa-Llah'* – easy for us!"

---

[92]That is, in conveying God's revelations to the earlier prophets.

The *sahabah's* hearts spoke, and they gave *kalimatu-l-ikhlas*, the word of sincerity, *"La ilaha illa-Llah."* For the one who says that truly, Allah Almighty opens in his heart an ocean from those Oceans. Now, therefore, when I am speaking to our Turkish sisters and brothers in their language, it doesn't matter; you are going to enjoy it a little. And they are also looking now when I am speaking English. So many sisters do not understand too much English, but they are also enjoying it. ▲

38: SINCERITY IS ESSENTIAL FOR FAITH

Today we are in the fifteenth century of *Hijrah*, which honors the last prophet of the world and of the universe, Sayyidina Muhammad (s), the Seal of the Prophets.

He came and carried out his trust; he gave us what he brought from his Lord perfectly. Now we are far from his time, fifteen hundred years, and, as he said, we are so many people now, more than one billion people of Islam, Muslims. *Wa lakinnakum ghutha.*[93]

We are Muslims, but in our time we have lost one thing – the most important thing in Islam, that one thing; while I was praying it came to my heart to say this. And since we have lost that most important thing in Islam, we are like a piece of rubbish – useless. What is that thing? I am listening now to what is coming to my heart.

That most important thing is *ikhlas*, sincerity. Finished, and if *ikhlas* is finished, *everything* is going to be rubbish. The most important thing for Muslims – that is *ikhlas*. *"Mukhlisina lahu din"*[94] – Allah Almighty is asking us to be *mukhlis* to Him, to be sincere. *"Ala lil-Lahi-d-dinu-l-khalis?"*[95] – Allah Almighty is asking for *ikhlas*, for sincerity. As we have lost that, we are going after painting the outside, making a good appearance, designing, decorating the outside part. But where is the place of *ikhlas*?

---

[93]But you are weak, meager, disregarded.

[94]"With sincerity to Him in religion." (7:29; 31:32; 39:2, 11, 14; 40:14, 65; 98:5)

[95]"Unquestionably, the pure religion is for Allah [alone]." (39:3)

Here; *ikhlas*, sincerity, is in our hearts. But we we are not looking at hearts; we are looking at outward appearances. *"Halaka-l-'alimu illa-l-'amilu. Halaka-l-'amilu illa-l-mukhlisu."*[96]

Now, as Muslims, we must learn which thing we have lost and how we can recover or obtain that lost thing. *We must return to taking care of our hearts.*

The Prophet (s) took the most care of the hearts of his Companions, and his Companions were never concerned about outward things, but their entire concern was for their hearts. They were so careful to acquire *ikhlas*. The source of *ikhlas* was the Prophet (s), and they tried to take, to drink, from that source as much as they were able, and they drank.

And that source is not going to be dry. As long as the *ummah* of Muhammad (s) is in existence, that source, like a spring, is always pouring forth. But you can't find that source or spring externally; you must find it in hearts. Even one is enough for billions, because the Prophet (s) was only one and he was enough for all the Companions. And his source is not decreasing, Allah Almighty giving him as much as his nation needs.

Therefore, in our time we are in need, most in need, to look for that source, in whose heart it is flowing. We must ask, the whole *ummah* must ask. We must find it in the heart of even one person, and he is enough to give everyone's heart *ikhlas*.

Once a *sahabi*, a Companion, asked the Prophet (s), "What is *ikhlas*?" And the Prophet said, "Let me ask Jibril," the Angel Gabriel. When he asked Jibril, Jibril said, "Let me ask the angel Mika'il." When he asked Mika'il, Mika'il said, "Let me ask the angel Israfil." When he asked Israfil, he said, "Let me ask Allah Almighty"; this is mentioned by Imam Shaarani. And Allah Almighty answered, *"Ikhlas sirru min asrari.*[97] That is a secret treasure from among My treasures, and I give it to those who ask and who

---

[96]"The knowledgeable one [or scholar] will perish, excepting the one who acts on it. The one who acts on it will perish, excepting the one who is sincere."

[97]Literally, "Sincerity is a secret from among My secrets."

are trustworthy for that treasure. If anyone asks for *ikhlas*, which is from among My secret treasures, I give it to him."

We *must* ask, because without *ikhlas* we are rubbish, going directly to the dustbin. Allah Almighty is asking only for *ikhlas*, and with *ikhlas* everything is going to be all right. Without *ikhlas*, everything that you are sending to your Lord's Divine Presence is like plastic bananas, plastic grapes, plastic oranges. Who gets any benefit from plastic fruits? Even if I fill this whole place with all kinds of oranges and bananas, but plastic, and leave a person inside, saying, "Eat these and don't die," will that person live if he eats all that plastic fruit?

Therefore, you must know: if we have *ikhlas*, that sincerity, no more quarreling. We will respect each other, because every divine attribute that Muhammad (s) was given may live in our hearts by means of *ikhlas*.

There is a pond here. If no water, no fishes live in it. *Ikhlas* is like an ocean. The Prophet (s) may give us every divine attribute that he was given, but he looks at our hearts, if there is *ikhlas* there. If no *ikhlas*, finished; he will never give, because it is going to die, to dry up. Every good characteristic, good attribute, good behavior, good manner, lives with *ikhlas*. Without *ikhlas*, nothing.

We have lost it and we are in trouble. The Muslim world's peoples are fighting each other. In Islam it is not right for two people to quarrel; a *mukhlis*, sincere, person is never going to quarrel, to fight. He says, "If you are quarreling for this, O my brother, take it. You are more valuable than this, because in the sight of Allah Almighty, the value of the whole world will never be more than one wing of a mosquito."[98]

---

[98] The paraphrase of a *hadith* stating that, if in the sight of Allah, the whole world's value was equal to the wing of a mosquito.

How much will you give me if I fill up this whole place with wings of mosquitoes? How much will you pay? Nothing! A wing, *one* wing; each mosquito has four wings, but even one – the whole world's value is less than *one* wing of a mosquito! And you are going to quarrel for this low world, while the *Shari 'ah* says that *iman*, faith, means to respect what Allah Almighty respects and to disrespect what Allah Almighty makes unrespectable. *Dunya*, this world, is unrespectable in the sight of Allah, but still you are fighting, you are quarrelling, for this unrespectable thing! *Where is iman?*

Iman is with *ikhlas*, dwells with *ikhlas*. Iblis, *Shaytan*, prayed in the Seven Heavens, in each one, for 40,000 years, and each year was like 40,000 of our years; you may calculate how much that is. But all his worshipping was without *ikhlas*.

Without *ikhlas* it was rubbish, *"habaan manthura."*[99]What does it mean? Rubbish; put it there, in the dustbin. Who was more of a worshipper than *Shaytan* was among the angels? No one. But it was all lost, disappeared. No *iklhas*; if he had had *ikhlas*, he would have kept it. No *ikhlas*; gone away, *habaan manthura.*

Therefore, the most important thing for every Muslim is to look for *ikhlas*, and then everything is going to go in the right way and heavenly doors are going to open to him. When you leave this life and the angels are taking your soul towards Heaven, there are coming orders: "See if My servant has *ikhlas* or not. If he has *ikhlas*, open for him to come in. If no *ikhlas*, let him go down," and he falls down.

You must acquire *ikhlas* during this life. *Ikhlas* opens to you eternal Paradise's doors forever. On the Day of Resurrection, you will be asked about *ikhlas*. It is *qalbun salim*, a pure, sound heart, full of *ikhlas*. A little *ikhlas* is more useful to you in bringing worshipping and prayers than the value of this whole *dunya*.

---

[99]"Floating particles of dust." (25:23)

Try to do everything with *ikhlas* – to do everything for the sake of Allah Almighty, for the love of Allah Almighty, not for anything else. "For You only, O my Lord. You gave me Your divine love and I am Your obedient servant." Nothing fills his eyes except his Lord. *That* is *ikhlas*. ▲

39: concerning trustworthiness

All the prophets came to make people believe in their Lord, Allah Almighty, and without believing in prophets, you can't believe in Allah. You must believe in a *person*. Then you may believe what he says.

Therefore, it is something related to our hearts. No matter how much you may listen, if your heart does not say "Yes," there is no belief. Your heart must say, "That is true." When your heart says "Yes" to a person, if that person is *amin*, trustworthy, then your heart is opened to him and accepts what he says.

All the prophets have some perfect attributes from their Lord Almighty. One of them is to be trustworthy. This means that those who believe in their prophet, his followers, must also be trustworthy. And when you are trustworthy, people's hearts are going to accept you, are going to be pleased with you, may trust you, can trust what you say, and then you can offer your way to them.

The Seal of the Prophets, Muhammad al-Amin (s), lived among his tribe, among the Quraysh. Allah Almighty was preparing to build Islam. He sent Muhammad (s) among an ignorant tribe and he lived among them up to the age of forty years. He was well known as trustworthy. From the beginning up to the age of forty, when prophethood came to him, he was called Muhammad al-Amin, "Trustworthy Muhammad," by his people, so that there was no doubt about his call, his saying, "Come to me. Come to Allah Almighty, come to your Lord."

Therefore, throughout his whole life he was trustworthy. And his Companions were given what he transmitted to them, and therefore, in our belief, all the Companions of the Prophet, 124,000 *sahabah*, were trustworthy.

That is important to know. We know that every Companion of the Prophet (putting aside anything that happened between them; that is not for us to judge) was trustworthy. The Prophet himself was innocent, and the Companions, also, Allah put under protection from evil and from devils. All of them took that attribute from the Prophet (s); all of them were trustworthy. As he said, "My *sahabah* are like stars. Whichever of them you may follow, you will have been guided on the right path." And we are *Ahl as-Sunnah wal-Jama'ah*;[100] we are followers of the Prophet (s), and we have also been ordered by Allah Almighty to be trustworthy people. ▲

---

[100]People of the [Prophet's] *Sunnah* [Practice] and Community.

40: the importance of being humble

Up to this day, man is an unknown territory belonging to Allah Almighty, such an unknown area. The True Man is *still* undiscovered.

People are writing so many books – thousands or even millions of books have been written – about man, but still man is an unknown being in the universe, particularly to himself. Who knows about man, about mankind? His Lord, His Creator, and He gives, He opens that knowledge to His prophets. And the inheritors of the prophets, *awliya* also know something about man, about the sons of Adam.

Man has something of his Lord Almighty; he carries a light from his Lord's divine light. That is our soul. And when the Prophet (s) was asked about the soul, he replied only, "It is by the order of Allah; it is only by the command of your Lord,"[101] and gave no further description of it; because it is something like an ocean, and man brings only a little cup and says, "Put the ocean into this."

"Wa ma utitum min al-l-'ilmi illa qalila."[102] However much knowledge we may have been given, it must always be within limits; as much as we may learn, there is more than what we have learned. Therefore, you can't put any limit on knowledge.

Abu Yazid al-Bistami, that grand-*wali*, said, "When you say 'I know,' you stop. When you ask for more, you improve. Divine knowledge opens

---

[101]Referring to 17:85: "And they ask you [Muhammad] about the soul. Say: 'The soul is by the command of its Lord.'"
[102]The continuation of 17:85: "And you have not been given except a little of knowledge."

for those who ask for more, but the one who says 'I know' remains on the same level, never improving." Therefore, the one who recognizes that he is always ignorant is given more, but the one who says, "I know, I am a scholar" – he has so many degrees from Oxford University – is finished and full-up; he stays there, no improvement. Therefore, even though your capacity is always going to be within limits, you must not deny the existence of that total knowledge, claiming that it is only *I* who know it. You must leave an opportunity for *everyone's* knowledge.

Therefore, we are saying that man is still an unknown being to himself. Allah Almighty knows him because He is the Creator. I don't know about this tape recorder. Who knows about it? The one who made it, he knows best. Therefore the Creator is the one who knows man completely, and, after Him, those who have been given knowledge by their Lord, they know, also.

During the Night Journey, when the Prophet, beloved Muhammad (s), ascended to the Seven Heavens in the Divine Presence, Allah Almighty granted him so much. And He declared to His Last Prophet, within view of all the prophets, "O Muhammad, if I were to give each one of My servants the chance or opportunity or authority which I gave to Pharaoh, no one would hesitate to be a Pharoah. But I am keeping it back, I am not giving that chance to everyone."

This is the Creator's statement to the Prophet during the Night of the Ascension; *He* is saying this. Therefore, when I say that every ego is proud, it is correct: everyone's ego is as proud as it can be. If there is even one stripe here – "Oh, look at that!" and he becomes a corporal; yes. If there are stars, so much pride; if an eagle, too much; if swords, even more than this. If a crown – *oh!!!* Yes? We know about pride from ourselves. None of us can cheat the other.

Therefore, humbleness is the most lovely characteristic of people. Everyone likes humble people and everyone dislikes proud people. Even if we are proud ourselves, we never like others to be proud. Yes – we are proud on *our* level, but if anyone above our level is proud, we are not satisfied with him, saying, "He is a proud person." *You* are also proud. Therefore the Prophet (s) said, *"Ijlis kama yajlisa-l-'abd wa kul kama yakulu-l-'abd.* I sit as a slave sits and I eat as he eats because I am also a slave to my Lord." And therefore Islam just fought against slavery, Islam came to make people free.

Now we may speak of the humbleness of Abu Yazid al-Bistami. He was one of the most humble people among saints and he said, "I respected everyone. I never expected respect from anyone, but I obliged myself to give respect to everyone and I never asked anyone to give his respect to me – 'Oh, I am a shaykh, a grandshaykh; you must respect me.' It never came to my heart to expect respect from one who was a young person – 'I am an old person, an old shaykh; you must respect me.' No. I respected him and did not expect, did not wait, for anyone to respect me."

He said this, teaching his disciples that you must respect an old person or one who is elder than you, and you must respect younger people, also. And people said, "We understand that you must give respect to older people, but what about young ones?"

"O my sons," he said, "you must respect elder people because you must consider that this old person began to obey and to worship my Lord so many years ago. He has had so many years more of worshipping my Lord than me. Therefore I must keep respect for him. Then you must say to your *nafs*, because it is objecting, 'I understand about old people, but what about younger ones? I am an old person. Why should I respect young people?' – you must say to your proud ego, 'Because they are young and their books have no dirt written on them, black marks. But *you* – so much!'" Therefore you must make much of children, you must respect them.

The loveliest characteristic to our Lord is to be humble, and all prophets' teachings were for that purpose: to make our egos to be humble, to accept. *"Wa khuliqa-l-insanu dhaifa"*;[103] it means that we are weak, with no

---

[103]"And man was created weak." (4:28)

power. *"Fa-subhana-l-ladhi bi-yadihi malakutu kulli shay"*;[104] — all power is in *His* hands. We are only between two breaths. If breath does not come in, if breath does not go out, you will die, leaving your life, so weak. He who is powerful is proud; to be proud is his right, not anyone else's. We must be humble.

Every *fitnah*, every badness or evil, appears from pride. The first sin itself came from pride; *Shaytan* was so proud, and pride caused that sin. And up to the end, every sin comes from being proud, while humbleness is from Adam.

Shaytan was created from fire. Fire goes up, like this; therefore he was proud. Adam was from earth, from clay, and he signifies humbleness, earth. Therefore, *Shaytan* said, "O Allah, *You* are making me to be proud and causing me to commit that sin, causing me not to obey Your order,"[105] while Adam expressed humbleness, saying, *"Rabbana, dhalamna anfusina;*[106] — O our Lord, we have wronged ourselves." Therefore, humbleness caused Adam to return to his first station, the real Homeland, Paradise, but pride prevented *Shaytan* from returning to his Homeland once again.

QUESTION: Are we actually mistaken, Mawlana, when we identify ourselves with our egos? Are we the same? Are we the ego, or is the ego something else? We are not the ego, are we?

SHAYKH NAZIM: The ego always represents itself, and the soul is always in the background, running to represent itself, while our ego is saying, *"I am. I am Shaykh Mustafa, I am Shaykh Ibrahim."*

Although in reality the ego is our horse and we are the riders, people now are generally horses for their egos, not riding on them but carrying them instead. Yes, now everyone is keeping his horse on his shoulders instead of riding on it.

---

[104]"Then glorified be He in whose hands is the dominion of all things." (36:83)
[105]7:16 and 15:39.
[106]7:23.

There is a tale suited to this subject about Luqman al-Hakim. Who knows about Luqman? He lived in the time of Prophet David (a) – Luqman, the famous doctor, *hakim*, who had been given divine wisdoms.

One day he was riding his donkey and his son was walking beside him, going along. And some people came by, looking and saying, "*Subhanallah*, glory to Allah Almighty! That person is riding on the donkey, leaving the little boy to walk. No mercy with that person! *He* can walk while that little boy rides on the donkey."

Then Luqman said, "O my son, you come and ride on it. I may walk."

And he was walking. Then some other people came and said to each other, "*Subhanallah*, glory to Allah Almighty! No respect in our time; respect is finished. We are always complaining now that our sons don't give respect to us."

And the other person said, "Oh-h! No respect in our time. Sons don't respect their fathers. That son is riding and letting his father walk. Not proper!"

"O my son, you come and ride, also, with me." And the son and father rode on the donkey and went along.

Then some other people came and they said, "*Subhanallah*, glory to Allah! Those people – no mercy! What cruelty! One donkey, two people. That person is like a giant, like a bear, and the son, also, on one donkey! What is this cruelty?"

Then Luqman al-Hakim said, "Get down. We may walk." The two of them walked, and the donkey was too happy, running around.

Then some people from another group were looking on, saying, "What foolish people! They have a donkey but they are running after it and no one is riding it."

Yes. And we, also. Such a person is showing us wisdom: that Allah Almighty gives mankind ego, *nafs*, so that, as the Prophet said, "Your *nafs* is your mount." (The Prophet said it elegantly. Just for understanding, I am saying "donkey".)

Everyone has a "donkey". If you leave your donkey, going on alone and not *after* it, it is more clever; but we are *carrying* it as well, a heavy burden. We are saying, "What a pity! Let me carry it," and then putting the donkey on our shoulders. "Poor donkey! So you won't be tired, may I carry you?" And you are carrying it.

That is so. Therefore, every day sufferings and troubles are mounting, problems are increasing, until people throw their donkeys off their shoulders.

Now, what is the connection between this and that? Yes, you *must* understand, because when you are carrying your ego, its desires are endless, never giving you rest, always asking. You can't find any limit to make your ego be satisfied and say "Enough"; no – always asking more and more. Therefore, troubles and sufferings are increasing. But when people take their donkeys and throw them down, each one will be satisfied with everything that he has been given.

If you are given a good job, you look for another one; if you are given a good business, you ask for another. I heard a person talking about someone who has fifteen hundred shops. I was thinking about how he controls fifteen hundred shops and then that person said, "This is just a small thing! There are more than these, all around the world."

If he is given a palace and he sees that Buckingham Palace is more desirable than his palace, he asks for it. If he is given a car, it must be a Rolls Royce; if the Rolls Royce is a black one, he asks for a white one (white is better, yes?). If you are given a beauty queen, you look for another. That is an *edebsiz*, ill-mannered, *nafs*!

Therefore, you may be given everything but yet you are looking for other things. You are within limits but your desires are unlimited. A person must be foolish, absolutely foolish, to ask for unlimited things with limited power. If you are given the whole of this country, can you keep that, can you enjoy yourself? Never! Therefore, the connection between these realities is that people are carrying their egos on their shoulders; they are obedient servants to their egos and their egos' desires are unlimited. Therefore, if anyone is given the whole world, he may ask for a way to the moon, to other planets, also, to get them, never saying "Enough."

Therefore, the prophets, including the Seal of the Prophets, peace be upon them all, were always calling people to *zohd*, simplicity. The luxurious life is killing people, destroying everything, going on without limits. Therefore, you must agree to a simple life, as much as you are able. Then you will be in rest and peace and satisfaction. Otherwise you will go into Suffering Oceans, making people sink down, falling and sinking and never getting out. ▲

41: the holy prophet's prescription for health

When physicians can do nothing for a pain or for an illness, we must do as the Prophet (s) advises us. He says that you must cure your illnesses by giving *sadaqah*, charity.

You may have a box. Each day you may put something in it and do as *Rasul-Allah*, beloved Muhammad (s) said: "O my Lord, I am giving this *sadaqah*." And when it becomes a bigger amount, if anyone is in need you may give it to him.

If no one is in need, you may send it to your country, your homeland. Otherwise, you ma give it to the mosque for charity. But you must do this every day, morning or evening. One shilling, two shillings, four shillings, ten pence, fifty pence, one pound; as much as you are able to give, give. It is important. When physicians can do nothing for illnesses, you must use this advice of the Prophet (s).

He also says, "'*Alaikum bi-shifa'ain, al-'asl wal-Quran.*[107] O my nation, you must take care to cure your illnesses by means of two health-giving things. One of them is honey and the second is the Glorious Quran." Therefore, you may also use honey for your pain [or illness] and you may recite the Holy Quran, as we are now doing, and keep this *sadaqah* box with you, also, in the hope that Allah Almighty may give you health. ▲

---

[107]Literally, "There are two cures for you, honey and the Quran."

42: how to give charity

A person may ask something from someone. It is *halal*, permissible to ask and take if he gives. But if he gives without being asked, that is excellent, the best. Therefore, the people of olden times did not let the poor come to their places to ask for something for the sake of Allah. Instead, they went around, for the sake of Allah, asking who might be in need in order to give their charities to them.

It is an incompleteness, deficiency, to make poor people come to rich peoples' doors to ask for something. Allah Almighty looks at His rich servants to see if they are taking from their *ni'mat*, the favors they have been given, to poor people, not waiting for poor people to come to their doors to ask something for charity, no. And the Prophet (s) says, "*Akhtanimu ghanimah*"[108] – when you give your charity to a poor person, you must take the opportunity to give it to him when he is very pleased with your favors, saying, "O my Lord, give him more." That takes away from you heavy burdens.

It is a very important point. So many people are not in peace, they can't enjoy themselves; no pleasure and no happiness for them, and they are not understanding what is the way. And they are going among physicians and psychiatrists, asking, "How can we be happy? So much tension, troubles – here, this kind, that kind"; so many millions, now.

It is only a very simple thing to do: give pleasure, take pleasure. Make people pleased with you and people will make you pleased; make your Lord

---

[108]"Take your booty."

pleased with you and He will make you pleased. The Prophet's saying, that one *hadith*, takes from people all their burdens, their heavy loads, their unhappiness: "Look, O people! Take your charity to poor people and make them pleased." And when they are pleased with you and they say, "O our Lord, make him pleased," Allah Almighty, the Lord, looks at their prayers for you.

Quickly those heavy burdens will go from you. No need for psychiatry; it cannot do anything, nor physicians. The chief of them, the Prophet (s), is teaching them, "*Akhtanimu ghanimah*" – *ghanimah*, the spoils of war that you take from the enemy, booty. You must look upon those prayers of poor people, when you take your charity to them, as booty. It is such a rare booty. This is so important for you, O people."

When there is less in your hand – when your own portion becomes less, your business goes down – quickly go and give charity. That makes the door open for you. When you feel something inside yourself making your heart imprisoned – unhappiness, no peace, no satisfaction, no mercy – quickly run and give your charity. No need for any new plans to make your business bigger; useless. Only this: quickly go and give charity, as much as you can.

If your certainty is perfect, you may give everything for charity and you may await what comes from your Lord. Abu Bakr as-Siddiq, may Allah bless him, brought everything to the Prophet, giving everything. And when the Prophet asked, "What is left for your family?" he replied, "*Allah wa Rasul-Allah*. I have left for them Allah Almighty and His Prophet."

Sayyidina 'Umar, may Allah bless him, also brought something, and when the Prophet asked him, "What did you leave for your family?" he said, "O *Rasul-Allah*, I have brought half of my money, my property. I have brought half of it to you and half I have left for my family."

Abu Bakr as-Siddiq's certainty was perfect, 'Umar's certainty was half. Therefore, you may follow the way of as-Siddiq: if you have complete certainty, you may give everything and you may wait. If you don't have such perfect certainty, give half to charity, or a quarter, or ten percent. But you *must* give charity. That opens doors. It is impossible for a person to give a charity and doors to close on him. No, charity opens closed doors. Whoever gives for the sake of Allah, Allah will give him more. ▲

43: Ramadan's Mercy Oceans

Now, *alhamdulillah*, the nineteenth night is finishing, and our egos are saying, "One more is gone, one more is gone of Holy Ramadan!" Our souls are crying but our egos are laughing, enjoying so much. "Oh, fasting is going quickly. Then, after Ramadan finishes, each day we may eat – two times, three times, five times a day, like animals; ten times – eating, enjoying." But our souls, our spirits, are crying. They are taking this divine manifestation, these Mercy Oceans, which are coming now.

When Ramadan goes, that will stop because it is only for one month. The one who may carry with him the same actions, the same intentions, as during Ramadan, will be in the same manifestation of mercy during the whole year. But the one who leaves them, that mercy will leave him, also.

Therefore, you must be careful when Ramadan is finished, asking from our Lord, "O my Lord, leave me, leave my heart, to be with Ramadan. Bodily I am going away from Ramadan, but let my soul be in those Mercy Oceans that You opened during Ramadan." Then you will swim in those Mercy Oceans until the next Ramadan, and that next one will be more than this one, because our Lord's giving is not like ours or like what we understand. His giving is out of our imagination, and this year's mercy is more than that which passed away one year ago. This *rahmah*, these Mercy Oceans, are so great that the past Ramadan's mercy is only one drop compared to the Mercy Ocean of this year.

He is Allah; He gives. You must understand from this *how* Allah Almighty gives – gives without end; yes. This year's mercy is only a drop beside the next Ramadan's Mercy Oceans, always increasing.

Allah Almighty never likes a person to be on the same route every day. Every day you must grow, must become more, must ask more. And we are asking, "O our Lord, give to us from Your Mercy Oceans. We do not know what to ask. As much as we may ask, it is nothing beside what You are giving us. Then *You* give to us, O our Lord." ▲

44: BEING FREE FOR YOUR LORD

We are asking our Lord Almighty to make us understanding people. The worst person is the one who never understands. And who has no understanding? The one who is a slave to his ego, never listening to his Lord or to His Prophet (s).

Look at that little boy. When you are going to be like him, you will be able to put one foot on earth, one foot in the Heavens. When your attributes will become as they were when you were little, when you are going to be as you were in childhood, you will be *awliya*, friends to Allah Almighty.

Children have the same status as prophets: they are *ma'sum*, innocent. Prophets grow up innocent, and children, till reaching the age of maturity, are innocent, also. Therefore, we must try to be as we were in our childhood.

What are children's attributes? That little boy is never going to have *hasad*, envy, which makes our faith useless, and, if quarrelling, after one hour that boy is going to be as before, forgetting and not keeping enmity in his heart; yes. But we are keeping, we are nurturing, we are feeding envy.

We people are feeding envy, feeding enmity, feeding pride, feeding stubbornness. Every bad characteristic we are feeding, and all the prophets just came to make people stop feeding the wild animals in themselves. Understand? So many wild animals we are feeding. In our hearts, dogs, foxes, wolves, oxen, not snakes but more than snakes – dragons, we are feeding, always. And all the prophets came to make people stop – to stop feeding.

Let them die. Then you will be free for your Lord's worship, because now you have, from morning up to night, from night up to morning, no work except feeding your wild animals. That is true; yes, no work for people except feeding their wild animals, they have so many. And scorpions and lions, leopards, tigers – every kind you can find; more than in the zoo you can find in yourself.

Then how can we be free for our Lord's service, always engaged, engaged? Sometimes you try the telephone. *"Dhu-dhu-dhu,"* it says – busy, engaged. Allah Almighty wants to be in contact with your heart all the time, but He sees always, "Engaged-engaged-engaged."

Yes, it is an important thing. And He says, "When is My servant going to be free for Me? I can't catch him for even a moment to speak to him"; because waves from the Divine Presence are always going around. If you are able, you may receive them.

The divine addressing never stops; it is going on from pre-eternity to post-eternity, never cutting off. His words are not like our words, no; *always speaking.* Therefore, at any time you may receive them. We are saying *"hatif ar-Rabbani,"* the divine 'telephone' – divine telephone, but always hearing, *"Dhu-dhu-dhu,"* never finding our heart without being engaged. And Allah Almighty is saying, "When is My servant going to be for *Me?* He is always for someone else!"

That is a shame for believers; we must be ashamed if Allah Almighty looks at us and asks, "Where is My servant?" Therefore, the Prophet said, "Throughout your days, *nafakhat Rabbikum,* divine addressings, are blowing into your ears. But you must be ready to receive some of His addressings to you, you must be ready to listen."

Therefore, meditation is important, even for a few minutes daily, and in the nighttime meditation is easier, so that you may be by yourself, not occupied as much as you are in the daytime. You must keep a few minutes to be with your Lord. Perhaps at any time you may catch His 'phoning' to you, or He may catch you free for Himself.

But, as They are saying to us, I have seen farmers going to the stable with candles to feed their oxen and sheep in the nighttime, also. We, too. We are seeing that all the time we are feeding – not our domestic animals, no; wild ones, also, we are feeding. At every hour of the day we are busy. Even when we are praying, our hearts are occupied; we are not free to be with our Lord even while praying. We are thinking about how we are going to feed our oxen, our wolves, our foxes, our dogs. We are *engaged*.

Therefore, we must try to make our hearts free from *khawatir*, stray thoughts, and the main purpose of all worshipping is to make our hearts free of everything except our Lord. You may pray once a year or once a month or once a week or every day, but still your heart may be occupied. Therefore, every day and every night, for every hour, we have a *sunnah* prayer, making us free to be with our Lord more and more.

And fasting especially makes us more free to be with our Lord. As much as you are hungry, you may understand that you are in need of your Lord, Allah Almighty, and you are going to think, if you should be in a situation where no eating or drinking is possible, how you are going to be.

At *that* time you are going to be with your Lord! "O my Lord!" you will cry, you will shout. "O my Lord, O my Lord, where are You?" – looking around, and He is with you, in you, outside of you, and He is all-in-all. And we are waiting to be with Him on the Day of Resurrection, but now we think that we are free from Him, that we are far away, so far away from Him!

Therefore, fasting is a very important worship, making people to be so close to their Lord, Allah Almighty. Allah Almighty says, "I spoke to Moses on Mount Sinai behind 70,000 veils. But when people are fasting, at the time of their breaking fast, I leave only one veil, I am so close to My fasting people."

That is an honor for us. If we knew that honor, we would want the whole year to be Ramadan. But we do *not* know, and we are saying, "Today is the fifteenth, the sixteenth, the seventeenth. Now twenty days more, fifteen days more, ten days more. Little by little," our egos are saying, "it is going by."

If we could understand what is given to fasting people during Ramadan, no one would want Ramadan to go but would want Ramadan to be twelve months. But Allah Almighty is making only one month for fasting, and He is giving to us, for each day, as much if it were ten days, so that, in thirty days' fasting, people are given the equivalent of 300 days' fasting. And as a *sunnah*, after Ramadan are coming six days more, and Allah gives us tenfold for each day of fasting during Shawwal,[109] equivalent to 360 days of fasting.

It is impossible for a person to be free from feeding his animals without finding someone who is free for his Lord. If you don't find such a person, you are never going to be free from feeding your wild animals. Therefore, Allah sent prophets, and, after the prophets, their inheritors, *awliya*, to look after people.

Awliya may be anywhere. One foot may be in the East and the other may be in the West, one foot in London, one foot in America. Doesn't matter; it is so short a distance for them. He who is free for his Lord Almighty is free from bonds.

Our feet are tied, tied with chains; we can't move more than one yard – like this, but *they* are free. He who is free for his Lord is free in his territories, in his sovereignty. Therefore, the highest honor for you is to be free for His service, for His worship, and with every worship, we are practicing being free from the hands of our egos. But you can't practice it perfectly until you reach and find some of them. And when you ask sincerely, a *wali* may step from East to West and come to you.

The whole universe is free for them, everywhere. Therefore, the one who is free for his Lord Almighty has been given divine authority to pass

---

[109]Shawwal is the lunar month following Ramadan, during which it is a *sunnah* to observe six days of voluntary fasting. The lunar calendar consists of 360 days.

freely, without hindrance, throughout the whole universe, and he makes *tawaf*,[110] circling around the *Holy Kaba*, may Allah give it more honor. And he is free to make *tawaf* of *Bayt al-Ma'mur*,[111] the Place of Security in the Heavens. Then, he is also free to make *tawaf* around the Divine Throne. When you are free, the chains are taken from your feet. Try to be free. *Don't be a slave!*

This is our way of practicing. That is the purpose of the whole *Shari'ah*, the Divine Law – only to make us free. But ignorant people think that the *Shari'ah's* laws are tying them down, chaining them.

That is the final, utmost degree of ignorance. If anyone understands, concerning the Divine Law, that he is going to be chained by it, that is the ultimate ignorance, because in reality it gives freedom to everyone, freeing them from the hands of their egos and making them a slave to their Lord, and therefore free.

No one can imagine what is the pleasure when you are free for your Lord. If a person is imprisoned in a prison – not like English prisons, no; a prison like that in which Prophet Joseph, Yusuf (a), was imprisoned, a dungeon; no one could stay there for even one hour now, so terrible it was in that dungeon – if a person is imprisoned in a dungeon, how does he look at being free? And when he is free, what does he feel of pleasure and happiness? You can't imagine what your pleasure will be when you are free for your Lord from the hands of your ego. *You can't imagine!*

Therefore, all prophets are free and all *awliya* are also free. But still they are asking to be free, completely free, from this body, also, and they are waiting for 'Azra'il, the Angel of Death. They are looking for him every day,

---

[110]*Tawaf*, the act of making seven circuits around the *Holy Kaba* while glorifying and supplicating Allah, is one of the principal rites of the major and minor pilgrimages (*Hajj* and *Umrah*). The spiritual bodies of prophets and *awliya* are also present at that holy place, circumambulating the *Kaba* as do the pilgrims at all times of the day and night.

[111]The celestial prototype of the *Holy Kaba* in the Seventh Heaven.

morning or evening – when he will come to take them away, to open the cage, opening the door and it will go *"Prr!"*

No one stays. When the cage is opened, no one stays in it, believers or non-believers. For unbelievers, also, *"Prr!"* But it is not enough when the cage is opened and the soul goes to Hell. For some of them, the doors will open and there will be a reception, a heavenly reception, for his sacred soul. But for some of them there will be no reception. No doors will open; only falling down for them.

I am asking forgiveness from Allah Almighty for everything, saying, *"Astaghfirullah."* And I am also saying *"Astaghfirullah"* for those who are not asking forgiveness on behalf of themselves, because the Prophet (s) always asked forgiveness for himself and for his nation. ▲

45: the prophet (s) and saints are living powers

I was at the tomb of Abdul-Qadir Jilani Sayyidi in Baghdad for *khalwah*, seclusion. He is a living *wali*. All *awliya* are alive, speaking to you or listening to you. And he is listening, can hear and can send from his heavenly powers to us, his heavenly power coming, blowing on us. And he was saying, "In every assembly, every meeting, where our name is mentioned and people are listening or speaking, those people are going to belong to us. On the Day of Resurrection, we will have *shafa`a*, intercession, for them in the Divine Presence."

The Prophet (s) is in his grave, seeing, hearing, speaking, understanding – a living power. That is our belief. And we also believe that every *wali* is a living power in his tomb; yes. If *awliya* were dead, they could never listen, could never hear. But they are not dead. When someone goes to the tomb of a *wali*, of someone who has been given such a living power, he must know that that *wali* can see, can hear, can know that person.

Subhanallah, glory to Allah Almighty! There was a well-known writer who was working on Islamic knowledge, John G. Bennett, a famous one. He has so many books.[112] He came to Damascus, and I said to him, in connection with finding our Grandshaykh, "You must go to Sayyid Muhiyuddin ibn al-'Arabi,[113] may Allah bless him." And he wrote in his

---

[112]Shaykh Nazim adds parenthetically, "He has a book called *Subud*. There are personal references in it to Grandshaykh."

[113]This great thirteenth century *wali* is buried in Damascus.

book that when he first went down to Muhiyuddin ibn al-'Arabi's tomb, he felt that he was just standing in front of a living person.

Yes, anyone may go and may feel that they are not like ordinary people. Therefore, you may find people coming and going at the tombs of *awliya*. All kinds of people, not only learned people, visit the tombs, the graves, of *awliya* and *sahabah*. At the least, they feel a sense of pleasure, of something different, as though feeling themselves to be out of this atmosphere. Yes, for all *awliya*. ▲

46: obedience to the lord

Our Lord has given us the honor of being His obedient servants. And *Sultan al-'Arifin*[114] Abu Yazid Bistami, may Allah bless him, said, "O my Lord, I am not surprised that we like You, but I am surprised that You like *us*."

That is honor enough for us: *Allah Almighty likes us*. That is the greatest good tidings. But what is this? For what would He like us? He has rights that we should like Him; yes. He has perfect attributes; absolute perfection is His, absolute power, endless Beauty Oceans, endless Mercy Oceans, endless favors, endless giving by Him. We *must* like Him; no one can deny that. But, "O my Lord," Abu Yazid said, addressing Him, "You like *us*? What are *we*? We are nothing."

But He says, "I have given you something from Myself." Allah Almighty gave to Adam from His Holy Spirit, blowing something from His Holy Spirit into him. Therefore, the sons of Adam were created at the end. The whole universe had been created and ornamented. Then Adam (a) was created, and Allah Almighty said, "I am creating Adam and his descendants as My deputies in the world."

No one else among creatures has been given the honor that we have been given. Endless happiness, endless pleasure, for those who understand that secret, who understand about themselves what Allah Almighty has given them. We must be the happiest people, the happiest creatures!

---

[114]Literally, the Prince of the Knowers (of Allah).

O people, O believers, ask an ant. It has an ear to listen, to hear, because it hears its Lord and it has a tongue to glorify its Lord. Be Solomon (a), and you may hear what it says. And now, such proud people, with their technology! Yes; if they have so much technology, so much science, so much knowledge, take an ant, one ant, and ask it.

What are you going to ask? Do you know? You must ask the ant because, although there is something smaller than an ant, you can't take it in your hands, and that ant is enough. Take an ant and ask.

But, because of our egos' wildness, it wants to run away from us. If there were no cruelty from our egos, none of the domesticated animals would run away from us and wild animals would never attack us. A lion or tiger or snake never attacks the sons of Adam except out of fear that they may kill him, because they have been ordered to be obedient to the sons of Adam: "As much as they are My obedient servants, you must be *their* obedient servants."

You understand? When you are obedient to your Lord, every creature is going to be obedient to you. But we are *not* obedient servants to our Lord; only for our egos we are saying, "Yes, sir, all right!" All the prophets came to teach us how we should be obedient servants to our Lord. And Abu Yazid, may Allah bless him, asked his Lord, "How can I come to You? How can I be Your obedient servant and reach You?"

And Allah Almighty replied, "Leave your ego and come to Me, to be My obedient servant and to be with Me forever." And we are trying to be with our Lord.

There is no happiness or honor greater than being with our Lord and our Lord with us – yes. And the Prophet (s) said, "Prayer is *mi'raj*.[115] It is the meeting of servants with their Lord," because when you say *"Allahu Akbar,"*[116] everything else is finished; you are in the Divine Presence. Allah

---

[115]Returning to Allah.

[116]At the beginning of the prayer.

Almighty makes an atmosphere around you and you are with your Lord. If there is any pleasure greater than this, who can imagine it? No one! But people are running away from praying. Even Muslims now are saying that prayer five times a day is too much: "We are too busy, we must work. And what is five times?"

They are understanding praying as a burden. A burden? *Do it as a pleasure for yourself!* Do it as if you are meeting with our Lord and you are escaping from everything to Him, as He says, "O people, escape from yourselves to Me – *fa-firru ila-Llah.*"[117]

We must escape. Leave everything. Leave even yourself, even your ego; leave and come. Escape from everything, because everything except your Lord is *nothing*. If you find your Lord, you find *everything*. If you lose Him, there is nothing for you. You have lost everything.

Now we will return to that ant. It tries to escape, as that ant in the Holy Quran warned its people, "Quickly, to your holes and hide yourselves, because King Solomon and his soldiers, his armies, are coming, so that they will not step on you."[118]

Is Allah telling a tale or speaking of Reality in the Holy Quran? That ant *saw* Solomon and his armies. You must believe what Allah says; yes.

Then, we shall ask the ant. You must give it a guarantee that you will not harm it but only want to ask it one question, to teach the sons of Adam, to let them to learn that they have been given perfection among all creatures. They must know, they must learn.

"What are you asking?" says the ant.

"O ant, O my Lord's creature, are you satisfied with your position – that Allah Almighty created you as an ant? Are you pleased with your Lord who created you as an ant?"

---

[117]"Then escape [or flee] to Allah." (51:50)
[118]27:18.

Listen to what it says:

"Glory be to my Lord who created me and gave me a chance to glorify Him, to say '*Subhanallah!*'"

And yet you, we, all of us – we are not pleased with our Lord. We are not saying that He gave us the honor of being the sons of Adam, of being His deputies, and that He has given us everything, making us governor over all creatures and promising us eternal life.

All creatures will go. On the Last Day, Allah Almighty will order them, "Be dust," and they will be dust, will be nothing. And He has promised us eternal life but still we are not pleased with our Lord, a shame for everyone!

Yes, it is true; we must think about that. We are not thinking about our Lord and His favors. We only know about running after this dirty life and its pleasures. *Astaghfirullah!* And we are saying, "Five times a day prayer, it is too much!" without feeling ashamed.

Allah Almighty is trying His servants, whether they are obeying Him or not. That is important, to be His obedient servants. We must obey our Lord. Yet however much He gives us, we are saying, "This is no good. Another one!" People now are living like spoiled children. No matter how much we are given, we are saying, "This is no good! Another car; that one is no good. Another set of furniture, another plane!"

If it were something that would make us more excellent, more obedient servants, then we could ask for more – more pleasure, more complete, more perfect things. But we are not looking at our service to our Lord, and yet we are asking for more perfect things, to be more pleased.

Give pleasure, take pleasure. You are too tight-fisted a person, not giving pleasure to your Lord but asking for more pleasure. No. Give pleasure, take pleasure. Give respect, take respect. Give mercy, take mercy, not just asking but not giving! ▲

47: following the prophet's (s) example

May Allah Almighty make us as He likes, not as *we* like. It is dangerous for a person to be as he likes, but rather he must try to be as his Lord likes. The one who is as his Lord wants him to be is going to be in peace and satisfaction and pleasure, here and in the Hereafter.

The greatest sin is to fight against Allah Almighty. Therefore, the Prophet (s) says, *"Man ramana fa-laisa minna;* the one who shoots his arrow against us is not from our nation." But it is not only for the one who puts himself on the enemy's side by sending his arrow against the Prophet's army. Rather, it has a very broad meaning: to be against the Prophet, and, if the Prophet liked something to say, "I don't like it."

In everything, we have been ordered to take him as the most excellent example. Therefore, if anyone is against what the Prophet liked, it means that he is leaving the Prophet's ways, not following the his ways perfectly. If anyone does this, it is also a kind of shooting of arrows against the Prophet's will and being against him in his desires. Even in his habits, a perfect follower of the Prophet must be in agreement with the Prophet's habits.

Once the son of Sayyidina 'Umar, may Allah bless them both, was riding on the way to *Hajj,* pilgrimage, going with people. Then he arrived at a place where there were two ways. One way was winding and the other was straight.

When he reached that fork, he turned and followed the winding way. Then his followers asked, "Why did you turn this way instead of going by that?"

He said, "I saw beloved Muhammad (s) arrive at this point and turn from here and then go on. And I like to follow his footsteps everywhere."

That is a perfection for Muslims, for anyone who wants to be a perfect follower, because *nur* lights every spot where the Prophet put his holy footsteps. But blind people do not see even the light of the sun – and the Prophet's light is more than the light of a hundred suns.

How could the son of Sayyidina 'Umar leave that *nur* and go by another way? It is impossible. The *sahabah*, the Companions of beloved Muhammad (s), saw his *nur*, his lights, and followed them. Therefore the *sahabah* reached to the lights of the Prophet, so that everyone who follows the ways of the Companions of Muhammad (s) reaches to his *nur*.

Now, we have been ordered to follow his ways because, in the ways of the Prophet (s), we may find lights which make our way clear for us, as the sun makes clear for people their way. We are in need to find our way through the darkness of the future through the lights of the Prophet (s); you can't find your way among the future's darknesses without his lights. Therefore, as much as you are able to be a real follower of your Prophet, you may acquire more lights, and as much as you acquire more lights, your future is going to be more clear for you; the ways to your destination are going to be more clear.

Everyone has a private destination, and you must make clear your way to your destination. And it is impossible for a person to make clear the way to his future or the way to his destination without taking a light from the Prophet (s). The sun never shows you the way to your destination, and you are in need of another sun to make your way to your destination clear: *shamsu nubuwwah*, the sun of prophethood. That is important.

Then whoever goes against the Prophet's steps, sending his arrows against the Prophet's ways, is not going to receive lights from the Prophet. Therefore, in every way in which the Prophet (s) is an example for us, we must be suited to being on his way, not being against his *sunnah*, even in eating, in drinking, in habits.

We must follow him. Even in simple things, if you know what you are doing and yet you go against his *sunnah*, you lose his lights. And inasmuch as something was liked by him, it was liked by his Lord Almighty, because if Allah Almighty had not liked it, the Prophet would not have liked it. That is impossible, because he was as his Lord wanted him to be in everything; then how could our Prophet consider being on a way other than the way his Lord wanted him to be on? Therefore, when anything, even of the customs of our Prophet (s), reaches us, we must keep it.

But now in our time, Muslims generally are losing the ways of the Prophet (s). Now most scholars and learned people, and most Muslims, are speaking about the customs or habits of the Prophet (s) and they are saying, "It doesn't matter if we leave them. They are not worships, they are not like prayers"; saying, "We will keep only what the Prophet brought us as worships, as prayers. But as for what he used to do as a custom, it doesn't matter if we leave that and if we follow new customs in eating, in drinking, in dressing. Accommodation – yes? We may do as we like now."

Yes, there is tolerance in Islam. But that is for *dunya*, for this world. If you are asking for *Dar al-Akhirah*, the Eternal Home, you must be closer to the life of the Prophet (s), you must be a more careful follower of his ways.

Arabs are running after new fashions, and Turks, also. Pakistanis, also; they like to follow new fashions. Yes, everyone who comes to Western countries is affected by the new fashions, and they are saying, "Doesn't matter, doesn't matter!"

That is suitable only for beginners, yet, *alhamdulillah*, those who are newly coming into Islam from Western countries are keeping the ways of Prophet Muhammad (s) firmly. Yes, we *must* keep them. We must not be against the Prophet, even in customs or in habits, because he always asked his nation to be the leader, not to be a follower. You must be guides, you must be the first, not imitating others, no; you must be in front and people following you. But in everything we are making non-Muslims first; then we are following *them*. And it is not suitable for us. If we have been honored by Islam and real faith, we must be the first.

What customs can be better than the customs of the Prophet (s)? But now we are following the desires of our egos and we are saying to our egos, "As you like." We are finding satisfaction in saying, "Those are only customs, not worships," and we are not understanding that even the customs, the habits, of the Prophet, are like worships. As much as we are following his customs, it is a kind of worship.

Therefore, if the Prophet said, "I like this," and you say, "I like it, also," it is a kind of worship; and if he said, "I don't like this," and you say, "I also don't like that," it is a worship, because we know clearly that the Prophet would never say for something, "I like it," without his Lord's making him like it. *"Hubbiba ilayya,"* he says. "My Lord made me like it, and if I like something, Allah Almighty made me like it." And when he disliked something, you must know that his Lord dislikes that thing. Therefore *he* disliked it, and you must follow him. That is perfection in following the Prophet (s).

Therefore, in the spiritual ways of Islam, grandshaykhs always advised people, believers, saying, "O *mumins*, O Muslims, you must follow someone, because it is an order from your Lord Almighty. You must have an *imam*, O Muslims; you can't be without an *imam*."

Imam means leader or guide. You can't be without a guide: that is the order of the *Shari'ah*, the order, the command, of our Lord Almighty, and the Prophet says what his Lord Almighty orders him to say. You *must* have an *imam*. If you take an *imam* for your prayers, how can you *not* be in need of a guide for your life? Therefore grandshaykhs are saying to believers, "You must take someone as your guide." But you must look for someone who is very careful about keeping the Prophet's *Sunnah*, his ways.

If you can find a person who is very careful in keeping the *sunnah*, follow him as much as you are able; as much as you can find a perfect person, you must follow him. If he is not perfect, it is useless. It is like a person down in a well, saying to a little boy, "Take my hand and pull me up from here," while he drags that boy into the well, also. Ask that a more powerful one than you should take your hand and pull you out.

May Allah Almighty make us find such a person, such people, so that we may take benefit from them in order to be more perfect. If he is more perfect than we, his perfection will come on us, also. Therefore, if we find such a perfect person, we intend to be his followers. ▲

48: BE WITH YOUR LORD

O my Lord, we are asking from Your endless favors. Give us from Your endless favors so that we may keep Your way, the path on which Your beloved people, Your beloved servants, are walking, to come to You, to be with You.

That is our aim: to find the way to our Lord and to be with Him. And all the prophets, peace be upon them, came to show the way to Allah Almighty for His servants.

They did not come to teach us how to get this life's pleasures, no. No need to teach; everyone knows by birth. No one is ignorant about this life's pleasures. Children are born and cry to eat and drink; they take pleasure in eating and drinking. And so on; each one of our physical body's pleasures is well known. Therefore, no need to teach them. But they came, all the prophets, to teach the way to Allah Almighty and to show the way to be with Him.

That is the ultimate desire or the most perfect or excellent thing that we can think of or we can want. And no one can imagine what he is going to find or to see or to feel or what pleasure he will be in when he is with his Lord, Almighty Allah. Therefore, those who know something about that – I mean to say, those who are with their Lord – left this life's pleasures and also the next life's pleasures. But we – our level has not yet improved from the level of the zoo. Every kind of animal you can find among people.

I was thinking about all kinds of animals, wild animals and also other animals, and my Grandshaykh explained to me that just as animals are different, every kind of animal is to be found among people, also, everyone's ego representing one kind of animal. You know what kind your ego is and you must keep yourself from that kind of animal, keeping yourself and keeping people from your ego's harm.

The people whose interests during this life are only with eating, drinking and dancing and playing (yes, too much!), their level is the first level. They are never asking for the next life's pleasures. They can't control their egos; therefore they are under their command. What their egos are saying, they are doing, and their pleasure is with this life's pleasures.

And the second level is for those who are asking for, who are believing in the next life, believing in Hells, believing in Paradise. They are keeping themselves from falling into Hells and they are asking for Paradise's pleasures in the next and eternal life. But the highest level for the sons of Adam is for those who are asking to be with their Lord forever. They are not interested in this life's pleasures nor in the next life's pleasures, never asking for them. That is the level of the prophets and saints and angels, those angels who are always in the Divine Presence. The Divine Presence is for prophets and *awliya* and angels. They are asking only for their Lord Almighty.

And holy books, particularly the last one, the Holy Quran, are showing the way for all the kinds of the sons of Adam. Those who are taking their pleasures from this life may find their way through the Holy Quran; and those who are asking for Paradise and its pleasures may find their way through the Holy Quran; and those who are asking for pleasure, endless pleasures, through being with their Lord, Almighty Allah, they are finding their way through the Holy Quran. Therefore, the Holy Quran is a divine feast for all the sons of Adam. Through it all of them can reach their desires, their aims, their goals. And the perfect one is asking to be with his Lord.

We are humble people, not running after perfection; we are asking for a simple thing, for the simple life and simple pleasures which common people ask. But we must ask for more than this, and we are practicing through worshipping because worshipping opens in our hearts the doors of desire to be with our Lord Almighty.

Every prayer, every worship, makes a way, closer, closer to our Lord, so that if you pray only once a year, you may find a way to your Lord. If you pray only once a month, you may find a way to your Lord. You may pray once a week, as Christians and Jewish people do, and Muslims are also holding Friday prayers each week, and you may find a way through weekly prayers. But Allah Almighty is calling His servants to daily prayers by day and by night.

You may pray once a day; that is a way to your Lord. Or you may pray five times a day, because Allah Almighty is calling you to be with Him five times. And you may also pray more than five times.

During the Night of the Ascension, when beloved Muhammad (s) was in the Divine Presence, Allah Almighty ordered prayers fifty times a day. That was an honor for us, and beloved Muhammad (s) accepted those fifty times of prayer with pleasure, with honor, because he was always asking for more honor and more pleasure for his *ummah*. But when he met with Moses (a),[119] Moses asked, "What did your Lord offer to your nation?"

And beloved Muhammad (s) said, "My Lord, Allah Almighty, honored my nation with fifty times of prayer during the twenty-four hours of the day and night."

And Prophet Moses (a) said, "That is the best thing. But your *ummah* is too weak to carry that. We know that you have been given the highest honor, but we are afraid that they can't carry that honor, can't carry such a responsibility. Because they are weak, ask Allah Almighty to make it lighter."

Therefore the Prophet, beloved Muhammad (s), asked to have it made lighter and still lighter. Then it became five times a day; otherwise it would

---

[119]In the spiritual world, as mentioned in 32:23.

have been fifty times. The chance was given, among other nations, to the nation of Muhammad (s) for his *ummah* to be with their Lord fifty times a day. But we love *dunya* too much, more than *Maula*, our Master, our Lord; we are engaging ourselves with *dunya* more than with our Lord. Therefore it was made only five times.

Therefore, Islam is the perfect religion. No other religion can compare with it. Which religion now can order people to be with their Lord five times a day? And all the prophets just came to make people be with their Lord, Allah Almighty, as much as they can.

Yes, we are not understanding why Islam is the perfect one. Allah Almighty is asking His servants to be with Him as much as they can, more than with this world's troubles. As much as we are leaving Him, we are falling into troubles and sufferings, and suffering is just going to reach the highest point after a little. We are not understanding what is the honor that we have been given.

Therefore, prayers after *fard*[120] are a divine order, Allah Almighty giving permission to beloved Muhammad (s) to make the *sunnah* prayers. And we have a *sunnah* for each time: *sunnah* for *Ishraq*, the sun's shining;[121] *sunnah* for *Duha*[122]; *sunnah* for *wudu*;[123] *sunnah* for *Awwabin* between *Maghrib* and *'Isha* prayer;[124] and *Tahajjud*,[125] the night's *sunnah*, so that, for whoever wants to be with his Lord more, that is open.

---

[120]Obligatory. A fixed number of *rakats* (units or cycles) in each prayer are *fard* and the others are *sunnah* -- that is, practiced and recommended by the Prophet (s) but not obligatory.

[121]Two *rakats* observed shortly after sunrise.

[122]Two, four, six or eight *rakats*, observed during the morning hours in sets of two *rakats*.

[123]The two *rakats* observed after making *wudu*, ablution for prayer.

[124]Six *rakats* after the *sunnah* following *Maghrib*, offered in sets of two *rakats*, for forgiveness for the sins of the day.

[125]Voluntary prayer during the night, especially recommended during the last one-third of the night, offered in four sets of two *rakats*.

Rabi'ah al-Adawiyah is a famous lady in the Muslim world; from the time of the *taba'iyin*[126] up to now she has been a well-known personality in Islam. She had the honor of being a beloved servant to her Lord, Allah Almighty, and we are honored to mention her name here. And we are asking for her *barakah* for us, also.

Look at those who are asking to be with their Lord, what is their way. (I am saying this so that when ladies say, "We are always in the background, men are always in front" – no, Allah Almighty gives you honor. Sometimes *you* may be in front, also.) That is Rabi'ah, may Allah bless her.

Every night, from sunset to sunrise, she would pray one thousand *rakats*. Yes; she had pleasure in being with her Lord Almighty always. But we are saying our prayers quickly, to escape, if we even come to pray. And now in our time, more ladies are praying than men; if you look, you can find that at this time they are more than men – double. Therefore the Prophet (s) said that when the time approaches for *Qiyamah*, the Last Day, you will find more religious people among ladies and more among villagers than among city people.

Rabi'ah prayed every night, never becoming tired. The Prophet (s) said, "My Lord made me love prayer, *salat*, as I love my eyes." As he said, "Prayer is *mi'raj* for Allah's servants. He gives them the honor of *mi'raj* when they pray."

These are those people who understand what honor is, the perfect honor, and perfect pleasure and perfect satisfaction and peace. When a person is with his Lord, he gives his whole life to be with Him. Therefore earlier people (among Christians more than among Jewish people) built monasteries on mountains. For what? To be with their Lord.[127] Therefore, the perfection of religions is in Islam, and perfect pleasure for mankind is in

---

[126]The second generation of Muslims – that is, those who immediately followed the *sahabah* or Companions of the Prophet (s).

[127]Shaykh Nazim adds parenthetically, "That was at the first. Later they enjoyed themselves and came down."

praying. As much as people are able to pray, are able to worship, that way is going to open to them.

Rabi'ah would sit in the desert, and around her deer were sitting and listening, yes; as a cat comes and sits in front of you, in that way they were listening. They know the good people and also the bad people, the cruel people, who they are. She sat reciting the Holy Quran and they were listening.

Don't be surprised that those deer came and listened to Rabi'at al-Adawiyah. Allah Almighty says in the Holy Quran that when David (a) recited psalms, mountains and everything on those mountains and the birds would come and listen to his heavenly recitation.[128] In such people there are examples for you, O sons of Adam, O believers. The path is correct; you may go on it. But we are *not* going on it, we are going after our egos. It is tasteful, going around after our egos!

Of what are we in need? We are in need to be patient. People have lost patience now; therefore they are not coming to pray. Praying needs patience; if no patience, you can't pray. You must be patient so that you may pray and you may taste; without being patient, you can't reach that pleasure. Everything is going to be difficult at first, not tasteful, but afterwards it is going to be tasteful.

Hu-u Rabbi![129] Rabi'at al-Adawiyah said, "At first, when my shaykh gave me '*Allah-Allah-Allah-Allah-Allah-Allah-Allah...*' to say for *dhikr*, it was so heavy. But I never gave up my *wird*, my *dhikr*, as my grandshaykh ordered me. And Allah Almighty sees when you are carrying that difficulty for the sake of the love of your Lord. He opened to my heart from His divine love. I left everything else when that pleasure came. No *dhikr* can be tasteful to me as to say '*Allah-Allah-Allah-Allah-Allah....*'" What does it mean? "O my Lord, I like to be with You – *to be with You!*"

---

[128] 21:79 and 34:10.
[129] O my Lord.

But people of no mind are objecting, "What is *dhikr*?" Animals do not understand about *dhikr*. There is a well-known saying, "The one who does not taste does not know." The one who tastes it knows.

All of you are mature people except this boy. This boy does not understand what mature people taste; as yet he does not know. Therefore, those people who are objecting to *dhikr*, to *tariqats*, are still like little boys, children yet, not understanding. May Allah make us to know, to taste.

Now, people are of two kinds. Some of them are reaching maturity and tasting during this life and going. The second kind of people are not tasting. They are going, they are dying, before maturity. They can't get into the first group.

The first kind of people are going to be with their Lord forever because they are saying, "O my Lord, I want to be with You." Therefore, we are saying, "*Allah-Allah-Allah-Allah-Allah...* " or we are saying, "*La ilaha illa-Llah, la ilaha illa-Llah....* "[130] And *dunya* is calling us, our *nafs* is calling us, "Come to us," and we are refusing, saying, "No! *La ilaha illa-Llah, la ilaha illa-Llah.* I am asking for no one else." When we are victorious, we will say "*Allah-Allah-Allah...* ," and everything will say with us, "*Allah-Allah...* ," the whole universe making *dhikr*. That is *sultan adh-dhikr*[131.] May Allah give us His *dhikr's* pleasure.

There was a lady, also, They are telling me to say for the pleasure of our daughters and sisters, Grandshaykh's mother's sister-in-law. She was always saying, "*La ilaha illa-Llah, la ilaha illa-Llah, la ilaha illa-Llah, la ilaha illa-Llah, la ilaha illa-Llah, la ilaha illa-Llah,*" not anything else, and if someone said something to her, she would say, "O my son, O my daughter, may Allah also make as tasteful for you as He has made for me this *'La ilaha illa-Llah.'* Tasteful, sweet. *La ilaha illa-Llah. La ilaha illa-Llah. La ilaha illa-Llah.*

---

[130]"There is no deity except Allah."

[131]The repetition of the Holy Name "Allah" is referred to here as the chief of *dhikrs* or litanies of remembrance and glorification of God Most High.

La ilaha illa-Llah. La ilaha illa-Llah," making *tasabih.*[132] Even at the time of sleeping, her fingers were like this, never stopping. And still she is in her grave like this. May Allah make His *dhikr*, His remembrance, tasteful for us also. ▲

---

[132]Glorification of Allah.

49: THE POWER OF REMEMBERING GOD

We must be occupied. Satan has such power to understand which person is engaged and which person is free. When you are sitting like this, he understands what you are doing. Therefore, if not doing any work related to this life, you must be with your Lord: *"Allah-Allah..."* Then there is no way for evil to come to you.

You may do any kind of dhikr: "Allah"; "La ilaha illa-Llah"; "Hu"; "Hayy"; "Haqq"; "Bismillah"; "Allahumma, salli 'ala Muhammadin wa 'ala ali Muhammadin wa sallim"; "Astaghfirullah, astaghfirullah"; "Alhamdulillah"; "Subhanallah wa bi-hamdihi, subhanallah al-'Adhim, astaghfirullah."[133] But, "Allah-Allah, Allah-Allah, Allah-Allah, Allah-Allah, Allah-Allah" – is so easy!

QUESTION: But can't evil come when we're doing work, also?

SHAYKH NAZIM: Yes, it comes if you are *ghafil*, heedless. When you are heedless, evil comes to you. Heedlessness is evil itself.

QUESTION: Is it more valuable to be doing *dhikr* than just to talk to Allah? Is it the same, or is it better to be doing *dhikr*? Or doesn't it matter?

SHAYKH NAZIM: *Dhikr* is one thing. Sometimes you are in *dhikr* and sometimes you are doing *munajat* – that is, addressing your Lord by praying alone, speaking to Him at night, saying, "O my Lord." But you don't do that always. Sometimes you do that and sometimes *dhikr*. ▲

---

[133]Please see the Glossary at the end of Book Six for the meanings of these individual phrases of *dhikr*.

50: advice for a successful marriage

Marriage is an order of God Almighty, and it is the way of the prophets, also, from the first man, Adam, and the first woman, Eve. They made their marriage in Paradise, and therefore Allah Almighty gives those who get married a sweet scent from Paradise so that they will be happy. But they must keep that good scent between themselves throughout their lives. That is important. And we are now asking our Lord Almighty to continue that good scent between them along their way, throughout their lives in this world, and we hope that they will also be together hereafter, in the Eternal Life. That is the meaning of making a marriage ceremony for a new couple.

We are thanking our Lord, who created men and women, and gave them from His divine love. If He does not give His divine love, no one can come together. And He orders for His servants an honorable life by being one for one, not one woman for all men and not one man for all women.

That is the honor of ladies. A lady is only for one man and a man is only for one lady; that is their honor in this life. Whoever breaks that law, Allah Almighty is not going to say that they are honorable people. Therefore, we are holding this honorable ceremony, and we are asking our Lord Almighty to make them successful in their life together.

You must look and see only your husband. Who is the most handsome person in the world? If you are asked, you must say that my husband is the most handsome person. And you, also. Who is the most beautiful lady in London? Your wife. If each one looks only at the other, there will be no more troubles – in London, in England, in Turkey, in Cyprus, in the East, in the West.

That is the most important advice for new couples. I am hearing about so many couples, going and registering with the registry clerk. After three days, after three weeks, after three months, after three years, one goes this way, one that way, because they are looking: the lady is looking at other men and the gentleman is looking at other ladies. Then it can no longer be successful.

You are now establishing a new "building", a marriage, and we are asking our Lord to make you lovely to each other. ▲

51: the importance of appreciating your wife

Bring your wife some jewelry, so that she may be pleased with you. Always, when your wife is angry with you, bring her something that she likes. You must know, all of you: *don't hurt your wives; don't hurt your wives!* Make them always pleased with you; otherwise, when you come, they will surely go out. Understand? Keep them happy, and in return they will keep you happy, also.

Women are very fortunate, here and in the Hereafter. Why? Because there will be no questioning for them. On the Day of Resurrection, all ladies will come with their husbands, and when the husband goes into Paradise, the wife will go in with him; no questioning for her. But men – there will be so many questions for you!

Understand? Showing your passport at the door of Paradise, going in, and your wife will come with you. "This is your wife?" *Allah 'Azza wa Jall*[134] will ask you.

You will say, "Yes."

"You are satisfied with her?"

If you say, "Yes," Allah Almighty will say, "Take her and enter Paradise." But if you say, "O my Lord, I was never satisfied with her. Too much talking!" then Allah Almighty will say, "Stop! Stand up. Why were you not satisfied with her? She was a barrier between you and Hell. If she

---

[134]Allah the Mighty and Glorious.

had not been with you, you would have fallen into Hell. Therefore, all of them are more valuable than you."

Yes, because if our wives did not serve as a hindrance, all of us would fall into Hell. No one would take us out except ladies, for they are our protection. So, when you go to work, take her hand [he simulates kissing hand] and do the same at night, also.

You must treat your wives - your ladies -very gently. Yes, that is true; definitely, surely, too true. Therefore, you must keep their rights. You men are often committing cruelty against ladies, in not upholding their rights. Everyone must keep their rights.

Allah Almighty will ask, "Why weren't you satisfied with your wife? She was the barrier between you and Hell! Didn't she keep your house, cook for you, do your laundry, raise your children?" Allah will ask.

There is no obligation on ladies to do anything.[135] *Men* must do it – washing, cleaning, looking after the babies. In the *Shari'ah*, Allah Almighty does not even order the mother to give milk to your, to her, babies. The provision of it is on you men. *You* must look after it, *you* must pay.

Are you men compensating your ladies? For every child she bears, you must give her jewelry, such as a golden chain. Yes, when she gives her breast to the baby, you must pay, not saying, "*You* can do it, *you* can find someone to give milk to your child."

No ordering work! Her God-given role is only to be a barrier between you and *haram*; that is her duty. Everything is the responsibility of husbands, but wives do all they can because they are grateful to us; they serve us voluntarily. Do *you* sometimes clean the house? Watch the children? ▲

---

[135]According to the Islamic *Shari'ah*, it is the responsibility of the Muslim man, not of his wife, to provide the means of doing the housework and caring for the children. If his wife does not wish to or cannot nurse their baby, it is the father's responsibility to secure a wet-nurse or make some other arrangements for its feeding.

52: women working outside the home

Shaykh Nazim gave the following advice to a woman
who asked whether or not she should work.

If you are in need to work, work. If what your husband does is enough, don't work. If a man works, we are not saying that his wife should work, because we believe that Allah Almighty gives a man more *barakah*, more blessings, if his wife does not work. If she works, less *barakah* comes for both of them. Therefore, we prefer that only the husband works and you be the keeper of your home. You are not asking for so much money; you are asking for *barakah*. Even if it is little money, more *barakah* is better than much money and both of them becoming tired with no *barakah*.

Your service is for your husband only, doing everything inside your house. And if you have more time and you want to do something, you can do some handiwork in your house. But don't be a slave to outside work.

People now are slaves because you can't find any limit for work or for desires. You are saying, "I must get more, I must get more." No – you are free not to be under the command of business people; you are free.

If you can find time, in order not to become bored, write, draw, do needlework – anything that is suitable. You may make ready for your future daughter so that there will be something in her house when she grows up. In earlier times every mother would prepare the *jihaz* for her daughter.[136]

---

136 The bridal dower. Preparing the *jihaz* for a girl's marriage was formerly a custom in many parts of the Muslim world, girls and women occupying their spare time with embroidery, crocheting and other handiwork to make ready linens and other essentials for the future

Do such things because it is important. If you do not engage yourself in something, your ego will engage you for its bad desires. There is no idleness in our way. Don't sit idly. ▲

---

household.

53: how a believer interacts with family members

The one who believes in his or her Lord Almighty's absolute attributes is beloved among the community, and particularly beloved within their family.

We are saying that a *mumin*, a believer, must be within their family at the very least like the cat: everyone likes a cat, everyone strokes it. But now we live in strange times. We are seeing that when believers go among their family, they are instead making themselves like hedgehogs. How can he be a believer and act like a hedgehog among his family? That is not true faith for a real Muslim, a real Christian, a real Jew. A real believer never harms anyone.

Therefore, is your wife happy with you? Yes, because your faith gives familiarity to the members of your family. When you are with them they are happy, and when you are far away from them, they are asking, "Where is our father? Where is my husband?" That is important, and we are praying for everyone to be in such a way with his faith. ▲

54: obligations to parents

As believers, as Muslims, we have been ordered to do our best for everyone, and it is asked of a Muslim to give his best to his parents before anyone else. Whatever is the best for them – you may see about that point.

As much as you are able to respect parents, that is their desire. Parents expect their children to respect them; that is the first thing. And, in addition to respect, as much as you may be able to look after their needs, their expenses, do; as much as you may give them, give. It makes them happy.

We have been ordered to make people happy, and the ones who are asking that from us more than anyone else are our parents. That is our way: to make everyone happy, as much as we are able, and to make everyone pleased with us, to give them pleasure. When you do your best with a person and give him pleasure, he will be pleased and happy with you. Therefore, as much as you may be able to do for your parents' happiness, do it. ▲

55: the inevitability of death

Allah Almighty created Adam, the father of the sons of Adam, in Paradise. Then, before his soul had yet come into him, he was lying, without soul. Then God Almighty ordered there to rain on him forty years' rain of sorrow.

Sorrows rained on him for forty years. Then that stopped and there came one year of enjoyment. Therefore, forty years of sorrows and one year of happiness: if a man lives forty years, for one year there should be all pleasure with him and forty years will come with sorrow; if eighty years, two years will bring enjoyment and eighty years are going to be full of sorrows.

We must be patient. But we can't be patient without belief. If anyone believes, believes in his Lord Almighty, his Lord carries his burden away from him; if he has strong faith, then Allah may carry it for him. If no beliefs, he is quickly destroyed.

Death comes to everyone. People crowd around him or her, and he or she is there in the coffin – everyone; that day is coming for *everyone*. She or he is in that coffin, and people are crowding around and crying.

Everyone has a day to mourn. We say, "Happy birthday," when a little baby comes – "Happy birthday!" But every baby mourns and cries. He knows or she knows what we do not know. He or she looks and sees what we can't see, and he or she, that baby, hears what we can't hear, but has no permission to speak, the Lord locking his tongue: "No, don't speak! Permission only to cry." And people around him are happy, saying, "Happy birthday!" and he is crying, *"Ah-wah, ah-wah!"* All of us cried.

Now, it must be that one day we will also go. We came and we must go. On the day of separation, people around us will cry, but that person must look to himself. When people are laughing around him, on the birthday, he must try to be happy, and when people are crying around him, he must be happy on *that* day, also. But only good people are going to be happy on that day when people are crying over him. Therefore, we must try.

That day is coming for everyone; no one can escape. The Lord's command is for everyone: Christians, English, Western people, Eastern people, oriental people, Pakistanis, Turks, Balkan people, Germans, Scots – coming for everyone. People now are in a queue. The Death Angel takes one. When he takes one, we go one step closer. When another goes, you must know that death is approaching one more person.

Everyone has come to go; no one has come to stay. There may be one million, one billion people, but you must know that each time it is one step less – one step, one step, coming to you. Each time you look at a dead person, you must know, you must understand, that now I am going one step closer to death. Yes, approaching.

That is the wisdom which holy books are speaking about. But people are like drunk, never thinking about it or never understanding it. ▲

56: facing difficulties

Difficulties come to everyone from Allah Almighty. Some of them come in spite of our will, and some of them come because of the action of our will.

Sometimes difficulties are from Allah Almighty's Will, to give you high degrees. They come to cover your sins, your wrong steps. Therefore, for the difficulties which come without our wills, by our Lord's Will, we must be patient.

Some difficulties come, also, according to the actions of our wills. Those difficulties that come to you because of your actions and will, *you* must take care of them. At that time, don't accuse anyone except yourself.

You must take care of your own actions and will; because of them, some difficulties and troubles and sufferings have come on you. Then you must correct your steps. It means that there is something wrong with you, so that you have left the right way and gone on the wrong way, and you must quickly correct the course, your way. ▲

57: Choosing the easier alternative

This talk was given in response to a question asked by a disciple about remaining in England after finishing his studies or returning to his homeland, which is a Muslim country.

Anyone may ask such a question about his life, about his destiny. We must be like running water - a river, a spring - flowing out. When it runs, water always follows the easy course, avoiding difficulties and passing through easy ways, not stopping. If it finds a deep place, a hole, it fills it and then runs again; if finding a rock, it does not try to cut through the rock but changes its way and runs, never stopping. If it stops, it fills that place and runs, also.

In our lives we must always see what is the easier way for ourselves. If people know this, they will be in rest and comfort, but they never think about that wisdom: to run as it is easy for them. If *this* way is going to be easy, you must follow it.

There is an Arabic saying, *"Al-'alamatu-l-idhn at-taysir"*[137] – the sign that Allah Almighty's Will is with this way, if it is easy. If you see that something is going to be easy for you, that is the sign that your Lord is pleased with it, that His pleasure is with that thing. When you see that there are difficulties, it means that your Lord is not pleased with that; therefore you must change your way to an easy one. Don't stop for a difficult situation, don't pursue difficulties. There are so many ways for the sons of Adam. Whichever one is easier, that you must follow.

---

[137]Literally, "The sign of permissibility is ease."

In our life, we may face so many difficulties. Allah Almighty makes difficulties to keep His servants from falling into a bad situation, putting a barrier in front of them so that they can't fall down into a valley, and you must change your course. In the *Shari'ah*, also, if something is difficult for people – for example, if a person can't pray standing, he may sit and pray; if not able to sit, he may lie down and pray. Or, on a ship, you may intend to face *Qiblah*; then, however the ship turns, it doesn't matter. As an alternative to every difficult way, there is an easy one. If there is a "No Entry" sign and you can understand that the road goes like this, don't enter it. If you do, you may find something that you are not going to be pleased with.

Therefore, it is an important thing for our lives to always follow the alternative to difficulties because the two ways run side by side. If no way, if a difficulty comes to you, change your way to an easy one; if *that* one is closed, you may find an open way. Therefore, don't be like a rock. Instead, you must be like water – running, always running. When you run, you will reach the ocean. Rocks stand in their places, but water runs.

Allah Almighty gives us will power, but you must know that His Will covers our wills. Don't be stubborn about your will; His Will is over it. You may know something, but He knows *everything*. Therefore, when you ask for something, perhaps from this side it may look good to you but you are not seeing what is behind it. But He knows what is behind it, also. Therefore, follow your Lord's Will.

How do you follow His Will? You must know that His Will is always going to be for ease for you.

QUESTION: Is there not a time to try to confront difficulties, to take on the challenge, so that you'll meet a difficult way but gain something through it?

SHAYKH NAZIM: As water does, you may do. If there is a rock not firm in the earth, water carries that rock, also; if such a powerful river comes, it takes it away. But if it is firmly in the earth, the river changes its course.

According to whether it is easy to move, you may understand. If not easy, if it is firm, you must understand that it is impossible. Then change and go; otherwise the rock will stay in the middle of the stream because there is no power for the water to carry every stone in its path. Therefore, the water leaves and runs.

This is a very good method for everyone's life. Don't be stubborn about difficulties. You must run; don't stay there – no. Don't be rock; instead, you must be like water. Then you will be in peace always, never complaining. The one who runs with events, he is in peace, but the one who runs against events is going to be amongst troubles always.

Agreement is the key to peace and satisfaction and happiness in the lives of people, but very few people understand that, and they are fighting, fighting, against the running of events. You can't stop events; you must run with them. You are coming like this and the river is running like this; you can't stop it but you can easily run with the river. I mean to say, the Will of Allah runs powerfully; your will can't stop it. You may try to make a way against it but you can't. However much you may try, it will take you like this.

Sometimes you must jump from one possibility to another. When you change doors and finally you see that every door is locked, then the matter is finished. Yes, finished. In such a case you must go back. It is a very fine line.

Most people are saying that this, my order, must be carried out, insisting. As Pharaoh said "My order must be carried out," our ego is saying to us, "*My* order must be carried out." *That* causes suffering to people. They are not like running water; they are like rocks, saying, "This Nile must run as I say," and the Nile is *never* going to run as you like but it runs as its Lord orders it to run. That is the main reason why people are suffering: they refuse to be soft.

You must be very careful about this point. You must follow Allah Almighty's Will, and the sign of His Will is to be able to follow events easily. We must run behind events, following them easily through difficulties. If you want easy ways, you may find endless easy ways, but if you say "No," everything says "No" to you, echoing. When you say "No!" everything says "No-o-o!" but when you say "Yes," everything says "Yes-s-s!" and when you say "Happy!" everything around you says "Ha-a-apy!" That is important.

QUESTION: But if you're saying that we should go with the flow, when now this time is like a flood of *harams* and bad thoughts and bad things coming on us, how can we at the same time not go with that flood but yet not come right up against it and get washed away? We don't want to go with it, but if we try to go directly against it, we aren't able, we don't have enough power. And it's difficult to know what we should do in our lives if we live, for example, in Western countries – in America, in Europe, in this culture. We don't want to go with it, but if we can't resist it, what should we do? What is our tactic?

SHAYKH NAZIM: We said that for every difficulty there is an easy way. You are asking protection from your Lord. You know that when the flood of Noah came, it did not come on all the people. Why? Some people took the Ark of Safety. If you were in it, the flood would never touch you.

When you go under the protection of your faith, you may be anywhere; no worry for you – you may run. All people are going, but some people are sinking and some people are swimming up to the end. The ones who are sinking down are finished, but others have a life preserver. The one who has one does not sink. If not, he will go down, finished, as at the time of Noah.

Now you are taking the life preserver. No worry about your being in London, in Western countries; no. Allah is keeping you from *haram*, *alhamdulillah*. You are coming here and sitting. All of you are young people, and outside there are young ladies, other young people, and you are sitting here.

Who is protecting you? Your faith in Allah Almighty is keeping you, or you could go to parks, to beaches, to discotheques; you could go to all such places to do as others do, jumping around, dancing – yes. Why are you sitting here?

It is miraculous. It means that Islam, the way of *tariqat,* is a living power. It is enough evidence that Islam is a living religion and of the power of *tariqat* that all of you are young people; even *one* young person proves that power. The power that takes away even one person from that flood, that is the divine power, the miraculous power, that Allah Almighty gives to real faith. ▲

58: communism and rejection of god

Our side in politics is that we must be with those people who are against Communism; that is our politics. We can't accept Communism or anyone who allies with Communist countries. We are going with those who have been given divine books; we are not going with those who are rejecting and denying holy books, heavenly orders or guidance, because they are against our Lord Almighty and they must be punished, and not in the far future – *soon* they must be punished.

Therefore, that is our main politics: not to be with Communists, with Communist ideas. People are one thing, but Communist ideas are making people fall into difficulties, fall into troubles, making them suffer. We are not agreeing with such ideas.

Muslims are followers of the *sunnah* of the Prophet (s). The Prophet made alliance with *Ahl al-Kitab*, with those people who had been given divine books, but he never made alliance with those who did not believe in God Almighty.

First of all, everyone should know who is his friend and who is his enemy. Whoever comes into Islam, whoever believes in his Lord Almighty, must know who is against his Lord. We know that our chief enemy, our biggest enemy, is Satan. And his followers, all of them, are Satans.

Communism is not only against *us*; it is against our Lord, fighting our Lord; you must know this. In Western countries, value is given to individuals; everyone has value. But in Communist countries, people are like herd animals: there is no individual life so that everyone may live his life, and Allah Almighty allows people to live their lives. Who can prevent it? Only those people who are denying that there is a God Almighty in existence. But people always are not thankful to their Lord – in England, in France, in Germany, in the United States, in every free country. They are asking for Communism to come to them and make them slaves, like herds of cattle. Then – finished! No one will be able to speak about anything.

The Communist leaders are laughing at people, pretending that these factories are for you, these shops are for you. They are putting forward one person [as their leader]; for one person, the whole world is going and coming, and they are not leaving off fighting against Allah Almighty, keeping back the rights that He has given us. Who has given them that authority? Allah Himself gives us those rights! *Alhamdulillah* that we are in London. In so many countries you can't speak about such things, you can't do *dhikr*, you can't do your worshipping freely.

Understand, or not? We *must* understand! So many people never understand and they are going with Communists. As a punishment, those whose hearts are with them will not remain on earth; the divine anger is on them. "We have sentenced God to death," they say. You must know that!

Therefore, your desire may be for the world not to be in two parts, but the Prophet (s) said that the world *would* be in two parts, that people would be in two camps. Fourteen hundred years ago the Prophet said this. You can prevent it? You *never* can prevent that! And it is not just that on one side there will be Communism and on the other side free countries, but now we may really consider all people to be believers and unbelievers.

All Communist people, those who accept Communism, are not believers, and standing in the face of them, against them, are all the believers. We are saying that they are *all* believers, whether they are Jews, whether they are Christians, whether they are Muslims; we are saying that all of them are allied against the atheism that Communism represents. You can't stop this. This is a time when people are divided into two camps, believers and unbelievers; there may be unbelievers in the west; there may be believers in Communist territories. We are only criticizing unbelievers, wherever they may live. ▲

59: keeping mercy in our hearts

We are in need of Allah Almighty's favors at all times. We are now in the last part of Holy Ramadan, in the last quarter, and we are expecting *Laylat al-Qadr*, the most important night in Islam, perhaps in any religion, to be during the last third of Holy Ramadan. And we are asking from our Lord to meet that holiest night.

The Prophet (s) was always in *i'tikaf*, seclusion, for ten days during the last third of Ramadan, and it is a well-known *sunnah* of our Prophet. Here, perhaps in Central Mosque, some people are observing that, or maybe in other mosques, so that the mercy of Allah which He keeps for every worship may come down on us, also. At least one man, one person, must do that in every town, in every place, where there are some people from the *ummah*.

We are intending to do that, but it is difficult for everyone to do. Yet we are asking for some part of those Mercy Oceans, and we may reach those favors and Mercy Oceans through our intentions. In Islam, intention is more important than deeds, the Prophet said, because Allah Almighty gave us a short life, and it is only to try His servants. And we have been ordered to do our best for everyone on every occasion.

We may *intend* the best in everything. Our physical body's powers or our financial capability may not reach that point, but our intentions may. Therefore, the Prophet (s) ordered the people of his nation to always be keepers of the best intentions. The place of intentions is our hearts, and Allah Almighty always looks at His servants' hearts and He likes there to be good intentions in them. Therefore, every worship is for the purification of our hearts.

Allah Almighty is not in need of our worship or praise. His heavens and His worlds and His universes are full of worshippers, and our worship is not even one very small drop in an ocean. Even though Allah Almighty has endless respect and endless worship and praise from His servants, He is not in need of their worship. Nevertheless, He ordered praise and worship and the whole of the *Shari'ah* and *tariqat* for His servants. The main purpose of all of them is purification. Because Allah Almighty looks at your heart, the best thing servants can do is to put their hearts in the best possible state by making them pure for their Lord Almighty.

Therefore, on the Last Day, on Judgment Day, Allah Almighty will reward His people, His servants, not according to their deeds but according to their intentions. Our deeds are only so small, but our intentions are wider and wider. And Allah Almighty wants to give His servants more and more from His endless favors. He is not keeping His endless Mercy Oceans and endless Favor Oceans for Himself because He is not in need of such things, but everything – every mercy and every favor and every grace – is only for His servants.

In our forms we are very small but by creation, by our inner forms, we are wider and vaster than all the universes. The universes may be so many. It doesn't matter; man is always more important and bigger than all the universes, and more valuable in the sight of Allah Almighty. Therefore, man has endless desires, never getting tired or fed-up with his desires, even during this life, which is a very short one; it is only like lightning, quickly coming and disappearing between pre-eternity and post-eternity. And our souls' desires in the post-eternal life are going to be endless.

Therefore, Allah Almighty created man as His deputy, so that, no matter how much he may ask, his Lord may give. And when He gives, He is pleased; when His servants ask more and more, He is more and more pleased. That is a divine attribute.

He likes to give, He likes to give endlessly. *Why are you not asking?* And He is angry with us when we do not ask, in contrast to His servants; when *we* are asked for more, we are angry, but Allah Almighty's attribute is to give endlessly. Therefore, honor to you and endless good tidings for you, O sons of Adam. You have been created for endless mercy; you have been created for *mercy*!

Therefore, we are the most fortunate of all creatures because we have been created for the endless Mercy Oceans of our Lord, Allah Almighty. And Allah Almighty is asking one thing from His servants. What is that?

"O My servants, I am merciful to all of you. Be merciful to My servants, be merciful to My creatures. That is what I am asking from you."

The last time that Gabriel (A) came to beloved Muhammad (s), the Prophet was about to leave this earth and go to his Lord's Divine Presence, and he was advising his nation, "O my *ummah*, keep mercy, be merciful." And the Prophet asked Gabriel, "Will you come after my death? After I leave this life and go to the Divine Presence of my Lord, will you come to earth again?"

And Gabriel answered, "Yes, on certain occasions, for certain reasons, I will come; I will come several times." And he mentioned some of them and said, "I will come again to take away mercy from hearts." There are other things that Gabriel (a) mentioned, but I am speaking now only about that point: that he would come and take away mercy from hearts. That has happened now in our time.

Mercy is just finished in hearts. Very few people are keeping mercy because mercy cannot be in a heart in which there are no beliefs. Whoever does not believe in his Lord, you can't find mercy in his heart. Therefore, although Allah Almighty orders us to be merciful to each other, we are living in a time when mercy has gone up, returned to the Mercy Oceans of our Lord, and mercilessness is growing on earth, growing each day because each day beliefs are decreasing.

And in our time, from every direction, there are attacks on beliefs, even within religions – even in Islam, in Christianity, in Judaism; unbelievers are growing from inside. Reformers are a new fashion among people. They are claiming that religion must be renewed, must be reformed, and they are completely foolish, no-mind people, engaged by the devil, by Satan, and devils are establishing their sovereignty on [the basis of] unbelief. Therefore, everywhere, people who do not believe in anything are increasing. *If they do not believe in a Creator, in what do you expect such people to believe?*

And then, in proportion to that unbelief, mercy is thrown out of hearts, finished, and now they are preparing themselves to destroy everything, everyone living on earth, so that no one will remain on earth. Earlier, people fought with arrows, with stones, with swords, with spears, but now people are trying to invent some bombs of death with which to kill everyone.

If a person is a believer, you may say to him, "Kill an ant," and he may think about why he should kill it. He may say, "That creature is also glorifying its Lord. If it does me harm I may kill it. If not, for what?" Then, how, with a bomb, can you kill everyone among innocent people, nothing-knowing people, without making any difference between armies and civilians? You can fight armies with armies, but what about others? <u>It is prohibited to kill anyone who is harmless, who does not do harm!</u>

But now people are not thinking about that. Both sides are preparing to kill each other. And Allah Almighty just sent all the prophets and ordered them to say to people, "Keep respect for your Lord. Be respectful to your Lord and be merciful to His creatures."

These are two pillars. Don't just say, "Not missiles."[138] That is correct, but it must be from both sides. Otherwise, one side must be totally with its Lord; then there will be no effect of that other side's bombs. But we are *not* with our Lord, and therein is danger for everyone.

Therefore, that lack of mercy among people is carrying them into the hell of this world; that mercilessness is carrying people into a fire-flood. At the time of Noah (a), Allah Almighty sent water, a rain-flood, but now He is

---

[138] Referring to earlier questions about nuclear disarmament.

sending, by the hands of His servants, a fire-flood. Only the one who has mercy in his heart will never be harmed, here or in the Hereafter. Therefore, we are in need of more mercy.

Take more mercy! *How* can we take more mercy? This fasting month is teaching us something about mercy because the one who is fasting tastes what the pains of hunger are, and mercy grows in his heart for those people, those millions, suffering with hunger. As much as you think about them, more mercy from divine Mercy Oceans comes to your heart and surrounds you. *You* can't see it, but there are some people who can see that certain people are surrounded by mercy. Even if the whole sky becomes like fire, it will never affect them; they are protected ones (even if some of our brothers are objecting to saying "protected," yet there *is* protection, divine protection, for some servants; yes). And as much as you may be merciful, you will be protected more.

There will be a blood-flood and a fire-flood, and more men will be killed and more women will be protected, so that men will be less. There will be one man for fifty women, so many men will die. What is the reason? Because men's hearts are like rocks; you can't find any mercy in them, but in women's hearts you can find more and more mercy. That is the reason why women should be protected. But men are like Nimrods, with their rockets, and so much punishment will come on them.

Therefore, make mercy to grow in your hearts. You must practice that; you must be merciful to everyone. Don't look at peoples' bad actions; perhaps that will make you hate them. But you can ask from your Lord mercy for everyone. Therefore, Allah Almighty is saying, *"Wa 'afu 'anna, wa ghfir lana, wa rhamna,"*[139] teaching us to ask forgiveness and mercy and His favors for all, for everyone. And as much as you are asking for everyone, mercy will come, covering and surrounding you.

---

[139]"And pardon us, and forgive us, and have mercy upon us." (2:286); note the plural, asking for everyone collectively.

It is impossible for all the armies in the world to keep you or protect you. People are making some underground shelters for atomic war. It is impossible. The only shelter for you is to be merciful to everyone, merciful and compassionate. That will keep you, that is a shelter for you.

And we were speaking about intentions. Just as rewards from Allah Almighty are coming because of good intentions, all punishments are coming because of our bad intentions. Don't intend or ask anything bad from your Lord for anyone. Don't curse anyone, because that curse will turn and come back on that person, landing on his head first.

We are asking our Lord Almighty to put us under the shelter of His mercy, and anyone who is asking for a mercy-shelter from his Lord must give his compassion to everyone. ▲

60: suitable words
for all occasions

Bismillahi-r-Rahmani-r-Rahim. When you begin with the name of Allah, All-Mighty, All-Merciful, you must weigh your words, not saying just anything under the title of "Bismillahi-r-Rahmani-r-Rahim." If you weigh or balance your words, you must know the suitable speech for every meeting, for every occasion or assembly.

People are sitting here. You must know what they are in need of, to give to them. But it is difficult. I am attending so many people's speeches, particularly religious people's. The people who are listening may be in the East but *they* are speaking about the West; people may be in the desert but *he* is talking about the poles.

For what are you saying *that*? It must be suitable for your listeners, and it is impossible to reach that point without using your spiritual power. You can't say everything to everyone. It is like a chemist.[140] The one who comes to him, asking about his sufferings, will take any medicine he may give. But a chemist isn't able to do this; only a physician can prescribe which of them is for him. Although he may be a chemist, the keeper of all medicines and drugs, he never knows which of them is for whom.

And now scholars, the doctors of the *Shari'ah*, are keepers of so many Quranic verses and *hadiths*. But it is not enough to make a speech or to give people what we know of verses, what we know of *hadiths*, giving whatever we know. No; for everyone there is a suitable speech which may be given.

---

[140]Pharmacist (British).

Therefore, the scholars of olden times, when they had finished learning *hadiths* and verses and other knowledge of the *Shari'ah*, would go to some knowledgeable people to practice how they might use those verses and *hadiths* on others, as now a physician finishes taking his diploma but afterwards he is an assistant to an experienced doctor. It is not enough to learn. He must get his experience by working with another doctor, a specialist, an experienced one; then you may trust him. Then why not for the *Shari'ah*?

Therefore, many times – not *some*times! – what they are destroying is more than what they are building, and our new scholars' interest is to destroy the old structure but they can't build a new one.

That is a catastrophe. Our time is a time of unbelief and everyone is destroyed, particularly religious people, in every kind of religion. Even in the three monotheistic religions, newly-emerging scholars are trying to destroy everything that was built by the people of olden times. New scholars and doctors of *Shari'ah* are going to destroy the old faith, the old beliefs, totally; their interest is only to make people not to believe in anything. They want to destroy all old things, what people believed in olden times, those beliefs coming to the present, so that they may no longer be seen. But they can't build new ones, no. The old ones are going and no new one is coming, and people are becoming lost. Therefore the disease of atheism is covering everything. People do not believe in anything.

Therefore, no one is taking any spiritual joy from our scholars, as if you are wood or straw. But you are not an animal. What are scholars giving to people except paper? There is a kind of Syrian feast with rice, meat and pine nuts. The doctors says, "Don't eat this. It will make you fat. Better to eat this straw. Then you are not going to be fat"; yes, something like this. Therefore we are saying always: "Encourage people to believe in something. Don't destroy their beliefs. *Guide them to believe.*" ▲

61: the darkness of the present era

The Prophet (s) said that there will be, among his nation, a group of people who lead the flag of haqq, of truth, of right. Everyone may speak against them but they will not change their way; they are on the right path. And the Prophet said that when the Last Day approaches, Muslims are going to be lonely people, alone. Among great masses of people, they are going to be scattered like stars in the sky: There is one here, one there; in the mass of darkness, they are little dots.

There will come a time when the world is going to be in darkness; there is sun but yet darkness. It is not the darkness of night. The darkness that will come on the earth will be because of peoples' dark actions.

Now, in Western industrialized countries, people are saying that the air is dirty, there is pollution. What is the reason? So many factories are causing it, making air pollution. This is as much as they are able to see. But there is another pollution, making darkness.

The whole world is in darkness now; you can't find *any* place without pollution. Darkness, heavy darkness, the Prophet (s) said, more than midnight's darkness in the countryside. At that time, Muslims will be alone amidst great masses of darkness, and if someone says, "This is white," and it *is* white, in the darkness people will not be able to see, saying, "No, it is black."

Therefore, you can't change the minds of people during this time. The Prophet (s) said, "Jewish people will be divided into seventy-one parties, groups, and Christians into seventy-two groups. My nation is going to be divided into seventy-three groups: Seventy-one Jewish, seventy-two Christian, and seventy-three, my nation."

We now have seventy-three different understandings, different ways of thinking, about Islam. And the Prophet said, "Except for one, all of them are wrong and their ways lead to Hell."

And the *sahabah*, may Allah bless them, asked, "What is that exception among the seventy-three groups?"

And he said, "Those who are on my way and on my *sahabah's* way."

Now, therefore, you can find Muslims with different understandings everywhere. Particularly in our time, people are trusting in their minds more than in traditions and they are understanding different things, asking for evidence concerning Quranic verses and *hadiths*; but they are such people as have no leg to stand on. Therefore, it is difficult to change a person's understanding. As the Prophet (s) advised us, if people have different thoughts and different understandings, you must follow a way that your heart is pleased with, with which it is peaceful or satisfied.

If your heart is not in peace with a person, don't listen, don't sit with him. Leave him. That is the main sign for us. If your conscience says that that person is sincere, it is enough to be with him to learn sincerity. That is the important thing; no need to learn anything else. Everything follows from sincerity. ▲

62: the need for patience

So many people are suffering now; there is suffering among millions of people. No management, not enough care for anything. And Allah Almighty is giving His servants one order, one command: to keep everything in the best way.

That is the command, the never-changing command, from Allah Almighty: "O people, keep everything that you have been given in the best way." But people have lost this. We are not keeping our Lord's favors in the best way but we are using them in the *worst* way. Therefore, suffering is always increasing.

If we can use everything in the best way, we will not fall down, always going up. We can use our money in the best way, we can use our bodies in the best way, we can use our minds in the best way, we can use our eating and drinking in the best way. But none of what we have been given as favors by our Lord Almighty are we using in the best way, but rather using them in the worst way.

That is the source of troubles. Only one order: "Keep My favors in the best way," but no one is doing that. "Use your youth in a good way": they are using youth in the *worst* way. The best time of our life, springtime, we are now using in the worst way, *the worst* – it can't be worse! Youth are passing from that age, and they are physically and spiritually finished, damaged, totally destroyed; all of them are in a state of sickness, ill people. And we are without hope for any government to do anything about that. They can't do anything. They have power but they can't use it because they themselves are ill, also.

Therefore, it is such a thing as, when autumn comes, the leaves of the trees fall down; no power can keep those leaves on the trees. Only certain trees are keeping them but most trees are dropping their leaves on the ground; from now until spring comes, never will the trees get their leaves back. We are losing everything that we had before, and it is impossible to get it back until spring comes. And we are waiting and expecting spring to be near, so that when it comes the naked trees will again wear leaves. Now it is impossible. Only some trees like you are wearing leaves, but generally they are going away. And everyone is waiting, expecting springtime.

You must be patient. People may say anything, they may object to anything, because they are ill people and an ill person loses his taste. If you give him a tasty thing, he may say, "Tasteless, no taste." *We must be patient.*
▲

63: seeking a leader from our lord almighty

Allah Almighty helped and supported His beloved Muhammad (s). He was alone when his Lord ordered him to call people, to say, *"La ilaha illa-Llah,* there is no God but Allah." No armies, no treasures, not anything of this world's powers was with him. That is the greatest miracle of the Prophet, the Seal of the Prophets, Muhammad (s). If anyone has a brain in his head, he must look at that basic point.

He was alone. Now, from being one, alone, throughout the fifteen centuries up to today, Islam has spread over the whole world. Now on this earth, on this planet, there are more than one billion Muslims. People are afraid when they are saying that there are one billion Muslims, but they will be two billion; will be three billion, also, because Allah Almighty has promised us that the whole world will say *"La ilaha illa-Llah."* And we are waiting.

O believers, we are at a time when we are in need of Allah Almighty's support. If He does not support us, no one can support us. And Allah Almighty is teaching the *ummah* of Muhammad (s) by mentioning an event concerning the Children of Israel.

When they fell, there was no support for them; they knew that it was impossible to rise up. Then they ran after their prophet, saying, "You must ask from our Lord a king. *Ub'ath lana malikan nuqatil fi sabil-Illah,*[141] make a king for us. The king will keep us under his command – such a king, such a

---

[141]"Send us a king so that we can fight in the way of Allah." (2:246)

strong person who will gather us under the flag of Allah Almighty so that we may fight against the enemy." And we are weaker than the Children of Israel, but still we are not asking Allah Almighty to send us a person who will be responsible, a leader!

Our teacher, Grandshaykh, was saying that now everyone who goes to *Hijaz*[142] is asking Allah only on behalf of himself and his family. Yes, we *must* fall down into the deepest part of the valley now; we are asking only for ourselves, we are saying, "*Nafsi, nafsi, nafsi* – me, me, me!" only, not anyone else. And the Prophet, throughout all his life, asked Allah Almighty on behalf of his nation, his *ummah*; and we must ask from our Lord what He promised for Islam, for every time that people may ask, and then He may send him to us.

Now we are in need of that person. He should be an extra-ordinary being, not from the common people, not from common presidents or kings; no. We are asking a divinely-empowered person to be sent to us to keep the *ummah*; otherwise, it is impossible. You look at the West, you look at the East; no more hope for our people. We are asking for a heavenly-empowered person, as Allah Almighty mentioned in this verse. Therefore, we must *at least* be like the Children of Israel: they asked for such a leader and Allah sent him to them. *You must learn what Allah is teaching.*

Then, the second point that Grandshaykh mentioned concerning support: we are in need of the support of our Lord Almighty, and He ordered the Prophet (s) to say, "*Wa Allahu fi 'auna-l-'abd ma dama-l-'abdu fi 'auni akhihi.*"[143]

We have forgotten this. We must write in golden letters and post everywhere that in the time of His Prophet (s), Allah gave such a *hadith*, because *hadiths* did not come from the Prophet's own ideas, they came from Allah; yes, he spoke as his Lord ordered him to speak. "O My servant, as

---

[142] That is, for *Hajj* or *'Umrah*.

[143] "And Allah is in support of the slave [of Allah] as long as the slave is in support of his brother."

much as you support My servant, I will support you. If you do not support each other, no support will come – finished." Therefore, we must be for everyone, we must support others as much as we can; we must give support for the sake of Allah Almighty to everyone.

O believers, we are responsible. We have been ordered by our Lord Almighty to raise high *kalimat-ullah*, the word of Allah, and to put down *kufr*, unbelief. Look! From traditions, we know that Nimrod made a fire, a big fire. For what? To burn Ibrahim (a), Abraham. That fire in Basrah could be seen from Damascus, so long a distance but so big a fire. For what? For one person! For one person one match is enough, but Nimrod was so afraid of Abraham. And you must be, every one of you must be, like Abraham. He was only one but he was like a match.

And everyone was carrying wood for that fire. Only one ant – you know an ant? – a black ant was running, carrying in its mouth a drop of water and running. "Where are you going?" it was asked.

It said, "I am going to extinguish the fire of Nimrod." Therefore Allah Almighty rewarded that ant and mentioned in the Holy Quran that Sulayman (a), King Solomon, spoke to ants, giving them honor.[144]

What is that ant? What is it able to carry? What is that gigantic fire? Allah Almighty is teaching us: "O people, don't say, 'What can I do?' You can do as much as an ant can do." We must try for this: to raise up the word of Allah Almighty and to bring down the word of our *nafs, hawa, Shaytan, dunya.*

Now, throughout the whole world, from East to West, from North to South, there is the sovereignty of *Shaytan*; he has established his sovereignty and people are serving him. And he orders everyone to help him with his sovereignty.

When, how, can we be safe from the fire-flood? You must think and you must act. *That is Islam.* ▲

144A reference to Surah Naml, the Chapter of the Ants, 27:18-19.

64: entRustinG ouR families to ðivine pRotection

I am saying to our Turkish brothers in London, in England, in Germany, in every place where they are living in Western countries, that they must be careful about their children. Yet it is impossible to safeguard our children in Western countries. We are trying to keep Islam and *iman*, but it is so difficult for our children because conditions are so heavy, so difficult, taking our children away from us. And my Grandshaykh reminded me today to speak on this point. It may be useful for all other Muslims also, because our children are a very important matter in our hearts.

Every week, every Friday (it may be best to be on Friday), you must gather your wife and the children who are living with you – the small ones, the big ones, all of them. Make them clean themselves, wash their faces and hands and feet, and sit around you, and you sit in the middle. And repeat *Kalimat ash-Shahadah*,[145] *"Ashhadu an la ilaha illa-Llah wa ashhadu anna Muhammadan 'abduhu wa rasulihu,"* three times, and then also three times, *"Astaghfirullah, astaghfirullah, astaghfirullah"* – if more, it doesn't matter.

Then give your *shahadah* and *istighfar*[146] to the Prophet (s), with your family: "O my Prophet, I am giving this *shahadah* to you from all of us, and I am giving my family to you, also, under your view, under your gaze, to keep them." And the Prophet is *amin*, trustworthy, one who keeps *amana*, trusts, and then he will take them under his protection, under his view. We

---

[145]The Declaration of Faith, "I bear witness that there is no deity except Allah, and I bear witness that Muhammad is His messenger."

[146]Asking for forgiveness.

hope that this will be like a protection for the new generation in Western countries, because Muslims are often asking me and complaining to me about their children.

In the time of Prophet Hud (a),[147] when people denied Hud's prophethood and would not listen, would not come to faith, Allah Almighty informed Hud that He would destroy the 'Aad nation by a strong windstorm, and Hud (a) gathered all the believers and sat down in a place, making a circle around them. Then, by the command of Allah Almighty, that storm came upon them, taking everything, everyone – and Hud's people were like the tower of a church or the minaret of a mosque; gigantic people they were – from the earth like leaves, taking them up and throwing them down, breaking them into pieces. But inside that circle where Hud (a) was sitting with the believers, that wind came softly, gently, like a wind from Paradise coming down.

Now, Grandshaykh said that in Western countries, and everywhere else also, there are heavy storms, taking people away. No one can make himself firm except the one who puts himself inside a circle of protection with Allah Almighty, and this is a strong means to keep the *ummah* in Western countries and everywhere else. Once each week you may do this renewal of your faith and ask forgiveness from Allah Almighty, and He may make a circle around you and your family so that stormy winds cannot enter or you will not be out in them.

That is a protection for us; otherwise it is impossible to keep the new generation. That is most important for Muslims, but it is also important for everyone, because non-Muslims, Christians and other peoples, are also affected by those stormy winds. Everyone is suffering, and there is no shelter for the sons of Adam except what Allah Almighty makes as a shelter for them. The one who comes under that shelter may be in safety and

---

[147]Hud (a), a prophet of ancient Arabia whose story is told in the Quran, was sent to the rebellious and unheeding 'Aad tribe, who were destroyed by a terrible windstorm after consistently rejecting the divine guidance.

peace, but the one who runs away is never going to save himself or anyone else. And all people now are suffering from their families, from their children. Nothing can be done now in our time except to come to the shelter of our Lord. There is no shelter except our Lord's shelter.

May Allah put us under His divine shelter, and everyone who belongs to us and everyone whom we are dealing with. And we are asking shelter for all the people who are living in this huge city. It is an obligation of gratitude for believers to pray for others, as well as to ask for them, also, a shelter with Allah Almighty, because a believer must ask for good. As much as he asks for himself, he must ask for others also. We will be pleased if everyone believes in his Lord, we will be pleased with anyone who is going to be his Lord's servant. And we are also asking to continue to be our Lord's sincere and humble servants. *Amin.*[148] ▲

---

[148] Amen.

65: events of the end-time

Factories are making the air dirty, but there is another dirty cloud, going from West to East, coming from East to West, from North to South, from South to North, covering the whole world. Now it is unseen *dukhan*, smoke, going around the whole world, just as the Prophet (s) informed us that when the Last Day approaches, there should be smoke, black smoke, covering the whole world. The unbelievers are going to be like drunk people from that smoke. It is a sign of Qiyamah, the Last Day.

Now in our time, that smoke, those black clouds, are unseen, covering the whole world, but after this there will also be *seen* clouds, smoke, covering the world. That is *fasad* – evil, wickedness. Good attributes have disappeared and bad attributes are increasing. People are leaving *fard*, religious obligations, and doing *haram*, prohibited, deeds; they are leaving the *sunnah*, the ways of the Prophet, and accepting *bid'ah*, new fashions, innovations. They are leaving *ittiba'*, obedience, leaving off following the orders of Allah Almighty and the way of His Prophet (s), and keeping the ways of unbelievers.

In our time, for every fashion that is against the ways of the Prophet (s), Muslims are looking and saying, "This is good, this is very suitable," while for the ways of the Prophet they are saying, "This is no good now. That has finished; leave it. Take from the new fashion. Leave the ways of the Prophet. They are old-fashioned."

Now people, the new generation, are 'brainwashed,' but in reality they are making their minds *dirty*, not washing them. Yes; making them dirty, with dirty thoughts and raising doubts against *Shari'at-Ullah*, Allah's Divine Law, and against the ways of the Prophet (s). They are following fashions, not following the ways of the Prophet. This is a general illness which has appeared among Muslims in the Islamic world. Our people are looking at Western countries and thinking that what comes from there is best for us and what we have is worst.

We must keep the way of the Prophet (s) on our eyes, on our heads,[149] but instead we are throwing it on the ground – and stamping on it, also, *astaghfirullah*! The Prophet (s) is not an ordinary person; he is *extra*-ordinary. He is perfect – in his feelings, in his attributes, in his spiritual powers, and in his physical, bodily, powers. Prophets are perfect; their vision is perfect. Therefore, when the Prophet said, "Just as I am able to see from the front, I am able see from the back of my head, also," that is something which he was saying humbly. Perhaps he was able to see in six directions, not only from the front and back but from every direction because he is *nur*, light, and *nur* shows everything. We have *nur* only here [in our eyes] but he is complete *nur*, complete light, so that he can look and see from every direction, even at midnight.

Therefore, don't suppose that the Prophet is an ordinary person; rather, he is a person of extraordinary power. And he said, "O my *ummah*, you are going to follow *Ahl al-Kitab*, those who have been given heavenly books – you are going to follow them exactly, *shibra min shibr, zira'n min zira'.*"[150] This means that you are going to follow them step by step; for *everything* you are going to follow them. Even if they enter a fox's hole, you will also try to enter that hole.

Now, there is a meaning from that coming to my heart. In our time, people are wearing such tight clothes, as if going into a hole, and, because it is a new fashion, all people are wearing it, men and also women. Yes, Allah's Messenger (a) spoke the truth; always his words are true. And, as he said, we are running after fashions that are coming from Europe, from

---

[149] That is, with the greatest respect, honor and obedience.
[150] Span by span, cubit by cubit.

Western countries, and we are throwing away our customs, saying, "No good!'

Yes; that is the sign of *Qiyamah*. But people are thinking about new buildings, new highways, jet planes; they are looking at that and saying, "Oh, *dunya*, this world, is going to be new, to be renewed." But this is an old *dunya*, very old, more than me.

And *Qiyamah* is approaching, silently approaching. And it will come suddenly; after its signs, it will suddenly come. But we are saying, "There is still so much time – doesn't matter! We must have so many new fashions. Then, when the signs come, we may take our care." And now all the small signs have already appeared. After this, there are going to appear the ten *big* signs of *Qiyamah*. When one of them appears, the rest will follow quickly; not much distance between them; no.

Therefore, now there is waiting a great war that will destroy three out of four parts; three-fourths is going to be destroyed and, out of seven people, six are going to be destroyed. The most terrible and the greatest war is coming now, and that is the bridge or mediator between the small signs and the big signs; when that war breaks out, the little signs are going to draw near to the big signs. And you know that the people of this world are waiting. Everyone is awaiting that war, morning or evening. There is a fear on the whole world.

When that begins – finished! The big signs will follow the war, and during the war, Mahdi (a) will say *takbir*, "*Allahu Akbar! Allahu Akbar! Allahu Akbar!*" and he will appear for Muslims, and then the great sign, *Dajjal*,[151] will come. After the second great sign, 'Isa, Jesus Christ (a),[152] will

---

[151]The arch-deceiver or Anti-Christ foretold by the Prophet (s), who will appear during the End-Time and lead people to their destruction by calling them to a false religion and performing miraculous feats.

[152]According to Islamic belief, the prophet Jesus (a) was not put to death on the cross but was raised to Heaven alive (see 3:54-55, 4:156-157). According to *hadiths*, he will return to the world during the period of the Mahdi (a), will live for forty years, and then will die, and the Last Day will follow soon thereafter.

come. Then three parts of this *dunya* will sink into the ground; then *Yajuj* and *Majuj* (Gog and Magog);[153] then *Dabbat al-Ard.*[154] Then *dukhan*; this whole world is going to be covered by thick smoke.[155] Then fire. Then the sun will rise from the place of its setting, the West. When it is all complete, *Qiyamah* will come. ▲

---

[153]Gog and Magog are a people mentioned in 18:94 and 21:96.

[154]The Beast of the Earth. The *hadiths* concerning the events of the End-Time can be found in several collections of *hadith*, such as *Sahih al-Bukhari* and *Sahih Muslim.*

[155] Mentioned in 44:10.

66: MORE CONCERNING the MAhDI (a)

Until Mahdi comes, things are not going to be straight. When he comes, he will put everything in its center. Now all people have left their centers. Women are not in their centers, men are not in their centers, children are not in their centers; learned people are not in their centers; universities are not in their centers, have left their centers. Therefore, it is the time of dhulm,[156] oppression, because justice means to put everything into its center. When people move out of their centers, they become oppressors.

This is not put on that, that is not put on this. This is not put on her head; this tea you can't put here. Understand? Allah Almighty created everything to be in its center. Therefore *fasad*, depravity, and *dhulm* are almost complete now, at the highest degree.

How are people of religion officials, how are officials people of religion?[157] How are people worshipping for their own selfish purposes? How are people doing what their egos are commanding them? All things except the sons of Adam are in their centers, but the sons of Adam have left their centers. Therefore we are in need of someone to say to us, "Get

---

[156]Dhalm (pronounced "zall-um"), meaning injustice, oppression, transgressing proper limits, or doing something inappropriate or incorrect, has also been defined as putting something in a place where it does not belong -- in short, to misuse or treat anything or anyone wrongfully or in ways that are cruel, unjust, wrong or inappropriate.

[157]That is, it is incompatible with sincerity toward Allah that a man of religion should agree to occupy an official post in which he may be subjected to pressures from a ruler, government or party, which has control over his means of livelihood, his ability to speak out for what is right, and even his life.

in, get in, get in to your centers." That is Mahdi (a), and he is commissioned by Allah Almighty.

No one can stop him; no power can stop Sayyidina Mahdi (a). He is coming to put everyone in his center, taking him by his ear and putting him there: "*You* – this is your center!" No one takes your ear *now*.

Then, when he comes, he will arrange everything. Now everything is going in so many different ways, like this, like that, from six directions, and accidents are happening with everything. When one has an accident, another comes, and another and another. Therefore the ways are closed; no one can move. All are waiting now. Sayyidina Mahdi (a) will come.

Therefore, officials will never like a Mahdi to come, and he is going to fight those people who claim that they are people of religion and at the same time officials. Official "religious" people can never like Mahdi (a), and, as they are fighting now, they are going to fight when he comes. ▲

67: patience to help reach our goal

O my Lord, give us from Your light. We are in need of Your light, in our hearts, in our bodies, *ya Rabb*.[158] Give us from Your endless favors. We are in need, we are in need! Give us opportunity, give us inspirations, for praising You, for thanking You, O my Lord, Allah Almighty. And accept us, *ya Rabb*. O my Lord, accept us.

This is the final day, the last day, of Your holy month for the nation of Muhammad (s). Give us from Your endless Mercy Oceans. Clean us, O our Lord, from every badness and from every trouble and suffering. Let our hearts be with You and You be in our hearts. And now Ramadan is finishing and going, saying good things and making intercession for some people, and complaining about others. Let us be with those people for whom Ramadan is interceding.

Yes, everything is going to be ended; nothing is going to be forever except what belongs to our Lord Almighty. Everything that belongs to our Lord is going to be in existence forever but everything in our life is going to be ended, and we must not be cheated by our egos, going wrong or understanding wrong or doing wrong. We are training how we can be right; we must take care of our wrong actions so that we can put them right.

It is a sign of *Qiyamah*, the sign of the Last Day, that a long period becomes short, that time passes quickly.[159] That is a sign of *Qiyamah*, because the heaviest load is on the people living in our time, more than on

---

[158]O Lord.

[159]A paraphrase of a part of a *hadith* concerning the End-Time.

any others who lived before and left this life. Even though you are seeing that it is the easiest time in terms of technology, in relation to our inner life, these are the most difficult conditions for everyone.

No one can be excepted from those conditions. You may live in a hut but you can't change the weather. One person may live in a hut and another in a palace, but the weather covers them all – winter weather, cold, snow; each one who lives in a palace takes his share of the weather or of winter. It cannot be for those people living in a palace to make winter into spring; you may use heating, a fireplace, making everything all right, but outside it is still winter. Therefore, in our time, all people are suffering because sufferings are transferring from one person to another, and therefore the number of psychiatrists will become more and more and more.

Therefore, we are saying that it is the most difficult time for everyone. There are only certain people who may be excepted from that, only a few people who are cutting a way, like a rocket going up to the atmosphere – so difficult to cut that distance. But when it is up, finished; no need to expend such power any longer. It goes by itself. Until gravity leaves it, it is in danger and difficulty, but when gravity leaves it – finished!

And for us, also, as much as our *nafs'* gravity catches us, it is so difficult to be on that level. That is the level of peace and satisfaction, and the level of pleasure, the level of familiarity. Yes, you may find so many Oceans. You may be on the level of love, you may be on the level of beauty, you may be on the level of mercy; they are Oceans. The one who reaches that goes forward from that level but does not come down. But, until reaching that level, this gravity of our egos catches us too strongly. *That* is giving us suffering; that is the suffering of people. When they reach there, there is no more ego with them. But they are only like stars; you may count them – just one, two, three, four, five. Yes.

Not too many people may be able to achieve that, but everyone is suitable for reaching *toward* that, to cut the way. But we have lost only one thing. That is patience; we need more patience. As much as you can acquire patience, it is going to be easier to reach that level.

Allah Almighty is teaching you by every worship how you may be patient. And this is the month of patience, to make people to be patient. If you can continue on that way after Ramadan, you may build your way to those levels: to the peace level and satisfaction level, the familiarity level, the love level, the beauty level; endless Beauty Oceans, endless Love Oceans, endless Mercy Oceans, endless Favor Oceans, endless Knowledge Oceans; yes, endless Light Oceans. You may find everything. ▲

68: living with certainty (yaqin)

Certainty gives power to people, while knowledge alone never gives them benefit. A person may be a big scholar but have no certainty. Another may be an ordinary person but if he has certainty about a few matters, he may be able to defeat evil, while that scholar cannot.

Yes, so many learned people can't keep themselves away from evil, while so many common, ordinary people may keep themselves away. Therefore, a little bit of certainty is more important than to be a big scholar without certainty. Anyone may acquire more knowledge, and, as Abu Yazid al-Bistami, may Allah bless him, said, [addressing scholars,] "You are acquiring your knowledge as if from one dead person to another," signifying no certainty. "But we are acquiring it from Allah Almighty." When Allah Almighty gives knowledge, He gives it with *certainty*.

Certainty, *yaqin*, is the soul of beliefs. You may say, *"Amantu bil-Lah*, I believe in God, and in the angels, in the holy books, in the prophets, in the Last Day, in *qadar*." That is how a little boy begins school, saying, "A, B, C, D... ," saying it without certainty, following his teacher. But afterwards, when he understands, he becomes certain that it *is* really "A" or "B" or "C".

Therefore, it is important for everyone to make himself improve in certainty, not remaining as he is. Everyone *knows* something, but not everyone has certainty about what he knows. Certainty comes through the heart of the Prophet (s).

The certainty which was with the Prophet came most of all to Abu Bakr, may Allah bless him. The certainty which came to Abu Bakr was not the same as the certainty coming to the other *sahabah*. Each one of them had certainty but not like Abu Bakr's certainty. And you can't get certainty from a person who doesn't have it. Understand? Not everyone can give it to you. If I don't have certainty, I can't give it to you. Only the one who has certainty can give it to you.

Therefore, it is important for a person to listen to lessons from the *Shari'ah* or from *tariqat* or from *haqiqah*, from Reality. If the teacher has certainty, he will give to you with certainty. If not, he will give you only some plastic forms. There are plastic roses, plastic fruits; he can give you those, but when you bite them, you understand that they are plastic. And even a shapeless fruit is more lovely to you than a house full of plastic apples.

What does it mean, to have a house full of plastic apples or grapes or bananas or oranges? Better this, even if it is a shapeless apple or grape or banana, because you can eat it; you can't eat those others. Therefore, don't be cheated by nice lectures, nice writers, no. Ask for someone who can give you certainty. Certainty comes from hearts and enters into hearts.

Therefore, the ranks of certainty are different. The certainty of Abu Bakr was much more than that of the others, but from every *sahabi*, the Prophet said, you can get certainty. And you must find their inheritors, *awliya*.

The certainty that the Prophet (s) brought to his *ummah* is not taken up. Still, among the *ummah*, his inheritors are keeping that. If you are in need of it, you can ask to find it. If not and you are saying, "Plastic is better for me now," you can have as much as you like and enjoy yourself.

Therefore, our lectures may be shapeless in comparison to scholars' writings and their lectures, but we have something that most scholars have lost, have never had, and that makes the servants of our Lord who are asking for certainty and sincerity come from East and West. The number of our listeners or readers is not important. Important is that, even if there are a lot of people, they may listen and accept and keep such jewels from

Reality. So many people are coming and going from the grocery store, but jewelers are not like grocers. People rarely come to the jeweler, and it is enough for him.

Therefore, don't be cheated, because there are so many famous people claiming that they have spiritual ways, a spiritual relationship to the heavens or spiritual powers. *Don't be cheated.* In our time, for the person who crowds around himself thousands of people, you can understand that it is empty inside, because people now are looking only at the outward view; they are cheated by the appearance of people. The one who is in need of showing himself makes too much noise but inside there is nothing, no relationship to the heavens.

QUESTION: Sometimes my certainty is very strong, sometimes not there at all, up and down. How can I get it to be stable, regular, continuous?

SHAYKH NAZIM: Regular certainty, *yaqin*, means regular walking in certainty. Sometimes still, as we are beginners, our ego is carrying us, and when you are walking on its path, your *yaqin* is going to be weak, reduced.

As much as you are keeping the relationship with your Lord in your heart, certainty is present and it will improve. But if you are seeing that sometimes you are going back, you must know that something is wrong with your actions, affecting your certainty, because our actions are like a mirror for our certainty. You may know everything about every action.

Our actions affect our certainty. Therefore, when your certainty is weak, you may understand that there must be something wrong with your actions – and wrong from inside, also, because certainty is related to our hearts, while actions come through our organs. If something wrong is done by any organ, it affects our certainty.

When we have certainty, we may keep our organs away from every prohibited action. If no certainty, you can't do that. Therefore, the heart is commanding our organs. If you can keep your heart, then you can keep your organs. And you can't keep your heart without certainty. ▲

69: doubt, belief, and spiritual and physical illness

Every doubt means a hole in your mind. If you fall into it, it is difficult to get out. Doubts are like holes in a field; if you don't fill them or put something on them, you may fall down. Therefore, it is important to take care of doubts because everyone's mind is suitable for accepting doubts.

A well needs two persons, one digging and the other one up, outside, carrying away the dirt. Don't leave your ego to make a hole in your mind, and Satan taking your ego and digging. If you do not take care, he will make a bottomless hole. If you fall down into it, you will never come up.

Particularly in our day, everything is running to make holes in beliefs, to cast doubts on beliefs, and the greatest thing that all beliefs have in common is the existence of God Almighty. Now in our time, all the powers of evil, all the powers of devils, are running to make people in doubt concerning the Creator, and that is the ultimate of foolishness and mindlessness and nonsense. If you see a person denying the existence of the Creator, you must know that he has to be someone who has escaped from a mental hospital.

QUESTION: Is there a way to fill up the holes?

SHAYKH NAZIM: Yes! They may be filled quickly because belief quickly fills everything. Belief fills the holes of doubt. Therefore, we are in need to believe. If one has no beliefs, then they are not safe from doubting, which may accelerate until a person denies himself. or is in doubt of his own existence. That is the opening to the mental hospital, making people crazy.

Such people are going to be in doubt of everything, because the one who doubts the existence of the Lord Almighty is going to have doubts about *everything*, even about himself, saying, "Do I exist or not?" Then he is going to discuss with his ego, sometimes saying, "Yes." and at other times saying, "No. I exist because now I am present with myself. I eat, drink, come, go, do, live. Yes, I exist. But after one hundred years I will not exist. Therefore, how can I say that I exist? It is only imaginary, an illusion, because I am between being and non-being. How *can* I exist?"

But belief fills that hole made by doubts, saying. "You were in existence both before and after. You were in existence before coming to this life, in a real existence, and this is only a manifestation by means of which you are now looking at yourself. This life is like a mirror for you so that you may see your existence now, but before you were secret, hidden, in Power Oceans. Now your Lord is giving you a form and you may look at yourself; you yourself are looking *at* yourself. Then, when you recognize yourself, you will return to your real station. You will have recognized yourself, that you are in existence." That is what belief says to you.

If there is no belief, it is impossible to remove doubts, and if anyone does not remove his doubts, he will never remove suffering. You may be in doubt about yourself, in doubt about your wife; the wife may be in doubt about her husband, her children, her parents; people may be in doubt about each other. You may sink into an endless Doubt Ocean.

Therefore Allah Almighty begins the Holy Quran, after al-Fatiha, the opening surah, by saying, *Bismillahi-r-Rahmani-r-Rahim. Alif lam mim.*[160] *Dhalika-l-kitabu la rayba fih.*[161]

---

[160]*Alif, lam* and *mim* are the letters of the Arabic alphabet corresponding to A, L and M. Many *surahs* of the Quran begin with such combinations of letters, about whose meaning there are various interpretations.

[161]This verse, 2:1, may be understood as, "This is the Book in which there is no doubt, guidance for those who are mindful of Allah"; or, "This is the Book; there no doubt in it -- guidance for those who are mindful of Allah"; or, "This is the Book without doubt; in it is guidance for those who are mindful of Allah." Each of these understandings is admissible

Three letters at the beginning. Allah knows who knows the exact meanings, for they are only a cipher, a code, between Allah Almighty and His Prophet (s). But sometimes Allah Almighty lets some of His beloved servants know the secrets of the letters. Each letter carries secrets, endless secrets; they are keys to the Holy Quran. The Holy Quran is endless oceans, not only one ocean – endless oceans. When Allah Almighty says *"Alif,"* the first letter of the Arabic alphabet, it indicates to us an endless ocean, and as often as He repeats *"Alif"* and once again *"Alif,"* each one of those *alifs* indicates another ocean and yet another endless ocean; you can't find the same meanings in each *alif.* In the Holy Quran you may find perhaps thousands and thousands of *alifs*, each one representing an endless ocean of divine knowledge.

Yet, according to our capacity, we may know something. As *sultan al-mufassirin*[162] Ibn 'Abbas (the son of the Prophet's uncle 'Abbas, may Allah bless them; he is the 'king' of those who have explained the Holy Quran) said, "*'Alif* signifies the name of Allah Almighty, *alif* beginning the word 'Allah'. '*Lam*' signifies Gabriel, and '*Mim*' signifies Muhammad (s)."

O people, that holy book which came from Allah Almighty by means of Gabriel to Muhammad (s), without doubt it has come from Allah Almighty, from His Divine Presence, through Gabriel to Muhammad (s) – without doubt. No one can have any doubt about that Book's being from Allah Almighty, Allah saying, *"La rayba fih"*, no doubt in it," so that it takes away all doubts from everyone; because man is full of doubts, and if he wants to fill every doubt by himself, he can't do that without using that holy Book.

Yes, it covers doubts. For all people, as many different doubts as there may be, they are going to be filled by the Holy Quran, the Glorious Quran. They are going to be like the holes of ants. When a river floods a place, which holes may remain? It fills them and goes.

---

and correct, complementing the other.

[162]The chief of the commentators on the Quran.

Therefore, we are in need, as believers, to always ask for one who has stronger faith than our faith to carry away every doubt from our hearts. And as much as you are able to believe in a person, he may give you benefit, may make you satisfied. Therefore, when you take part in a grandshaykh's association, you are feeling satisfaction. If you are not feeling satisfaction, it means that you are still in doubt and that that Grandshaykh can never give you anything. You must know this sign: if you are finding satisfaction, you must know that he has more spiritual power than you and is able to fill the holes of your doubts. Otherwise, leave him.

Therefore, faith or belief begins by believing in individual persons. If your patient does not believe in you, you can't cure him; finished. Therefore, first came the prophets, and we have been ordered to believe in the prophets so that it is possible to believe in God Almighty. If you do not give your trust to an individual person, you can't have belief in God Almighty. Therefore, Allah Almighty says that you must believe in My prophet, beloved Muhammad (s), that he has been given a Book from his Lord Almighty through Gabriel – *this* Book, "*dhalika-l-kitab.*" Without any doubt, you must believe that he brought you that holy Book, the Glorious Quran, from My Divine Presence through Gabriel, and you have trust in his personal existence as a prophet. Then everything is going to be all right. Otherwise, it is impossible.

At every time you can find the same illness, doubt illness, occurring among people, coming from their doubting, their mocking, at believers – yes, making them a substitute for entertainment. You can find that illness during every period, and in our day, beliefs are the subject of ridicule for all people. They are drinking, getting drunk and entertaining themselves at the expense of those who believe. That is the illness that is going to destroy humanity on earth – from both sides, destroying it spiritually and destroying it physically.

QUESTION: Could you please speak about the relationship between disease and the soul? If you become sick or have an operation, does that actually affect your soul or is it a reflection of some illness in the soul? If you have doubt in your soul, could you become physically sick? Or, if you are physically sick, does that show you have doubt in your soul that you weren't aware of?

SHAYKH NAZIM: When we say "illness," it may be physical or it may be spiritual. Each of them is different. Spiritual illness is always going to give troubles to the body, but bodily illnesses do not give trouble to our spiritual body.

When we are ill spiritually, it is going to have effects on our bodily life, but if our souls are healthy, our bodily suffering never affects them. The proof is Ayyub (a), Prophet Job. He had so much bodily illness but it never affected his soul;[163] his soul was always thankful to his Lord, saying, *"Alhamdulillah, alhamdulillah, alhamdulillah."* But when the soul is ill, people are going to be ill spiritually. Then the body is going to go down, to be destroyed.

Therefore, the doubts that we are seeing now among people have reached the utmost, the ultimate point, and they are destroying them spiritually and physically, from both sides. That is terrible!

QUESTION: If all psychiatric illness comes from disbelief as its root, does all physical illness come from disbelief, also?

SHAYKH NAZIM: No, it does not necessarily come from disbelief, because prophets sometimes bore illnesses; *awliya*, saints, also. But that is another thing; there are divine wisdoms in that. Sometimes prophets were carrying heavy burdens for their nations; *that* made them ill. For example, sometimes parents may be ill for their children; when they are carrying so much sorrow within themselves, their physical bodies may become ill. But prophets and *awliya* are never ill in their souls.

When the soul is ill from doubts and disbelief, that makes the physical body weak and there is no resistance to keep away illnesses. But when the

---

[163]See 21:83-84 and 38:41-44.

spiritual body is strong and ordinary illnesses come, it may resist them, as in the case of prophets' illnesses and sufferings for the sake of their nations, which their bodies bore and were not destroyed. If they were going to be destroyed, Job's body would finally have been destroyed, but that did not happen. He bore it but was not destroyed. ▲

70: make time for god's service

Endless praise and thanks to our Lord Almighty that He is granting us to complete the holy month of Ramadan once again. This is from His endless favors to us. You can't get that with money. It is something from our Lord, given to His servants.

We are claiming nothing. We are saying only, "O our Lord, we are Your weakest servants, and we are ashamed to say that we fasted or we prayed. Everything that we did was through Your favors, by Your Will, by Your power. Grant us from Your endless favors.

"If you leave us in the hands of our egos, only badness and evil will appear from ourselves. Therefore we are asking forgiveness for every bad deed, and we are also ashamed to say that we fasted and prayed during Holy Ramadan, because it is not suitable, O our Lord. O our Lord, it is not suitable for Your most high Divine Presence to bring such fasting and prayers, while there are in Your Divine Presence countless servants of Yours presenting to Your Divine Throne excellent and most beautiful praises every day, every night, at every hour, every moment, every time."

In spite of that, Allah Almighty shows His angels the fasting people of the nation of Muhammad. Angels are glorifying Allah Almighty; they are giving the most beautiful praises, excellent praises, to their Lord. But they are free for that; they are free only for that purpose. But the sons of Adam are surrounded and occupied by their *nafs* and by *dunya*, and at the same time attacked by *Shaytan* and his armies.

We are in a difficult position. Therefore, when we present something, Allah Almighty knows that we are presenting our respects to His Divine

Presence under such difficult conditions. Therefore Allah Almighty is showing the angels and saying, "Look at My servants. My servants are fasting and trying to keep My command, trying to give their respects to Me. And they are totally occupied by their egos, surrounded by their egos' desires, and they are sought after by *dunya* at every moment. In spite of that, they are trying to fast and to give their respect to My command. Look!" Yes, He gives honor to the *ummah* of *Muhammad,* and we have been honored to be from His beloved Prophet Muhammad (s).

Allah Almighty is one who gives endlessly. He is one who has endless favors; He is one who has endless Mercy Oceans and endless treasures; He is one who has endless Beauty Oceans; He is one who has endless Pleasure Oceans. And He is not in need of His endless Oceans, but the endless Oceans are all divine grants from Him to His servants.

Therefore, there is an endless Paradise. In Paradise you are going to find His endless Mercy Oceans and His endless favors, His endless lights; your Lord's endless pleasures, your Lord's endless Happiness Oceans and endless Satisfaction Oceans. And in Paradise you are going to find your Lord's endless Peace Oceans and His endless Power Oceans and endless Beauty Oceans. You are going to find everything that you can desire in Paradise endlessly.

That is endless good tidings for the sons of Adam. *You are not going to be nothing!* Inasmuch as He is in existence from pre-eternity to post-eternity, He is going to give you eternal life, to be in existence eternally, and you have been granted to be with Him Almighty.

O *mumins* and *muminahs*, you must think, for such endless favors as our Lord Almighty is granting us, what is their value. If you buy only a hut here in London, you will be a slave to a mortgage throughout your life; you will work to pay a mortgage for a hut, and in a no-good locality, also. Then what do you think about an eternal Paradise, a territory for yourself forever?

You work hard, you and your wife, from morning to night, from night to daybreak, and you say, "We are paying a mortgage on a hut." But do you ever think of paying a mortgage for your Paradise?

We may say that if people believe, they will be hard workers, more than ourselves, but I am seeing that we are so lazy in working for our mortgage in *Akhirah*, in the Eternal Life. Now, we must know what is the value of Paradise and of Eternal Life, and we must give more time to our Lord's service; otherwise, we must be ashamed in front of our Lord. On the Day of Resurrection, when He gives us from His endless favors, so much shame will come upon people that everyone will ask to disappear from the Divine Presence. O *mumins* and *muminahs*, give more time for your Lord's service or for the Paradise mortgage, if just a little more – a little more.

We think about giving it but our egos are not letting us give more. Our ego is saying to us, "You must work for *Me*, you must serve *Me*, you must do everything for *Me*, not for anyone else. I will never accept a partner!" Our ego is terrible! Therefore, don't let your ego command you and carry you as it likes. Instead, you must ask divine support to fight, to defeat, your bad ego and to bring it under your Lord's service.

Your *nafs* has been given to you only for your Lord's service; you must use it for serving your Lord. But people are receiving the horse of the king and are not receiving the king; they are receiving the donkey but are not receiving the guest on the donkey. We are receiving the horse – I mean to say, our *nafs* – but we are refusing the holy guest that we have been given by our Lord Almighty, our soul, putting the donkey on the chair and putting the guest in the stable!

It is enough for today, and this, at the end of Holy Ramadan, I think is for everyone – for every believer, without making any difference between Muslims or Christians or Jews. For those who believe in God and His prophets and His holy books, this lecture may give them a power, may give them a pleasure, may give them a support from their Lord Almighty.

When They are making me sit in this chair to speak, my heart is always in contact with my Grandshaykh's heart, and his heart is in contact with the Prophet's holy heart, and the Prophet's heart is in the Divine Presence. I am not speaking to you with excellent English. They are able, my Lord is able, to make me speak in a way that surprises people, but it is enough for everyone, and we are asking forgiveness for every mistake, for every misunderstanding. Your souls are understanding what I mean to say; doesn't matter if my English goes like this, like that. We have a saying in Turkish, "Wrong ship, right course"; it is something like that.

Endless praises be to You, O our Lord, *ya Rabb.* Our Lord, make us to continue. Falling, standing, we have walked thirty days. *Hadha min fadli Rabbana, Jallahu A'ala.*[164] ▲

---

[164]That is from the favor of our Lord, may His glory be exalted.

71: the difference between pride and spiritual satisfaction

When you look at your soul, you must be pleased and in expansion, you must be smiling. But when you look at your *nafs*, you must be solemn, sad.

Your soul gives expansion, your ego gives contraction. Therefore, as much as you are with your ego, you are in contraction, you can't smile. Yes, that is true; everything related to our egos is full of sadness and contraction. But everything related to our Lord, from our souls, gives us expansion and pleasure and peace and satisfaction and lights.

QUESTION: You're saying that everything related to the soul gives pleasure. Then is it right for us to feel pleasure in our souls? For example, if you do something for the sake of Allah that you feel good about, and you're pleased with your action or you're pleased with what you feel about it, isn't that pride? How can we tell the difference?

SHAYKH NAZIM: That is related to Allah; the source of expansion of souls is from our hearts. When we feel this from inside, it is from the side of Allah Almighty and never, never from our *nafs*.

There is the verse, *"Maraja-l-bahraini yaltaqiyan; bainahuma barzakhun la yabghiyan."*[165] These are two different things; pride can never enter in the side of the soul. Pride is always with ego, and ego takes its pleasure from outward things. And you may understand when your ego is proud, but,

---

[165]"He [Allah] has released the two seas, meeting; between the two is a barrier which neither of them transgresses." (55:19-20)

from the side of Allah, when you are with your Lord, that expansion comes directly from heavenly rays to you. No pride there.

Ego takes everything from outside, and you may know that it is the pride of your ego. Even if both of them occur in a person, they are never mixed with each other, just as Allah Almighty says that two seas run beside each other but never without a barrier; they are not going to be mixed. What you feel when you do a good action is not pride because that feeling comes to you from Allah Almighty.

Grandshaykh said that every night Sayyidina 'Ali would put his actions in front of him, good actions on the right, bad actions on the left, and then he would address his ego: "Look! All goodness is from your Lord, Allah Almighty, and all badness is from you. If your Lord leaves you, you are not going to do any good actions. Therefore these good actions don't belong to you. Don't be proud of these. That badness is *your* work!"

Then your ego will come down, will not be proud. It knows that every goodness is from Allah Almighty, by His *tawfiq*, His divine help, because if your Lord does not make you successful in doing those good actions, your actions will always be such bad ones. "Who did that," you may ask yourself"; "you or Someone Else? *How* did you do that?"

Then pride will never come to you. That is every day's *muhasabah*, accounting; that prevents that pride of the *nafs*. ▲

72: following a holy man

The thing which is important for people is to follow a holy man. A holy man means someone who belongs to the Divine Presence, what we call a shaykh.

It must be well-known that everyone is in need to follow a holy person in order to be a holy person himself. If you do not follow a holy person, you are never going to be a holy person yourself, and if you are not a holy person, you cannot go to divine or heavenly stations. For holy ones, the heavens, and for holy ones, the Divine Presence. Therefore, we must know who is a holy one.

All prophets are holy people, and the inheritors of the prophets, *awliya*, are also holy ones. Therefore, you must ask for a holy man, and the description of a holy man must be well-known.

Holiness does not mean to be a 'religious' man or to be a learned man. No; holiness is something else. But we *must* follow such a holy man. You may ask from East, from West, from North, from South; from England, from Russia, from Caucasia, from Damascus, from Baghdad, from *Hijaz*, from Jerusalem, from Egypt, from Marrakesh, from Africa, from Yemen, from the Philippines, from China, from America. You may ask from anywhere and there must be, *must be*, some holy people. Don't suppose that they live only in Mecca or in Medina or in Jerusalem or in Baghdad or in Tibet, the Himalayan Mountains, or only in monastaries; no. They are free people.

Holy people are free people; the whole world is under their footsteps. No need for passports, no need for visas, also; they are free, moving from

East to West, on the seas, on the mountains, in the skies. Nothing prevents them because they are holy people. Because they are deputies of the Lord of the universes on earth, they must have super powers, and they are in heavenly stations and in the Divine Presence.

Which thing gives them holiness? Holy people's holiness has been given to them because their hearts are always with their Lord. That one is a holy person whose heart is empty of everything except the love of his Lord. His heart is occupied or engaged by his Lord Almighty.

That is a holy one, like the prophets, like the *awliya* and angels. But a person whose heart is occupied, engaged, by this life's pleasures – he is not going to be a holy one, even though he may be the most famous scholar, even though he may be at the top rank of a religious *silsila*, chain. He may be at the highest point of the hierarchy among Muslims, among Jews, among Christians; there are some titles that we give them. That is not important; you can't call *that* holiness. If Allah Almighty does not give a person holiness, it is not something that can be given by wearing special clothes or by crowds of people; no. But we are asking our Lord Almighty to give it to us. *He* gives holiness to His servants, and He is not going to give a person holiness if he does not give his heart to Him. That is important.

You must not be cheated, deceived, by the titles that we have been given in the hierarchy, that *man* gives; no. You must follow a person who has been given holiness. You can't buy a ruby from a grocery shop; you can buy tomatoes. A tomato is red also, and a ruby is red, but a tomato is a tomato, not a ruby. You can find tomatoes, potatoes, in a grocery shop but not rubies and emeralds. Therefore, if you are asking and you know what you are asking, you must look seriously into where you can find it. If you are not in need of a ruby, take a tomato and go!

Anyone who believes in holiness and anyone who believes in eternal life, anyone who believes in the existence of the Lord of the universes, the existence of the Creator Almighty, must ask for a holy man in order to follow him. But, as we said, you must not be cheated by someone because he may be a scholar or a religious man, but instead you must ask your heart.

If you are satisfied with a person, don't look at whether he is a scholar or a learned person or a shaykh, a rich one, a poor one. Leave that. If your heart says to you, "That person is a holy one," keep him and take from him. You may take your holiness through him; he is a door, opening and giving to you. But if your heart does not bear witness, if there is no tranquility, no contentment in your heart, leave him. Look for another one.

In our time, people are running after empty titles, after the titles that other people give them, not asking for the titles that their Lord gives them. "I am the first, I am more important than you!" "No, *I* am more important!"

Doesn't matter! *You* are important also; if you were not important, you would not be in existence as a man, a human being. Man is the most important one, but heedlessness is not allowing us say and accept this, and we are running after the empty titles, nonsensical titles, that we are giving to each other. *Why?*

The one who knows realities during this life is always free, and the one who does not know is a slave. Therefore, I am not running after titles. It is enough for me, enough and more than enough, one million and trillion times enough, endlessly enough for me, that Allah Almighty, my Lord, is giving me the title of being His servant. If you give me all the universes with all their treasures, I will not give up or change that title.

Therefore, people are running after being *something*, and I am saying to the people who are coming to me, "I am nothing, and you are going to be nothing, also. If you are satisfied, you may come to be nothing," but so many people are running away. I am saying, "*Alhamdulillah!* He will never come back because he is asking to be *something*, but I am nothing and making people to be nothing."

That is what we are trying to do: to make people agree to be nothing. But they are quarreling with me, saying, "We must be something!" And every trouble is coming through that point, that claiming, "*I am....*"

73: BEING WITH YOUR GUIDE

If we are separate, we are like parts of a *tasbih*,[166] beads. If there is no string, they will be lost, scattered, but when they are on this string, that can never happen. And for each person, if alone, there is danger of being lost, but if coming with an *imam*,[167] on a string, he is protected.

Look, everyone! (Shaykh Nazim shows his *tasbih* - rosary.) Sometimes this string is strong; sometimes it is very weak and quickly breaks. Therefore, you must be careful. A silver one is stronger – you know? Then anyone who is with a shaykh, with a guide, the guide keeps him. If not with a guide, they are often lost.

We must be humble, as much as we are able, to be in agreement with a shaykh, with a guide. The guide is the most important person throughout our lives, because everyone must take a guide, either on a good way or on a bad way.

Everyone takes a guide. If a person does not take a guide on a good way, another guide is waiting for him, quickly taking him to a bad way. For bad ways there are so many guides, so many devils, dressed like men and taking them. Therefore, everyone is in need of a guide, but you must be careful to take a guide throughout your life for goodness, not for badness.

Everyone knows that, for all people, this life is going to be either with good things or with bad things; everyone knows that. But so many times we are so weak in the hands of our egos, running after our *nafs*. When you run

---

[166]A string of beads used for counting the phrases of *dhikr*.

[167]Referring to the *alif* or long terminal bead of a *tasbih* or *subha*.

and make your ego or someone who is from devils as your guide, you quickly fall into dangerous, terrible places, hells. You must choose that way which is going to be suitable for you.

A strong guide keeps his followers; they may be in the East, they may be in the West. When Yusuf (a), Joseph, was in Egypt, his father Ya'qub, Jacob, was in Palestine or in the area around Damascus. And when the wife of the ruler of Egypt called Yusuf to her bed, and he himself was ready for that, his father showed himself and said, "O Yusuf, keep yourself."[168] Ya'qub (a) could have been in the Far East; doesn't matter – he could have been as far away as you can imagine. Nothing keeps back that power; distances never prevent that power from reaching.

Awliya have miraculous powers like prophets, but prophets' miracles are more perfect. *Awliya* do not have such power but they have the same attributes as *anbiya*, prophets; then that power goes through them, also. They can do miraculous things, and a true shaykh may keep his *murids*, whether they are in the Far East or in the Far West; they may send their spiritual power with every *disciple* so that they are not alone or solitary. When you remember him, that remembrance makes your shaykh's spiritual power to be ready with you, to be present with you. That is a miraculous power which every true shaykh has been given.

QUESTION: How can we make contact with our shaykh, not just for asking help but for being with him?

SHAYKH NAZIM: If a boy falls in love with a girl or a girl falls in love with a boy, they are occupied, they are always in contact with each other. If you have such love for your shaykh, you may be in contact sometimes.

Some people are engaged by their Lord, Allah Almighty. They are the *anbiya*, prophets, and *awliya*, saints. Never does anyone get into their hearts except their Lord; they are *always* in contact. Some people are always engaged with the Prophet (s), some people with their shaykhs. Some people

---

[168]An interpretation of the words, "If he had not seen the proof of his Lord" (12:24).

sometimes, maybe when they are in need, ask for their shaykhs. According to your need, you may ask, you may be in contact.

And it is so easy. When the remembrance of him comes upon you, you are in contact. No need for protocol. Quickly, when you think about your shaykh, he is with you; when you forget, you are far away. When you remember, he is with you, quickly.

You must understand this point. Then it is going to be more easy for our brothers and sisters to be in contact with their shaykh. Any time they may be in need, if reciting a *Fatiha* and sending it to the Prophet and their Grandshaykh, it is all right.

QUESTION: Why don't we always remember him?

SHAYKH NAZIM: Heedless, *ghafil*. The Companions of the Prophet (s) said to him, "O *Rasul-Allah*, when we are here with you, we are like on the Day of Resurrection, we are living as a person lives on that Day. But when we go from here, we are not as we were when we were with you."

And the Prophet said, "If the same condition continues with you when you are outside, away from me, the angels will come to shake hands with you. But heedlessness comes over you so that you may do something for your earthly life, also."

Only certain people, only a very few people, have been chosen to be for their Lord always. Even though they may be in markets, buying, selling, going, coming, building, planting, working with their physical bodies, their hearts never leave their Lord; they are always with their Lord. That is true. But it needs practice to be always with your Lord with your heart. ▲

74: tasting the sweetness of faith

A disciple raised the issue of difficulty talking about Islam to his non-Muslim family members. Shaykh Nazim responds:

Yes, because they are still slaves in their egos' hands – slaves, but they do not know that they are slaves. They imagine that they are going to be slaves when they come to Islam but it is the opposite: when they come to Islam, they are going to be free. Before Islam they are slaves. But you can't give any proof to them because as yet they are not tasting. However much you may say, "Honey, honey, honey," people are saying, "What is honey? Let us taste!"

Therefore, particularly in our time, if Allah Almighty does not give a chance to taste, no one can be in Islam. The hardest conditions for Islam are in our time. During the first period of Islam, Islam was new, like a new almond. A green one you can eat, yes?[169] It has a good taste. But when it is dry, you can't bite it; your teeth will be broken.

Now, this is an almond and *that* is also an almond. If you do not crack its shell and take out the inside, no one can taste it. But we are giving the 'almond' in its shell and people are putting it in their mouths, trying to bite it – with no teeth, also. Up to the end of this world they will be unable to eat it. But if you crack it and give the kernel inside, they will be pleased.

We can't do this. Only Allah Almighty does that, and as much as people are engaged by their lives' pleasures here, they are not free to look

---

[169]In some parts of the world, almonds, plums and the like are often eaten green, as a fruit, before the outer shell and inner kernel harden.

for their Lord. And their Lord is keeping that honey to give to that servant but he is not interested – interested in something else. When a person is interested, he or she will quickly come into Islam, quickly taste.

Therefore we are saying now that if all the scholars from the Muslim world come to Europe and speak to just one person – not a young one; we are saying any person of intermediate age – they can't convince that person to come into Islam, and for the young generation it is even more difficult. Therefore, in Western countries, people come into Islam if they can taste something of the inner life's pleasures in Islam.

If they can find, if they can taste, that pleasure, they may come to Islam through that pleasure; otherwise, it is impossible. No scholars whom I now know, specifically know, can be successful in calling people to Islam by their way, but a person who has reached a station through his spiritual life and has tasted may bring others. The one who tastes may make people to taste. If he himself hasn't tasted, if he doesn't have it but only says, "Honey, honey," never taking any pleasure, what is he going to make people taste? There must be something with him for people to taste. If he keeps, if he has made honey in his heart, he may give it, may make people taste.

What is "honey"? Honey in hearts is *ikhlas*, sincerity. The one who has sincerity may give sincerity to people; the one who has sincerity within himself is one who enjoys it, while the one who doesn't have *ikhlas* never enjoys it.

The one who has sincerity does not spit the almond out of his mouth but keeps it. But not everyone keeps it, particularly new Muslims. They may try it once or twice and then say, "We do not taste anything," and throw it away. But for the one who tastes the seed, the kernel, that is all right.

When you find something, you are pleased with it and you think that everyone may be interested in it. When you eat, when you taste something, you feel that everyone may be pleased with it, but then you give it to a person and he says, "I don't like it." Yes, some food which you may like, he never likes. Spiritual pleasures are different among people. Some people are interested in another way.

Now, as we are believers, we are going in different ways. Moses (a) struck a stone and twelve springs came, and each of the twelve tribes of the Children of Israel drank from a different spring. But it has a secret meaning, also: that everyone has a private spring for drinking, and that is best for him or for her. When you ask to change it, he or she refuses. And sometimes, when a person is ill, you may give him honey, sweet honey, but he says, "It is bitter."

He is wrong. Honey is honey but he cannot taste it. Finished; leave him. Allah says to the Prophet (s), "Leave them. If they do not taste, leave them. *I* am looking after them." There must be a divine intervention so that can change.

At the time, leave it; don't discuss it. Discussion brings hatred. Therefore, we have been ordered to say to such people, *"Lakum dinukum wa liya din*[170] – your way for you and ours for us; keep what you like and we will keep what we like, but don't come to discussion." Only to those people who ask you, you may speak. ▲

---

[170]"For you is your religion, and for me is my religion." (109:6)

75: false guides

We have a saying, that a person may be going on the wrong way and he sees that he is losing, but he says, "Perhaps I may gain." He is losing but he hopes to gain or to obtain something. And people are saying, "O our brother, leave this. You are on a losing way. Turn back!" And he says, "No. I must continue because now I have lost. Perhaps I may regain what I lost." But they say, "O brother, turn back, because anywhere you may turn, that is your gain. Don't think, 'Now I have lost so much, therefore I must continue.' If you are asking for benefit, turn from the losing way. That is your gain, your profit."

Therefore, a person may follow another person and each time he sees that there is no benefit in the relationship, but he says, "I followed him at the first and I must keep him." But if, even after years, long years, he turns back, he has turned to the way of benefit. As much as he may have lost, it doesn't matter. At any time he turns, that is his benefit. Therefore he must say "*Alhamdulillah.*"

If he were to go with him forever, *that* would be losing, but when he turns back, even after ninety years, he gets benefit. If continuing on his former way, he will always be a losing person. But if he turns back from here, it is good for him; if continuing and turning back even from *there*, it is good for him. Any time a person turns back, it is good for him; any time a person can turn from badness to goodness, it is good for him.

One point we must be most careful of, particularly new Muslims. Old Muslims also must know; everyone must know, because Islam is for everyone. Islam is such a huge 'supermarket,' and there is a private, personal place, private, personal things in it, for everyone. It is important to find the one who knows where is your special *amana* that you have been given by your Lord Almighty – where it is, to know it, and to take it.

For everyone there is a portion, for everyone a share, and it is important to find the one who can guide you to it so that it is not such a huge distance away, further than from East to West. And new Muslims are more interested in their spiritual shares. When they are coming into Islam, they are first asking for their spiritual shares because they have had so much of the physical, bodily shares. But you must know how to take the treasures that you have been given.

You can't take another's share as you can in this life; no, you must take your own share. If not, you are not going to be given that other person's share. Therefore, there is no jealousy among *awliya*, among real believers, among sincere people, among the sincere servants of our Lord. No jealousy, because everyone has been given treasures by his Lord, and one person's share is not going to be less than another's; rather, perhaps each of them is going to shine more, charming treasures. If you see your share, you are never going to look at another's. Your treasures will occupy you sufficiently; no need to look at this or that one. Therefore, no jealousy.

But some people have so much anger. For what reason? Some people, who are slaves to their egos, when they are cheating others, are becoming angry; fake people – they are not even the doorkeeper but they are claiming to be the treasurer and are cheating people. And every new Muslim is asking for his hidden treasures. They have the right to ask, "Where are our treasures? We are coming into Islam. We have a share in Islam, we have a share in the hidden treasures that Allah Almighty gave us on the Day of Promises. Where are they and where is they key for them?"

When Ahmad al-Badawi, a king-sized *wali*, asked his Lord to give the key to him directly, Allah Almighty said, "My divine practice is that whoever comes by himself is not given. The one who comes to Me through his guide, I give it to his guide and his guide gives it to him. That is the divine protocol: no one comes to My Divine Presence without a guide. Go! Take your guide and take the keys of your treasures from him."

Now people, particularly Muslims, are proud; they are not accepting a guide. Some of our European, Western, brothers are asking for a guide, but among our native Muslim brothers, only very few people are asking for a guide. I mean to say, among scholars; common people easily take guides, but scholars are looking to themselves and they are proud people. They are claiming that they know everything in Islam, that they know everything in the Holy Quran and in the *sunnah*, and they are saying, "We do not need to take care about a guide."

The Prophet (s) took a guide to Allah Almighty, the angel Gabriel (a). Then, what about scholars? And what about Ahmad al-Badawi, may Allah bless him, when Allah said to him, "You must come with your *murshid*, your guide; you must come with your shaykh or not come at all. I gave the keys of your treasures into his hand on the Day of Promises. That is My rule and I do not change My rule. Go and take from him."

Therefore, everyone must take the keys of his treasures from the hand of his shaykh, from the hand of his guide. If he has no guide, Satan will take him. Allah Almighty was going to give Satan a guide and He created Adam, but he refused; Satan refused to take a guide – too proud, and then he was gone. Therefore, whoever does not agree to take a guide may fall as Satan fell.

But, in our time, so many people who are not spiritually authorized are claiming to be guides and are guiding people on the wrong way. This is an important point to be clear for us. About non-authorized people, Grandshaykh, may Allah bless him, was always saying to me, "O Nazim Effendi, I will give you a simile concerning unauthorized people. A simile for them is that of a person looking at a beach and seeing a sailor taking people to the other side in his boat. Another person also comes and brings a boat, saying, 'O people, I can take you, also. Come into my boat. We can go to the other side.'

"And people are getting in and then little by little going out to sea, going away. But that person has never passed through that sea; he does not know how to use a compass. And the people reach the middle of the sea.

Then, no more eating, no more drinking, no more knowledge about how they can go on, to which side they are going. And the people are calling to him, 'Why are you not going?'

"He says, 'I can't.'

"'If you aren't going forward, go back. Take us back to our place.'

"And he says, 'I can't,' neither forward nor backward. They are going to perish, to drown, to die there, finishing, destroying themselves."

Therefore, don't suppose that anyone, any non-authorized person, can be a guide. You can't become authorized by reading books. That is something else; you can't be an authorized person that way. There are so many captains in boats, in ships. How many years do they study in a college and then come on the ship? So many long years of watching the captain, learning, practicing. *Then* they are entrusted to take control. ▲

76: how to Recognize a true guide

A person may fall into difficulties, because our life is just encircled by difficulties. If we save ourselves from one, the second may catch us. Everyone has difficulties, according to his or her faith's power. But no matter how many difficulties we may face, we must not be hopeless of divine help. The wrong thing done by anyone who gets into difficulties is to lose hope. He must try to keep his hope in his Lord, Allah Almighty, and try to face the difficulties as well as he can.

We are weak; without divine support it is impossible. But our life is always like this for reaching the top, for climbing. Everyone has been given something, some treasures, by his Lord Almighty, and that is at the topmost point. Therefore, everyone must face difficulties; without difficulties, there is no taste for life. But it is important to make difficulties pleasure.

Glory to Allah Almighty, *subhanallah*! In Western countries, difficulties are mounting, mounting. When people who are not from the West look at the outside, at television, they see that the people of Western countries are all happy: they are living without any difficulties, no problems for them; so much work, so much money, so much enjoyment. But it is the opposite; my head is going to be like *this* from hearing about the difficulties of people. They are all asking, "What is the solution? What can we do? How can we get out?" and everyone is caught in a trap. If you take off the chains from here, after a little, he or she is going to be caught by another; the same conditions, so many traps. You take off one and after a little, another comes, and he or she is caught again.

The one who is hopeless about life, every way locked on him, looks, at that time, towards the heavens. If there is no way out and he is surrounded from every side, at that time he looks up at whoever is reaching out his hand to take him out of there, asking for help. And when they are asking for help, so many 'businessmen' are coming from Eastern countries to the West to do business – worldly people, not heavenly people, and they are cheating people, making them fall down more deeply than before.

So many different people are doing business on that point; in order to satisfy their egos, they are making a business out of spiritual or heavenly ways. But they are not holy people. Mostly they have been cheated by *Shaytan*, by their egos; they belong to this earth, not heavenly people. They can't do anything except to deceive people and make more troubles for them.

Therefore you must be very careful of such people. If your heart is troubled when you meet one of them, your conscience signaling a red light, leave him and go away. If you go to a person, thinking that he is a holy man, but your heart is not in pleasure, in peace, with him, if pain comes to your heart, you must know that that is a trap, catching you. Then leave him and run!

QUESTION: Is it possible for a person to call people to God or to Islam, but yet his power is from *Shaytan*?

SHAYKH NAZIM: You must see who his God is. Some people are making *dunya* their God. *"Arayata man ittakhadha ilahahu hawahu?"*[171] Allah is saying; not everyone makes Allah his God, but some people make their desires their God. Therefore, we must see, if someone is calling, to what he is calling: to our Lord or to his *nafs*, making himself Lord over people.

---

[171]"Have you seen the one who takes his desires as his God?" (25:43)

To what is he calling? So many people are saying, "We are calling to Allah." *Who is your Allah? Tell me!* The Lord of the universes? Are you a humble servant, an obedient servant to Him or not? Tell me! When you are going from here, from your house, up to the Central Mosque, are you looking at girls, at ladies, or not? If you are keeping yourself, I understand who your Lord is. If you are looking, your Lord is your *nafs*, your ego. Allah knows well! ▲

77: accepting and consulting a guide

May Allah give us more light; we are in need of it. If we have more light, our way, everything, is going to be more clear to us. Therefore, we are in need of such people whose hearts are lighted by real faith.

There was a custom in our countries. So many neighbors were Armenians, and when they had a wedding ceremony and came out of church, everyone carried candles. Then they would take fire from a sacred place and go out. If there had not been such a fire, everyone would have carried a candle in his hand, but unlighted.

Everyone is created as a creation which can be lighted. If we take a piece of iron, it cannot be lighted, but a candle may be. And each one of the sons of Adam, of mankind, is in a condition suitable for lighting.

In our time, those people who are carrying divine lights through the Prophet (s) are still in existence. Therefore we are in need to follow a holy person, to catch one of them, in order to acquire divine lights. And who is a holy person?

The one who is carrying divine lights, he is a holy person. Don't think that just anyone who is a scholar, who is a learned person or a religious figure, is a holy one. Particularly in our time, religious people are officials, functionaries, and most official people can't be holy people, and those who are following them are just following them officially. Therefore, official people can't give you holiness.

In Islam, scholars and religious people are of two kinds. One kind are traditional scholars or officials. The second kind are holy people – heavenly people, heavenly scholars. They are carrying divine lights, and if you can follow them, you can take from them holiness and divine lights. Otherwise, you will remain in darkness here and in the Hereafter.

Therefore, Allah Almighty says in the Holy Quran that on the Day of Resurrection, those who have not acquired lights during this life will call to those people who are carrying lights, "O brothers, sisters, O believers, stop for us and give us from your lights!"[172] And they will be in darkness; they will not be able to see their way because they never asked for lights during this life.

If anyone is asking for lights, he may be given. But don't ask for rubies from a grocery shop. You must know where they can be had and you may take them from the one who has them. Otherwise, you will waste your life and go in darkness to darkness.

Therefore, every believer must follow a holy man. If you can find a holy man among Christians, that is all right. If finding him among Jewish rabbis, that may be, also; the real aim is to find someone who has heavenly lights and he may give to you. Or you may find him among Muslims.

We are not saying that just *anyone* is a holy person, no, but holy people may be found among all people. In every part of this world, among every nation, you may find them. The aim, the main purpose, is to find a holy person and take your light from him. Let him light your candle, whether you find him among Christians, among priests, among rabbis, among shaykhs. Yes, if you find him, go and take.

But to find those holy people is so difficult, because religious people now are mostly officials with diplomas, so proud of their diplomas, putting them here, showing people this. Therefore, you can't find holiness among official religious people; no.

---

[172]See 57:13.

You may try. Try, and come and tell me. Come and say to me that I found an official; he is a holy man. And you are free. But if you can take lights from an official, it will be a strange thing.

Yes, it is so difficult. But, if you believe that on the Day of Resurrection there will be no sun or moon – it will be a very dark day and everyone will need light on that day – don't be like those people who will go to the Day of Resurrection without getting *nur*, lights, from this life, and who will ask on that Day to get lights from those who have them. Here your not having lights may be hidden, but on the Day of Resurrection it will be clear who is carrying lights. On that Day, every secret will appear.

This means that if a person is asking for heavenly lights, he must go where they are, must go and get them. Don't wait to go on the Day of Resurrection, and when you see the divine lights which people have, you say, "Give to us now." No. You must get your lights here; otherwise you will waste all your life and go away dark, without lights. The one who believes in the Last Day must look after himself *here*, *now*. That is what Allah Almighty is asking from His servants: to get lights and come to His Divine Presence.

Now we are living in the last part of the period of the *ummah* of Muhammad, the nation of Muhammad (s). Therefore, everything is going to be easy and, at the same time, so difficult. Getting our light may be so close to us; if we turn like this, we may find it. It is so easy but it is also so difficult because our ego, our *nafs*, never wants to turn its face in that direction. Instead, it closes its eyes and says, "It is in that other direction," and runs after itself. Therefore, it is so easy and at the same time so difficult to acquire lights in our time.

When conditions are more difficult, Allah Almighty's mercy approaches His servants more. But we are running away. According to our egos and their desires, we are leaving what is near at hand and running after distant goals. It is easy, it is only one step, yet our egos will never agree with us to take that one step; so proud, our ego, saying, "You must follow *me*."

We are asking it to follow for only one step but it is not agreeing with us. If our *nafs* agrees to take one step with our soul, it may be caught. That trap will catch it; it can never go around it. Therefore, *nafs*, our ego, likes to escape.

That is important now. Don't say that perhaps only a very few people have lights; you may count them on your fingers. No worry. If all the holy people on earth are finished and you are asking earnestly, from the heavens, not an ordinary angel may come, but Allah Almighty may send Archangel Gabriel to take you from here to the heavens.

Therefore, this is something relating to our desire for spiritual development. As much as we may be serious in asking lights from our Lord Almighty, it is going to be easier. But if you are a follower of your ego, you can't follow a holy man.

Leave your ego, leave your *nafs*, and come. Come! It is so easy. Then holiness will come upon you as a garment, your Lord dressing you. And the Lord Almighty, Allah, never leaves the sons of Adam without holy people.

When all the prophets had come and gone, no more prophets, Allah Almighty made for the nation of Muhammad (s) as many holy people as *anbiya*, prophets. There were 124,000 *anbiya*. Then Allah Almighty made for the nation of Muhammad (s) 124,000 holy people, *awliya*. They are on earth; one foot is on earth and one foot is in the heavens. *That* is a holy one! They are not those people who do not yet know how to walk on the earth; the one who is not yet able to walk on the earth and to walk on the seas cannot put his footstep into the heavens. The one who may walk on the seas, on the oceans – *that* is the one who puts his footstep in the heavens. That is the sign.

Don't ask, "Who is that?" You may know who he is. They have signs, but in our time they are keeping back their signs from showing to people. They are keeping back their powers, and the only signs are that you may find light and also you may be in satisfaction with them, you may feel refreshment with them. Yes; if they were walking around performing miracles, it would be a show and people would turn away, but if you can take that refreshment into your heart, into yourself, from a person, that is a holy man. *Keep him!*

May Allah give to us from His divine lights; we are praying for that. But then, how can we find them? As much as you may be humble, you are going to find them easily. As much as you are proud of your worshipping, of your knowledge, you are going to be late in finding them ("late" means you will never find them if you are proud).

And when you find such a person, you must try to follow him. Don't do anything without consultation. Consultation in everything is for those people who are like shadows for that holy man, who follow him like his shadow. But if a person is like us, he must agree to follow that holy person in three things. *Important!*

Whoever claims to be a follower of a holy person must ask him at least about three important questions. One is about marriage. When he is going to marry, he must ask his permission, must consult with him. Even after finding someone, he must bring her to his shaykh and say, "I would like to marry this one." At the least he must *inform* him.

And secondly, as a follower, he must ask if he is going to divorce. Before the official registration, before going to court for a divorce, you must consult about it with your shaykh or with your holy person.

And third, for a long journey you must ask permission. Without permission, it is prohibited in our *tariqat* to move from one country to another. Even for visiting your shaykh, you must ask permission by phoning or writing, and if he gives permission you may come. For business, for visiting other countries, for pilgrimage, also, *Hajj*[173] – yes, for all of them you must ask. If he gives permission, it is all right, because he is not going

---

[173]Since the performance of *Hajj*, the pilgrimage to Mecca, at least once in a lifetime if conditions permit, is one of the five or religious obligations prescribed by Islam, what is to be consulted about with one's shaykh is not *whether* to go, since this is obligatory, but the advisability of going during a particular year or under specific circumstances.

to give permission by himself. He will ask from the Prophet (s) and *he* will ask from Allah Almighty. ▲

78: Reaching the state of genuine peace

When is a person going to find peace within himself? That is the question; yes, that is the thing that our sister has in her heart.

Rivers run until they reach oceans, struggling, running, until reaching an ocean or a sea. Then, finished. And whoever is asking to find peace within himself must also reach an ocean or a sea, or at least a lake (doesn't matter, because a lake is also firm in its place). But moving, struggling. Therefore, everyone is running, every day. Everyone, from morning up to night or from night up to morning, is running, struggling.

There are two ways in which a person may attain rest. One of them is through natural death. Until death, a person is struggling. When he dies, his arms and legs are spread out, no more struggling. Depending on his station, he has reached peace.

Yet his peace by natural death is only for his physical body, but still he has not reached real peace in his spiritual life. Therefore, we must ask for peace from both sides – for our physical bodies and our spiritual bodies. Our physical bodies are going to reach peace by death, natural death, when the body is going to be in peace, no movement, no struggling. But we must look after our soul, whether it has reached peace or not, whether struggling is still going on or not.

Therefore, the Prophet (s) says, *"Mutu qabl an tamutu."*[174] *That* is what makes a person reach spiritual peace and satisfaction, real peace and satisfaction. Our physical body may die, but as yet we haven't reached our

---

[174]"Die before you die."

spiritual peace. Therefore, the one who is asking for real peace within himself must try the ways of those who have reached real peace in their spiritual bodies, and the Prophet's advice to his nation, to ourselves, is to die before natural death comes upon us.

Only few people may be equal in their bodily peace and spiritual peace, because most people are destroying their spiritual peace by running after the physical body's peace, and it is impossible for a person, without reaching his spiritual peace, to reach bodily peace until natural death comes. But there is no benefit at that time; you are finding peace in your physical body but your spiritual body is still struggling and suffering. And then, from the day of one's death up to the Day of Resurrection in his *hayat barzakhi*, his life in the intermediate existence between the Eternal Life and this world's life, those troubles and struggles may continue. Perhaps they may continue even on the Day of Resurrection, and that may not be enough, also. He may be in Hell, struggling and suffering for a period until he reaches the Ocean he was given in pre-eternity.

Therefore, the most important thing that we must know concerns our absolute peace – when it is going to be. Until you reach that Ocean which Allah Almighty gave you in pre-eternity, you are going to struggle and suffer; and you may be in hell during this life and in the grave and on the Day of Resurrection, and then, finally, in Hell itself, also, because it is impossible to find peace without reaching your Homeland in that Ocean, and you are always running.

We are giving sufferings to ourselves because we are using wrong, wrong methods to acquire peace or to reach peace. Sometimes scientists are preparing a rocket to go up but it turns and falls back. So many people are using wrong methods, so that instead of going up, they are coming down – a crash landing, falling back. Only some small thing, even a simple wrong thing, can do that. Therefore, we must be very careful, when we use a method, about whether it is perfect or not.

We are trying to give a perfect method to everyone who is asking to reach peace, real peace, real satisfaction, and we mean to say that peace is everyone's destination. You may take a train from London up to Edinburgh and on your way there may be one hundred stations, and at each station some people are getting out because everyone knows his destination. If you get out before Edinburgh you will not be satisfied; you will say, "Oh, we came to some other place. This is not my destination." And if you get caught and remain in that station, you are going to suffer forever because you have reached a wrong destination.

Therefore, we must know our destination, and then we must take a ticket for that station, not before it and not after it. Both kinds of those who lose their destinations are suffering, here and in the Hereafter. Then a person must do something to save himself from that first wrong station; he must do something, he must suffer long, in order to find a way back to his original destination. It is therefore terrible and dangerous for a person not to look out for his destination; he must look out for his destination and must use the right method to reach his destination. If not reaching his destination, he will not attain peace; he will *never* attain it.

And in our time, people are using so many wrong methods. They are not understanding or they do not even know what is the beginning and what is the end; from where they are beginning and to where they are reaching, as a blind person never understands where he is or where he is going to be. And most important for a person throughout his life is a true guide.

A true guide may be known when your soul is in peace and satisfaction with a person. That is the sign, the real sign: to feel peace and satisfaction with him in your heart. If you are still in doubt, hesitant, it means that something is wrong with that person and you must look for another.

If your heart is not in peace with his method, you must not follow that way. There are so many ways, and you must try for another one until you reach peace in your heart, so that it should be all right for you.

Then, this is the way to reach peace, to die before dying. This means that when you find a guide, you must be with him. You must not carry a different personality from his but must agree to be one with him, one unit. You can't carry another personality from your guide's; you must melt your personality in his personality and you must appear as himself. *Then* you will be all right.

Once a person came to a grandshaykh and knocked at his door. The grandshaykh asked, "Who is there?"

"Ibrahim," the man said. "It is I. ("I, I, I," always saying "I.")

"'I?'" the grandshaykh said. "My place is only for one, not for two. Go away!"

And that person went away. After one year he tried again, coming and knocking at the door. "Who is there?" the grandshaykh asked.

"You, you."

"If you are saying, 'You,' now you may come in."

Therefore, the first condition for a person who is asking to reach real peace is that he must give himself, all that he is carrying, to put into his guide. His guide can take it and carry it. When you are going to be in your guide, that is the way to reach your destination.

There is an airplane. It can hold one hundred or two hundred or three hundred passengers, but when it is flying, you see only one jet plane. You do not see five hundred persons inside; you see only that it is a plane, flying. The plane is taking all those people into itself; finished.

Therefore, when you take a guide to your destination, you may be in him; you may give yourself, your selfhood. You must consider yourself as a drop. Then it reaches its ocean and no more drop – finished; you are leaving that drop and are going to be ocean.

That is peace. When that drop falls into the ocean, can you take it out, can you find it? Finished; it is all ocean. Therefore, peace is not to be found without leaving your drop in that ocean. And your guide may be a lake or he may be a sea, but *they* are running into oceans, also.

That is important, to say "Die before you die"; that is the meaning of how we may die before natural death. You give your personality to your guide, you throw your personality into your guide's personality, and then you say, "I am no longer in existence, finished." When you look at your guide, you see yourself in him, and when he looks at you, he looks at himself. And we – we reached our spiritual peace.

You may find it during your short lifetime in this life. But if you do not use true, correct methods and you go wrong, you will always go far from peace. Instead of running towards oceans, you will be running towards deserts. Therefore, anyone who thinks about peace and happiness and satisfaction and pleasure and endless enjoyment must look after his spiritual life's peace, and this is impossible for a person if he does not find an ocean and run into it, because our egos are always too proud to surrender.

That is the most difficult proposition that can be made to our *nafs*. The most difficult thing for the *nafs* is to put its personality aside and agree to be with another's. It holds onto its personality very strongly, never liking to lose it. Therefore, we are fighting.

Between our souls and our egos a fight is raging, our souls wanting to reach that Ocean and our egos saying, "No!" It is like a bottle containing water, which is thrown into the ocean: the water wants to reach the ocean but the bottle is preventing it. And our *nafs* is just like that bottle, never agreeing to be broken and to be nothing, and to let that water go into the ocean. Therefore, quarreling and fighting is going on between our soul and our *nafs*. The one who may be successful in defeating his ego and making it agree to take the same personality as his guide is happy and has reached final peace – real peace, eternal peace, eternal happiness and eternal existence.

We are happy or we are taking enjoyment from our existence. The greatest grant of our Lord to us is existence, but real existence may be gained only when we give up our false existence or being. If we give up our *fani*, transitory, temporary, existence, we can acquire permanent existence.

As much as we are holding on to it so strongly, not agreeing to give it up, it is difficult to reach the permanent and real existence.

Therefore, we must try to reach our destination, and the one who reaches his destination has truly reached real existence, eternal existence. And you must give this life in return for eternal life, in exchange for eternal existence. As much as we are holding on to this temporary existence, real existence departs. Then natural death takes that temporary existence from us. But there may still be a long way for us yet to travel to reach eternal existence, a way of suffering, in the grave and on the Day of Resurrection or in Hell so that we can reach the ultimate existence. But if you agree here, during this life, to use true methods that are coming from our Lord to His servants, it is the easiest and most simple way to reach real peace.

We are living during a time in which there are hundreds and thousands, maybe millions, of ways, but they are altogether wrong ways, ways of suffering, perhaps taking people to a wrong destination, bringing them to wrong stations and saying, "This is yours." And then that person takes out his address book and looks here, looks there, but, no – wrong! In our time there are millions of wrong ways.

Therefore, the one who is asking seriously about his destination must be serious about his guide and his guidance; otherwise, his life is going to be full of sufferings. And those sufferings will continue after he leaves his physical body because such sufferings belong to our souls, and the soul is going to suffer because he has never reached his Ocean. Until he reaches it, he must pass through so many wrong courses.

Finally, this is so important for anyone who is not drunk, since people now in our time are mostly drunk, not only by drinking liquor and wine, no, but most of them are drinking and are drunk on this world's life, on this temporary life's works and deeds and problems and troubles. Problems of livelihood particularly are making people preoccupied by heavy conditions, and then they are like drunk people, with no time to look after themselves because they are struggling, they are fighting. No time for millions to ask for a guide.

Therefore, up to the end, their troubles are continuing, and when they die their bodily struggle is finished. Their physical bodies are in peace but not yet their souls; their souls cannot reach peace and happiness. Therefore their troubles and sufferings continue after death, also, until they reach their real destinations in the Divine Presence.

Allah knows best how a person may reach his destination after death, also, when he sees that he has disembarked at a wrong station. Then people are running like this, running like that, to find a way to get out, but it is not easy. Therefore, take your care as much as you may be able during this life, if you are not drunk (if drunk, you can't take care, you can't look after anything).

You may ask from your Lord: "O my Lord, I am asking from You. I am asking for a guide to reach to You, the Ocean of Oceans. I am asking for *You*." Ask from your Lord sincerely. When you ask sincerely, He may send you one of His beloved servants to take you to your destination. ▲

79: Restfulness in our hearts

When a person feels restful, in comfort, he may be able to follow everything easily. Now we are sitting restfully, but restfulness is in our hearts. It is not something related to sitting on a throne or in a comfortable place. When your heart feels rest and comfort, then, if you are sitting on a stone, if you are sitting in prison, if you are sitting on fire, no worry. Doesn't matter.

What gives comfort to people? Their hearts. And people now are leaving their hearts. Most people are interested in their physical bodies and physical pleasures, while all the prophets, from the beginning up to the end, just came to arrange our hearts. They are the engineers of hearts. No one else may look after hearts except prophets and their inheritors, *awliya*. ▲

80: the light of a believer's faith

Allah Almighty gives us sufficient honor during this holy month, and we are saying, "*Alhamdulillah*, thanks to Allah Almighty." It is a grant, granted by Allah Almighty to us. Among millions of people, we have been chosen to be here and to listen to the holy words that are granted to us by our Lord Almighty. May Allah fill our hearts with the light of faith, with divine light.

We are asking for divine lights, and divine lights never come to a heart which is engaged by this world. Whoever gives his heart to his Lord, his Lord sends His divine lights to his heart, because Allah Almighty always looks at our hearts, not looking at your hair, your turban, your moustache; no. If you are a black one, a white one, a brown one, a yellow one, a red one, hearts' color is the same.

Allah Almighty is looking at our hearts and asking, "My servant's heart – by whom is it engaged?" If He looks and finds Himself Almighty in the heart of His servant, then He sends lights. It is like an airport, with flights always coming down. Then, in the hearts of such servants, angels are always coming, always coming. We are saying about Heathrow Airport that every two seconds one plane comes or one plane goes, but heavier traffic than this takes place in our hearts by angels.

Angels are coming from the Divine Presence, landing on your heart – and your heart is not like this [he gestures to show the form of a heart]. This is only its physical shape; yes, just this. But our heart – *Hu-u-u*! Our Lord's Throne is in our heart; He chose the hearts of the sons of Adam to be the place for His Throne. The whole universe is too narrow for Allah

Almighty to be in it, but the hearts of the sons of Adam are *so* wide . You can't see the side, you can't see the end, of the hearts of the sons of Adam.

We do not know who we are; *we do not know*. We are ignorant until Allah Almighty opens our hearts to us, giving us a key for opening. But if He is not pleased with you, He will not give you that key to open. You must make your Lord pleased with you, and when He is pleased with you, you are going to be pleased with Him. Yes. We must be pleased with Him so that He may be pleased with us. Then He will give us that key for opening.

Allah Almighty says, *"Inna fatahna laka fathan mubina."* [175] This was for the Prophet (s), but he asked his Lord whether it was for his *ummah*, also, or not. He always asked every honor that he was given for his nation as well.

"Yes, if they go in your footsteps, they have *fathan mubina*, also. They are not deprived or prevented from attaining that. Everything you have been given, O My beloved Muhammad, peace be upon you, is for your nation, also."

Then, when Allah Almighty looks at your heart and sees that it is engaged by anyone other than Himself, He is *not* pleased with you. When you are giving your heart to your Lord, His Throne is in your heart, and Allah Almighty *'ala-l-'Arsh istawa;*[176] on that Throne you may see a divine manifestation, a divine appearance, specially, privately, for yourself. And likewise for everyone, because the manifestations, *tajalliyat*, of our Lord are endless, and He appears to each one of His servants according to their faith and love for Him.

Then, those angels are always coming, coming, in your heart, and your heart becomes lighted. Therefore, *awliya* say, if the lights in the heart of a *mumin* were to appear, there would be no darkness in all the universe. It would be filled with lights, if the light of a single *mumin's* heart were to appear. But it has been kept in our hearts, sometimes giving off from your

---

[175]"Indeed, We have granted you [Muhammad] a clear opening [or victory]." (48:1)

[176]"[Allah] is established upon the Throne." (20:5)

face. If you are walking in darkness, you may be seen as a figure of light passing through.

Therefore we are asking from our Lord a little bit of light so that we may see in front of us, where we are walking. If you are asking to follow the Prophet's steps and you are sincere in your intention, you may find light in the footsteps of the Prophet (s). If those who have lights in their hearts look at the places where any prophet has walked, in their footsteps there is light, *nur*.

For *awliya*, also. Once people sent *Sultan al-'Arifin* Abu Yazid al-Bistami, may Allah bless him, from his town to the capital, and they said things that were not good about him, because sometimes *awliya* are speaking about Reality. The outside view is one thing, but when you enter inside, there is a new view; the inside view is not like the outside one. Therefore, those who go inside see certain things and sometimes they may speak about it. Then the outward-looking people say, "Oh, what are you saying? We never saw, we never heard of such a thing! From where is this? We do not accept it!"

Therefore, in Abu Yazid's time, also, scholars accused him of being a heretic. They put chains on his feet and sent him to the capital for the *sultan* to execute him, to cut off his head. And he walked along slowly because of the chains.

That night the *sultan* dreamed that the Prophet (s) said to him, "O *sultan*, now *Sultan al-'Arifin* is coming from among my *ummah*. He is on the way, coming to your palace. You must go and receive him and bring him here. You must respect him as you would receive and respect 124,000 prophets, including myself."

Then the *sultan* got up from his bed and ordered two horses, and let the horses go into the dark night. In the darkness he saw a lighted figure approaching. When the *sultan* reached it and saw a person coming with his feet in chains, he quickly broke those chains, giving his respects to Abu Yazid and taking him by horse back to the palace. And he put him to rest.

The *sultan* sent away the guards and he himself guarded *Sultan al-'Arifin*. Then, after one hour – knock-knock-knock, knock-knock-knock, knock-knock-knock! – so many people were coming. "Who are you?" the *sultan* asked.

They said, "We are *murids*, students, of Abu Yazid."

"How did you know to come here?"

"O guardian, O *sultan, you* are asking such a question? How did *you* see him?

"I saw him as a lighted figure."

"We saw lights where he had walked and followed his lighted footsteps. We saw that the light of those footsteps finished here and we know that he is here, our grandshaykh."

It is enough. May Allah give us from His divine lights so that our hearts and our bodies will be in light. ▲

81: preparing our hearts for our lord almighty

May Allah Almighty teach us good manners. We are in need of that. Because we are going to His Divine Presence, we must have good manners. If no good manners, you can't enter the Divine Presence.

Satan had so much knowledge, so much worshipping, but no good manners. Then he was thrown out. Therefore, we are asking from our Lord, humbly, humbly, to grant us good manners. And Allah Almighty sent His prophets, all of them, with good manners, and the most excellent one for good manners was the one who said, *"Addabni Rabbi fa-ahsana tadibi,"*[177] the Seal of the Prophets, Sayyidina Muhammad (s). We may acquire excellent good manners from Muhammad (s), Allah Almighty making him the most excellent example for the sons of Adam in everything.

Therefore, the one who may acquire good manners, *adab*, is going to be in peace during this life and the Eternal Life. On the Day of Resurrection, no discussion, no argument, with him, all the doors opening for him to enter. Therefore, argument is no good, neither among ourselves, nor between you and the prophets, nor between you and your Lord Almighty, because the one who is accustomed to arguing, his argument will go up to his Lord Almighty. Therefore, we *must* stop argument.

My Grandshaykh, may Allah bless him, was saying, "O my son, don't argue with anyone. Even though you may be in the right, don't argue,

---

[177]"My Lord trained me in the most excellent good manners."

because argument extinguishes the light of faith." Therefore, the Holy Quran, the Glorious Quran, says, *"Lakum dinukum wa liya din."*[178]

"Don't argue," Allah Almighty says to the Prophet (s). If people accept, they accept; if not accepting, don't argue. Through argument no one accepts anything, no. "I never force My servants," says Allah Almighty. He gave us will, will power, so that, "O My servants, you are free to do as you like, but you will never do as you like except as *I* like. But I give you freedom through your will. As you like, go ahead. Don't force."

Allah does not force us; we are free in our actions. If a person accepts your way, you may tell him about it; if not accepting, leave him alone. Even with the Prophet (s), although he brought heavenly powers, miraculous powers, from his Lord in his hand, yet Abu Jahl, who was the *imam* of *kufr*, the leader of the disbelievers, never accepted, and the Prophet never had an argument with him; he left him alone. But whoever came to the Prophet (s), asking about *haqq*, Reality, the unchangeable realities – if asking, no one left the Prophet's presence without faith.

Whoever asked for something, the Prophet *had* to give, but to those who did not ask, closed-up people, nothing was given. They said that our hearts are locked up; they meant to say that no matter how much you may talk, it will never come in, locked. But the one who comes open may take everything from the Prophet (s) and from *awliya*.

Therefore, in our time you may meet all kinds of people. They may object to you, but don't argue with them. If someone asks, give him; if not asking and rejecting you, leave him alone. Allah Almighty said to His Prophet (s), "O My beloved Muhammad, you are going to destroy yourself because of those people who do not believe in you or in Me. But don't do that. Leave them. You must give to whomever asks from you. If they do not ask, don't give. To those who take, you may give. Those who do not take, leave them. *Don't argue with them.*"

---

[178]"For you is your religion and for me my religion." (109:6)

And in our time so many people are arguing with each other. They may be friends but when they argue they are becoming enemies. What is the benefit? No. "O my brother, you believe in that way. Keep your belief. You are going to your Lord's Presence. I am free, also, to believe or to reject. My beliefs are these. If you accept them, it is all right. If not accepting, I am not going to believe as you believe. *Lakum dinukum wa liya din*' – your faith to you, my faith to me; your beliefs to you, my beliefs to me.

"And you and I, our destination is the same. If you believe in Him, I believe in Him, also. One day we will return to Allah Almighty, to His Divine Presence. And we have been informed that, when we return to His Divine Presence, He will ask us, 'What did you bring?' And you may tell what you brought to Him, and He will look at what you brought and will also look at what I brought to His Divine Presence."

We must know what Allah Almighty is asking from everyone – when He will gather everyone in His Divine Presence, what He will ask from them. We must know it so that when He asks we may give it. "I made this ready," you may say. It is not something to make an argument, to make a quarrel, to make a fight about among us here. Important is to make ready that thing which Allah Almighty will ask from you, from us, from everyone.

You may claim anything during this life; you may say, "I am on the right path."' Yes, continue. We will see you, and everyone will see himself, on the Day of Resurrection when the scales are balanced. Then Allah Almighty will address you: "O My servant, come. Give Me what you have brought."

He is asking from His servant the *best* thing, and we must present to Him Almighty our best, not simply anything that is going to be available; no. The most excellent manners that the Prophet (s) taught his nation was to bring into the Divine Presence to present to their Lord their best, the *best* thing that they may take from here to His Divine Presence.

We are here, quarreling, fighting, arguing: Muslims, Christians, Jews, everyone; every *madhhab* or school of thought,[179] and every *tariqat* or Sufi order, or other groups. We are saying, "I am the best." You are saying, "No, I am the first one." He says, "*I* am the first one, *I* am the best one."

Those claims never give benefit. You will understand this when the Last Day comes and you are in the Divine Presence. Therefore, the Seal of the Prophets (s) taught his *ummah* to make ready their best thing for Allah Almighty. And the best thing is *qalbun salim* – *qalbun salim*,[180] the golden, golden heart, the pure, pure heart. That is what Allah Almighty is asking. And all our actions are only means, not ends. The end is *qalbun salim*, to bring to the Divine Presence a pure heart.

Do, don't argue! Use every means to make your heart a pure heart, so that Allah Almighty may give to you from His divine lights and illuminate it, so that your heart is going to be the Throne of your Lord Almighty. The hearts of the sons of Adam were chosen by their Lord to be His Throne because they are the deputies of Allah Almighty, and He gave them such a heart that, if the whole universe is thrown into it, it will be lost, becoming such a small thing compared to the wideness of our hearts. Therefore, Allah Almighty chose our hearts to be for Himself.

Imam al-Ghazali, Muhammad al-Ghazali, may Allah bless him, was a king-sized scholar and also a king-sized *wali*. He is a well-known scholar in the Muslim world and in Western countries, also. In many Western universities there are chairs for his teachings.

He stated in his books that no one can put a limit on knowledge. Only our understanding or our capacity is within limits, but there are no limits for knowledge because knowledge goes on and on, and ends in the main Source from which it came. Knowledge is a grant from Allah Almighty to

---

[179]School of Islamic jurisprudence or *fiqh*.

[180]A sound, pure heart, as mentioned in Abraham's prayer, "And do not disgrace me on the Day they are resurrected, the Day when neither wealth nor children will benefit [anyone], except one who comes to Allah with a sound heart" (26:87-89).

His servants, and as much as He is pleased with His servants, He is going to grant them more and more.

Therefore, don't suppose that knowledge is only written in books, no. That knowledge which is written in books is concentrated in the hearts of the obedient servants of our Lord Almighty. You may carry a seed, a little seed, but you can't carry that big tree. Therefore the concentrated knowledges which Allah Almighty grants to His sincere and beloved servants is never-ending, and it is impossible to write it all and finish.

Qul: Lau kana-l-bahru midada li-kalimati Rabbi, la-nafida-l-bahru qabla an tanfada kalimatu Rabbi, wa lau jina bi-mithlihi madada;[181] that is a verse explaining something about our Lord's knowledge. As an example, Allah Almighty says that if all the oceans were to be ink for writing down the knowledge of your Lord, those oceans would be finished, and if you brought another ocean, it would not be enough, also. It means that, because limited things cannot write unlimitedly, our mental capacities are within limits. But our spiritual power extends on and on.

Therefore Allah Almighty grants to His *awliya* such knowledge that, if anyone were sitting and telling about it, it would be impossible to write everything. Sayyidina 'Ali, may Allah be pleased with him, said, "O people, if I were to sit here and talk about the meanings of *al-Fatiha*, the *Surah* of Opening, consisting of seven verses, I could say so much about the meanings of those seven verses that you could load one hundred camels with books and it would not be finished."

We are saying that we are scholars, very knowing people. One hundred camels – how would they enter this place? Full-up, yes? Therefore, we must know that we have been given *something*, but, as our Lord says, *'Wa ma utitum mina-l-'ilmi illa qalila.*[182] O people, don't be proud of your knowledge.

---

[181]"Say [O Muhammad]: 'If the sea were ink for [writing] the words of my Lord, the sea would be exhausted before the words of my Lord were exhausted, even if We brought the like of it as a reinforcement.'" (18:109)

[182]"And you have been given only a little of knowledge." (17:85)

However much you may have been given, it is only a little. It will always be like a drop in an endless ocean, or in endless oceans. Don't suppose that you have been given so much. No, you have been given within limits always."

Therefore, Imam al-Ghazali, may Allah bless him, was saying, "Why am I saying such a thing as this?[183] Because there are some people who are arguing on such a point; if a person does not know, he says, 'We do not accept that.' But instead, you may say, 'This is the limit of knowledge which I have reached,' and you must leave the matter for someone else with more knowledge. As Allah Almighty says, *"Wa fauqa kulli dhi-'ilmin 'alim,*[184] over every scholar there may be one more knowledgeable than himself."

Imam al-Ghazali was saying that if a dead person is carried in a coffin, people putting it on their shoulders or carrying it like this with their hands or carrying it by car, during his journey to his grave Allah Almighty will ask that person forty questions, without using any interpreter. And he said that one of the questions which Allah Almighty will ask is, "O My servant, you always used to make your outward appearance elegant, so smart" – everything is all right, looking like this, like that; ladies and gentlemen, all of them making themselves look good. "You did that for My servants because they were looking at your outward appearance. Yes. Did you ever think about *Me*, that I was looking at your heart – to make it suitable, the best, for My gaze? *Did you ever think about that point?"*

That is the first question that Allah Almighty will ask His servants. You are working hard; *you are working hard.* When Allah Almighty asks you, "What about for Me? Any ornaments for *Me* on your heart?" what your answer will be, you may know. Yes, it is important. And it is enough for anyone who may think about himself. ▲

---

[183]Referring to his earlier statement that no one can put a limit on knowledge, but it is rather our capacity to grasp and comprehend which is limited.

[184]"And above each possessor of knowledge is a knower [of more]." (12:76)

82: "qalbun salim",
the pure heart

Allahumma, alhimna rushdana wa a'idhna min shurruri anfusina.[185] This is
the Prophet's prayer, asking from Allah Almighty and teaching us. If a
person has even a little bit of mind, he may understand that that word, that
saying, that prayer, could never come except from a prophet. And who is a
prophet? We shall see what is coming down from our spiritual 'Central'.

Who is a prophet – you or I or he? No, a prophet is one of the sons of
Adam in his physical form, but he is completely different from the inside.
He *must be different from us*, because a prophet must have a relationship to the
heavens. If the wires are broken, he can't bring tidings of the heavens.

The one who brings tidings of the heavens is going to be a prophet.
And our Prophet, Muhammad (s), the Seal of the Prophets, is the last one.
By creation he is the first one, but in the order of his coming among people
he is the last; he is the first of the prophets by creation but in relation to
when he was sent, he is the last one. The first must be perfect and the last
must also be perfect. Yes; that perfect one must be at the first and must
also be at the last so that all the other prophets may be kept between the
two powers.

And he is the most perfect one, also, because his prophethood, his
absolute prophethood, is for all time and for all space. And all the prophets

---

[185]"Our Lord, inspire us with our guidance. And we take refuge [with You] from the evils of
our egos."

are students of the Seal of the Prophets (s) because our Prophet has been given *'ulumu-l-awwalin wa-l-akhirin*, the knowledge of the first and of the last.

That is the proof that the Last Prophet, beloved Muhammad (s), was given knowledge which extends from the beginning of creation up to his death, as well as from his own time up to the end – the knowledge of what was before and after himself. When man was created, when creation was just taking place and creatures were being created, that knowledge about them, and after himself, also, he was given.

Therefore, each one of the prophets was given something of knowledge. Other prophets were given it before the Last Prophet came. And he was sent at the end of our period, the period of the sons of Adam, when the last period of the time of this world had arrived and the Last Day was approaching. And because his time is the most difficult time, he is *Nabi al-Akhir Zaman*, the Prophet of the End-time.

We are not philosophers to speculate whether there may be millions of years more for this world. Rather, it is going to end, our period in this world, because for every beginning there is an ending. But even if Muhammad's period were to go on after our time, also – even for millions or billions of years – his prophethood would be over people like the skies.

No one can pass above the skies' space; we always see that covering us, on us, over us. Therefore, even though the minds of people and their knowledge may improve, however much they may be able to know or to become more intelligent or intellectual, they are still on the earth. The heavens are over them; the earth down, the heavens up. Therefore, however much peoples' knowledge or technology may improve, it will still be impossible to reach the heavens. The heavens are something else. They are not a material thing, no. They are something else.

In the same way, our Prophet's, beloved Muhammad's, prophethood is absolute, and even if the world goes on for a billion years, we will be in need of keeping his method and ways and *sunnah* for reaching the heavens, the divine territory. Science is not suitable for that, just as our bodies are not suitable.

We have been given authority to reach the heavens through our spiritual power. Although you can't reach them through science, you may reach them through spiritual authority. And spiritual authority has been given through the prophets, not through scholars and scientists and technology.

And the last one, the perfect one, beloved Muhammad (s), is inviting people, "O people, come and take your authority"; yes, calling, inviting, "Come and take your authority for reaching." But people are drunk, heedless – *heedless*! They are drinking the wines of *dunya*, the wines of Satan, the wines and spirits of ego, their heads turning. They can't look up, always sitting down below, saying, "This is a good place, full of wine. Drink and sleep here! No need to get up."

Each of the prophets, peace be upon them all, called and invited people: "Take your authority or take your ticket and go. Take your invitation and go into the Divine Presence." And the last one, also; he came with universal, absolute prophethood. He called not only Arabs or Turks or Eastern people, but his prophethood is for all people, for all the sons of Adam. "O people, come here. Christians, Jews, Buddhists, Confucians – come here! Take your authority and go." Don't say, "I am a Christian, I am Jewish. What about *my* heavens?" The Prophet is inviting *all* people to reach their stations in the Divine Presence.

We recited a *du'a*, a supplication, at the beginning. The Prophet (s) was indicating something important in that *du'a*, *"Allahumma, alhimna rushdana, wa a'idhna min shurruri anfusina."* That is a key for people, taking them to the way of the heavens.

You may understand that our Prophet is teaching all people and that he knows everyone's secret, the secret of the sons of Adam. He knows their situation very well, and he is the chief one who knows perfectly how to arrange our inner lives for reaching the heavens. By this *du'a*, he is indicating to us that, firstly, O people, you must know that you have a friend. Your friend is a never-leaving friend. It is your *nafs*, your ego, and you must know about that ego, your *nafs*.

You must know that it is the source of evil. If you don't know what a person is, you are never going to keep yourself from his traps. Therefore, you must know about your ego and you must ask protection from it from your Lord, Allah Almighty. If you do not ask protection from your Lord Almighty, by yourself it is impossible to keep the *sharr*, evil, of your ego from harming you.

And secondly, you must ask your Lord Almighty to give you from His divine inspirations to your heart, to make you hear His divine inspirations, because the divine addressing is always going on. Now, there are some stations broadcasting the Holy Quran twenty-four hours a day; at any time you open them, you may listen. Just like that, Allah Almighty's 'broadcasting' from the heavens is coming among people – in the East, in the West, in London, in Mecca, in Medina, in Istanbul, in Baghdad, in Syria, anywhere you may be. In the Pacific Ocean or the Atlantic Ocean's depths, in deserts – everywhere you may be able to hear that divine or heavenly broadcasting.

But we have some new stations here in London called pirate radio, broadcasting but people cannot understand. Who does that? Some stations are coming in and preventing people from listening, also during wartime coming and jamming. You cannot understand what they are saying. If they say "Go straight," you are understanding "Go back."

If you do not guard your most precious organ, your heart, then Satan comes and makes too much noise in it, so that you can't understand anything, you can't hear. If you are even listening to your heart, you must at least hear that your heart is saying, *"Allah-Allah-Allah-Allah"*; if anyone is able to listen, he must hear that his heart is going on with *dhikr*: *"Allah-Allah-Allah...."* Without *dhikr*, without *tasbiha*, glorification, our hearts cannot work. Don't suppose that blood makes our hearts to work. No; that *dhikr* does.

If you leave your heart without guarding it, then Satan and his volunteers come and make an assembly inside, making more noise in it than a discotheque, so big an assembly. If no one is inside and no guardian, they are entering. Then how can you hear the divine broadcasting?

Therefore the Prophet (s) says, "Ask from your Lord. His heavenly broadcasting may come to you, making you hear." But you must put a guardian to guard your heart.

The most precious organ of a person is his heart, yet we are leaving it without a guardian. When you are saying "Allah-Allah... " in your heart, angels come to protect you. Then Satan and his volunteers cannot approach you. And therefore, purification is the first fard, command, of Allah Almighty. He is asking, "O My servant, make your heart clean and pure. Make it pure because I am coming." He does not walk; no need to walk, to sit, to get up. But He says, "I am in a pure heart, a clean heart; I am there. Whoever is asking for Me, 'Where is my Lord?' he may find Me in pure and clean hearts. I am there."

Therefore, the Prophet, the Seal of the Prophets (s), taught all the sons of Adam, "O sons of Adam, leave da'wat ananiyah"[186] – leave egotism, leave off claiming anything, saying, "I am this one, I am that one. I am a bishop, I am a patriarch, I am a pope, I am a priest, I am a shaykh, I am a scholar, I am a big man." Don't claim anything. It is not acceptable.

Allah Almighty is asking from you a golden heart; He means a clean and pure heart. He is asking His servants to cleanse and make pure their hearts because He is going to be there. No claiming that we are Christians, we are Muslims, we are Jews; Allah Almighty is asking from everyone, from every kind of person who is claiming anything, "Where is your clean heart? It is not enough to say that I am Muslim, I am a shaykh; I am a Christian, I am a pope; I am... , and so on. I am asking you, 'Did you prepare for Me, did you clean your heart and make it pure for Me, or not?'"

---

[186]Calling attention to or making claims concerning oneself, self-aggrandizement.

That is *one* question. Don't have so many questions. It is one question only: *"Where is your heart for Me? I am saying that I am with you."*

Therefore, we must know about our Prophet and about his prophethood, and because of what it is the absolute prophethood; because from the sons of Adam is wanted, wanted by their Lord, a clean and pure heart, not anything else. *"Yawma la yanfa'u malun wa la banun, illa man ata-Llaha bi-qalbin salim"*[187] – this verse is saying that Allah Almighty will ask you, "Where is *qalbin salim*, the golden heart, the pure heart, the clean heart, made ready for Me – *where is it?"* On the Day of Resurrection, Judgment Day, He will ask it from everyone.

Everyone must think about himself and he must think about his Lord Almighty. "To *where* is my Lord coming to me? Coming to my *heart.*" Make it clean and pure. And we have means.

If a person wants to wash his hands and his body, there are now so many soaps and shampoos. So many shampoos – apple shampoos, egg shampoos, banana shampoos. (I am understanding that they are for drinking. For what are they saying *"Apple Shampoo"?*) Yes, they are using so many kinds. For what? For washing, for cleaning? But for the heart – *no means, nothing?* Or must we drink?

Therefore, everything needs some means, and all the prophets just came to teach people how they may be able to prepare their hearts, to make them clean and pure. And fasting is one of the strongest means for making our hearts pure and clean.

It is a short time, only one month, and three weeks have already gone. Now we have only one-and-a-half weeks left. We must take as much as we can from the *barakah* of this holy month, and ask from Allah Almighty to give us the means to act for the sake of His love alone. ▲

---

[187]"The Day when neither wealth nor children will benefit [anyone], except one who comes to Allah with a sound heart" (26:87-89).

83: attaining perfection during this life

In our life there is no long time. All of it is a short time. Even one year is a short time because during this life *everything* is short. What is long is endless. Therefore, it is a good tidings for the sons of Adam to know that it is a short life and that everything that comes to them of either happiness or of troubles must be ended. On the one hand, it is a warning, and on the other, it is a good tidings for those people who have troubles in their lives, and troubles may be of any kind. The one who knows that they are not going to continue forever, that they must be ended, who knows that troubles, also, are going to be of short duration, finishing, is the one who makes his troubles tasteful.

It only makes troubles long from our side because we are without patience. *That* makes time long; but for good things, for the greed of the *nafs*, for asking for more, it makes it shorter. Maybe our egos are saying, "*This* is too long," and at the same time, "*That* is too short," but ordinarily, all *dunya* is a short time. And we are in need to be patient in our lives. The one who may be patient during his life, his life is going to be sweet or tasteful, because all patience is bitter in the beginning but finally it is tasteful.

And, as we are believers (you can believe in God Almighty in any religion; every believer believes in his Lord Almighty), the true belief is that we must believe in the absolute perfection of the Lord Almighty from every direction. If you look at your Lord, you may see Him in absolute perfection: being merciful, being just, knowing, seeing, hearing, acting, willing, being powerful. Every absolute perfection is for Him Almighty in His attributes.

And the one who knows his Lord in the absolute perfection of His attributes, that is enough to make *him* perfect, because perfection is a possibility for the sons of Adam; everyone may reach perfection. But the way lies in belief in his Lord's absolute perfection.; then that perfection comes from the Lord to His servant. The one who does not believe, or who believes but does not have certainty, is going to be late in reaching perfection during this life; perhaps it will go on after this life into the next life. But he *must* reach that point here or in the Hereafter, because no one can be accepted, no one is going to be acceptable, in the Divine Presence without being perfect.

Therefore, some people are reaching perfection during this life. As much as a person knows his Lord in the absolute perfection of His divine attributes, it is going to be easy for him to attain perfection during this life. Otherwise, he is going to attain it afterwards.

We have been ordered to reach upwards. In front of us there is a hard, steep mountain, and lower down there is also a valley. We have been ordered to reach that mountain because we have our treasures and our destination on it. But when we look at the difficulties, we are escaping and enjoying ourselves by running down into the valley and playing there.

But you must not suppose that we will be left without climbing that mountain. What we are doing is only to make the short way long. When we go down into the valley, one day we will be ordered to go from down below up that mountain. Then it will be so difficult; at that time we will be ordered by force.

Now we have our will power to use for climbing. But when we stop climbing and use our will to go down to the level of the valley, to be there to play, to enjoy ourselves with our 'zoo,' our will power is not going to give us any benefit. Then the way will be twice as long, starting from the valley up to the first station where we were at the time of maturity.[188]

---

[188]That is, puberty, the time at which Islam assigns adult responsibility to an individual,

People are now choosing, when they reach maturity, to go down to the valley to be with the zoo, to enjoy themselves, to have enjoyment with their egos, and only a very few people are choosing to climb up to their destinations. Therefore, it is foolishness, complete foolishness, to choose to go down, because when the time comes, you will be *forced* to go from the bottom of the valley to the first stop where you were, and then from there up to the mountain, also. It is impossible for the sons of Adam to be left to their wills except for a short time, and then by force, they must turn and go up. ▲

---

considering him or her as capable of distinguishing between right and wrong, and thus being accountable for his or her own actions.

84: obedience to our lord

We shall look to Allah Almighty, what He is granting for us today, and what His holy prophet, beloved Muhammad (s), is granting to us, and what is coming from Grandshaykh. It is easy for Them to make me speak excellent English; it is so easy, and to give strange [esoteric] knowledges. But for our level, as we are beginners, not more, when beginners begin school, they begin with A, B, C. Now it is only something about A, B, C we are saying.

About what are we speaking? How we can be a servant to our Lord. That is the main aim for the sons of Adam: to learn how they may be obedient servants to their Lord Almighty. But we have left off knowing, learning, how we can be an obedient and sincere and beloved servant to our Lord, and we are quarreling and fighting for nothing – *for nothing!*

All the world is going to be *nothing.* All things, all properties, are going to be nothing; all our works, our deeds, are going to be nothing. *We* are also going to be nothing in our physical bodies. But we are not going to be nothing in our souls. We are eternal creatures because of our souls.

Allah Almighty created the sons of Adam, first creating Adam (a) from clay and then blowing into him from His Divine Spirit. Whoever belongs to Allah Almighty is eternal, everything that belongs to Him. He blew into Adam and his sons, his descendants up to the end of the world, from His holy Spirit.[189] Therefore, our souls came from the heavens, from the Divine Presence, and when we are going to be nothing with our physical bodies,

---

[189]This is stated in 15:29, 38:72, 32:9.

that soul and spirit will return, going back into that Ocean from which it came.

Everything is going to be nothing, and we are working, we are tiring, for *nothing* now. We are working hard and tiring – for what? For this life's temporary enjoyment, although it is impossible to make a person's life wholly full of enjoyments. He may be the richest one, he may be the most honorable person, he may be the most powerful person, he or she may be the most handsome or the most beautiful person, he may be the most majestic person; but he will never be the happiest person or the one who is able to enjoy himself the most during his lifetime.

There is a tale about Yazid, the son of Sayyidina Mu'awiyah. We are asking our Lord to give us authority or power and to use us for good things, for goodness, because we are living in a life in which there is goodness and badness. Some people have been employed, engaged, for goodness and some for badness.

Yazid was a king, a caliph. He was able to enjoy himself with everything. Nowadays you can't find such possibilities for a person to do everything; therefore, Yazid was able to enjoy himself. He was a powerful and majestic emperor, ruling from China to the Atlantic Ocean, one of the most important empires of his time. And he thought of enjoying himself, but he was never able to enjoy himself without some suffering coming on him. Something always came which caused him to suffer, which gave him trouble.

One day he ordered, "Today I must be free from every care, and I am going to sit in my assembly with every means of enjoyment. Today I must enjoy fully, completely! I shall leave everything outside, every problem of the people. This day is only for my enjoyment. I am not going to listen or to look at anything that gives me sadness or makes me suffer. All day long there must be enjoyment, gathering together everything for singing, all kinds of music, all kinds of girls, every kind of drink, everything – sitting for enjoyment from morning to night and no trouble for this day." That was what he was intending.

Allah Almighty is teaching His servants, making some people examples for others. That person, the powerful emperor who thought of doing everything for himself and enjoying fully that day, toward the end of his assembly someone brought him a pomegranate. It was not their season; it had come from some distant place and was very beautiful.

He broke open the pomegranate and took out the seeds. There was one slave girl whom he loved too much; she was the most beloved person to him. He put the seeds in her mouth, and Allah Almighty's Will was working. He gave her those seeds and one seed got stuck, not going down and not coming out, and, falling down, she died.

The person who had intended to spend a day enjoying fully, such an emperor – you can imagine what sadness came on him at the end of his enjoyment. And after three days he died, also; yes, Yazid died as well.

This whole life that people are running after is going to be nothing, and enjoyment from this life is so difficult. Enjoyment is only what you may find in your soul. *That* is enjoyment, not anything coming from outside of you.

As much enjoyment as you are able to get from this life, it is going to decrease. Only for the one who gets enjoyment through his soul does it improve and increase, but bodily enjoyment is always becoming less. It is not the same as the first night. We are imagining that everything is going to be like the first night, but, no – the second night is less, the third night is less; the third year, the fourth year, less.

Therefore, don't be cheated. Everyone is cheated by this life except the ones who are listening to the call of the prophets and their inheritors, *awliya. They* are happy. Don't be worried. If your soul is enjoying, you are always at the first night. I am not accepting it to be the second night; it must always be the first night's enjoyment because the soul is enjoying, and the body, also. If you are not accepting the first night, it is more than the first night, even!

But people now are running. They are like drunk people, never understanding, never listening or realizing. But we gave our promises to our Lord on the Day of Promises: "O our Lord, we are your servants." And if we keep our promises, He says, "I will keep My promises to you."

You *must* improve, you *must* develop. Obedient servants, sincere servants, do not go down, they always go up, in their physical bodies and in their souls because enjoyment comes through souls. Yes; look at those who are fasting. Allah Almighty gives to fasting people in such a way that each day they do not feel less enjoyment; each day it is *more*. Physically it seems the same, but, if you are not at the level of animals, spiritually you are feeling more enjoyment each day; because animals enjoy themselves by eating and drinking, but for human beings, although they may enjoy that physically, their real enjoyment is with their spiritual life. Therefore, for a fasting person at the time of breaking fast, his enjoyment is not with eating and drinking.

Don't reduce your level to the level of animals! No, our spiritual enjoyment must be more. We are being refreshed, Allah Almighty sending refreshment on fasting people. Don't think, "What is there to eat this night of soup, of *kebab*, of sweets?" You must be careful, because at the time of breaking fast there comes a mercy, *rahmah*, refreshing our bodies, our hearts.

Wait for that mercy to come on you, for lights to come on you. Only fasting people may feel that, not others. They may sit at the same table with you but they can't feel it. It is forbidden. Only fasting people may feel that.

▲

85: making spiritual progress

QUESTION: I'm thinking of how to advance – to more freedom and knowledge, happiness, wisdom and effectiveness.

SHAYKH NAZIM: You are asking for so many things. And everything you acquire carries a responsibility; Allah Almighty never gives something to you without a responsibility: "If We give you eyes, you have a responsibility. If We give you a tongue, you have responsibility for it."

If you are given ears, you are given responsibility; if given hands, feet, heart, every part of your body that your Lord has given you as a grant, you are also given, at the same time, a responsibility. If you have been given honor, you are given responsibility for as much as you have been given. Some people have been given so much; their responsibility is more than any ordinary person's. You understand? Therefore, for what are you asking?

QUESTION: For enough strength to obey Allah.

SHAYKH NAZIM: Not enough strength; you need more. *Hu-u, Rabbi,* O my God! Give me more power. For what? For worshipping You, for obeying.

QUESTION: And to understand.

SHAYKH NAZIM: The one who is going to be Solomon understands. *"Fa-fahmna Sulayman,"*[190] Allah Almighty says. "We gave Solomon exact understanding." Therefore, you must be Solomon so that you may be given.

Solomon (a) was given the whole world; all kinds of creatures from among mankind and jinn and wild animals were under his command. And you may ask, "How can I be like Solomon?"

Yes, he had been given the whole world; no one had been given the like of his kingdom, his incomparable kingdom.[191] But in spite of that, he was the most ascetic person of his time. The whole world was under his hand, under his dominion, but in his heart there was only One; in Solomon's heart, on his heart's throne, was only his Lord. That is the meaning when we say, "Be Solomon." Then Allah may give you divine knowledge and wisdoms from among His wisdoms.

Our hearts are still too dirty, dirty with this *dunya*, with this life's pleasures; occupied, engaged, by this life, no place in our hearts for our Lord. Therefore we have not been given an understanding. But Allah says, "I gave exact understanding to Solomon," because, even though all the world was under his dominion, he kept his heart only for his Lord. If you can keep that, *you* may be given, also.

QUESTION: How to begin?

SHAYKH NAZIM: At the beginning. The beginning is intention: to intend, to ask. When we ask for such a pure heart, that is a beginning; when we intend to have a heart privately, solely, for our Lord, Allah Almighty, that is a beginning. And when you begin, *"Wa 'ala-Llahi-l-ikmal."*[192] When

---

[190]21:79

[191]See 38:35.

[192]"And the completion rests with Allah."

you intend to make a beginning, Allah Almighty brings completion – *He* brings completion.

Therefore, when you intend, it means that you are asking. You must continue on your intention every day, at every time, keeping your heart on the same intention: "I am asking for my Lord." Then you will be given an improvement.

Once Abraham (a) was in the desert, walking, and he was thirsty. Then he looked around to find something to drink. And he saw a shepherd, a black slave.

Abraham went to him to ask for something to drink. Then that shepherd addressed him, saying, "O Abraham!"

He was surprised. "How do you know that I am Abraham?"

And the shepherd replied, "The one who knows his Lord knows His servants." Understand? The one who knows his Lord knows his Lord's servants. "It is not so big a thing for me. You are Abraham. O Abraham, do you prefer milk or water?" and there was nothing with him.

And Abraham (a) was even more surprised. There was *nothing* with that shepherd, neither water nor milk. And he said, "I prefer water."

Then the shepherd stamped his foot and, whsh-h! – a spring came out. And he said, "Drink!"

Abraham drank from that spring. He said, "Never have I tasted such fresh, cool, sweet water." And he was astonished, saying, "O my Lord" (he was *Khalil*, the Friend of Allah), looking at that shepherd.

"O Abraham," said Gabriel, coming to him, "you are astonished at My servant.[193] He is My servant, a colored one." (White people think that they are better. But it is Allah Almighty who colors people, not *you* that are

---

[193] Here the angel Gabriel, the transmitter of the divine revelation to all the prophets, is conveying his Lord's divine words to Abraham (a).

coloring yourself. *Sibghat-Allah*,[194] Allah's dye, is the best.) "He is a slave, a colored one, but I am looking at his heart and I am not finding anything in his heart except Me. I am the only One, alone in his heart. Therefore he has been given such a miracle. And to anyone who keeps Me alone in his heart, I give *karamat*, miracles, granting them to him by My favor."

Therefore, the important thing is to keep our hearts for our Lord only. But we are putting everything into them, like a dustbin; you can find everything *except* Allah in our hearts. That is true. Therefore we will never be given a correct understanding. We can recite the Holy Quran, we can recite holy *hadiths*, but understand nothing.

For each verse of the Holy Quran there are 24,000 meanings, and all *awliya* are given 24,000 different meanings. You are given 24,000 meanings of a verse, and *you* are given another 24,000, and he, 24,000 other meanings, because each verse is an ocean of meaning. You can't write it all so that it is finished. Those wisdoms in the Holy Quran have been given to *awliya* for their improvement in heavenly stations. If you are in need, you will be given. If you are not in need, you are not given.

Now, for a rocket, how many people are putting something into it to give it that power to go up? It is not a simple thing, like your car going to a petrol station, in two minutes filling up and going. A long time was needed to put the power into it to send that rocket up. Therefore, the one who is asking for an improvement in the Divine Presence is taking that power from Allah Almighty, and if he is not asking for that, if he is not in need, he is not given. Each verse has such powers, miraculous powers; each verse is a miracle of miracles and contains divine power. The one who is prepared may take it and go.

Understandings have been given to people so that they may know and obey. When you know, you *must* obey; if knowing and not obeying, that is terrible, dangerous! *Shaytan* was given knowledge but he didn't obey. He

---

[194]2:138.

obeyed when it pleased him; when he was not pleased with that order, he didn't obey it. And he was not pleased with making *sajdah*, prostration, to Adam; therefore he didn't obey his Lord. His obedience was not for the sake of Allah Almighty but for the sake of his ego. Therefore he fell and was thrown out.

When you are looking at those people who have reached heavenly stations and you are asking to be one of them, it is that *intention* which begins to give you power. Step by step, step by step, you may continue to improve. And as much as you are improving, understandings are coming proportionately. ▲

86: GIVING up something to get something

In relation to spiritual pleasures, our physical bodies, our egos, are never satisfied. If we take care of our physical bodies' pleasures, our spiritual life goes down. Physical attractions cover it and do not allow a person to taste spiritual pleasures.

Everyone must pay something to get something, must give so that he can receive. You must give up something of physical pleasures so that you may get spiritual pleasures; otherwise you will give up spiritual pleasures and get physical, bodily pleasures. If one side comes down, the other side goes up. As much as you give up, you may receive more; if no giving, no taking. It is the same road from the beginning up to the end, the same road in the Torah (ols Testament), the same road in the Injil (New Testament), the same road in the Holy Quran: *you must give so that you may receive.*

Understand? Everything has a value; for everything there is a price. I go sometimes to Dalton Market. There are these rings and chains. For five pounds I can buy a lot of rings and earrings. And there are jewelers' shops. If you show them five pounds, they will say, "Go away!"

You can find everything in this life: a cheap one, an expensive one; low price, high price; valuable, of no value. And you are free; as much as you are able, you may buy. And everyone will finally see what he has bought.

The prophets, peace be upon them, are like a person with a caravan. At nighttime it stops in a place. Then that person shouts to the others, "O people, don't sleep tonight! You are in a valley full of diamonds and jewels, but it is up to you to take them."

Since it is dark, no one can see whether they are diamonds or just stones, but he calls out, "Take as many as you can because this whole valley is the valley of diamonds."

And then those who believe in him fill their bags and take the diamonds away. Some of the others say, "We can put in half from our own goods and half from these stones." Some others take only a little, saying, "We can put some of these stones in our pockets. We will keep our own goods and we can take some of these. They may be real diamonds."

And that person calls to them, "When it will be morning and the sun rises, finished! You will leave this valley. You can't return to take any more. Take as many as you can now."

And the people are watching. Night goes away and the sun shines. Everyone quickly looks at the stones he has gathered. "What is this? Real diamonds! Why, *why*, did we leave them instead of taking?"

One of them says to himself, "You're a big donkey! Why didn't you take more? Only one pocketful you took. Why didn't you put them here, also?" The ones who took half say, "What? What a foolish person I was not to leave my own goods and only take these!" And happiness is only for those who have taken all diamonds. ▲

87: the significance of knowledge

No one can live in this life without knowing *something*. Therefore, knowledge is the first order from Allah Almighty to all people, and for this Allah Almighty sent His prophets, from the beginning, to be teachers for the sons of Adam.

Adam (a) was the first man and also the first prophet – I mean to say, the first teacher of mankind, because without teaching, without knowing anything, we are not human beings. The sons of Adam have been honored by knowledge. Allah Almighty gave them more knowledge than any other of His creatures, even angels. He gave Adam that portion of His divine knowledge that is meant for creatures, for there is certain knowledge specifically for Allah Almighty which no one can know.

That is *ghaibu mutlaq*, the absolutely unknowable. There is some knowledge reserved for Allah Almighty which it is impossible for even any angel or any prophet, including the Seal of the Prophets, to reach because it pertains to divinity. But there is knowledge that has been given to creatures for *m'arifat*, so that they may know their Lord, and, from that knowledge, even atoms have been given.

All things in existence have lives, seeing, hearing, speaking and living – everything, even atoms. If not seeing or hearing, how are they coming from non-existence into existence? When everything was invisible in endless Power Oceans – *everything* – their Lord called them and they appeared in existence.[195] If not hearing our Lord's call, inviting us, no one would have come into existence.

"Wa in min shayan illa yusabbihu bi-hamdihi."[196] For everything there must be a language, a tongue, a speech; there must be a speech for saying, "Glory be to my Lord, who brought me into existence." Yes, for *everything; they* know. Allah Almighty gave to everything, to every creature, from that part of His knowledge which pertains to creatures. But, *la y'alamu-l-ghaiba illa-Llah;*[197] *that* knowledge belongs specifically to our Lord Almighty.

But then, in order that every creature might know its Lord, its Creator, and give its respects and praises to Allah Almighty, certain knowledges must be for everyone. And Allah Almighty gave Adam knowledge for *m'arifat*, knowledge of Himself, which He did not give to the angels and by which Adam was honored over the angels. Therefore, the rank of knowledge is the highest rank, and therefore the Prophet (s) says, *"Rutbatu-l-'ilmi 'ala-r-rutab."*[198]

We have been ordered to learn, to teach and to learn. Without learning, we can't keep the honor of being the sons of Adam. By knowledge, divine knowledge of our Lord Almighty, we have been crowned, and Allah Almighty ordered the angels to make *sajdah* to Adam because he had been given divine knowledge. ▲

---

[195]That is, even in seeming non-existence they were alive, possessing every faculty, and when their Lord called them out of that state, they became apparent or manifested in the particular material forms in which He clothed them.

[196]"And there is not a thing but that it exalts [Allah] by His praise." (17:44)

[197]No one knows the Unseen except Allah.

[198]"The rank of knowledge is above all [other] ranks."

88: Respecting Allah's Beloved Prophet (s)

We are not in a classroom, and you are not students and I am not a teacher, but [rather] all of us are humble servants to our Lord Almighty.

We are nothing; we must know this. The beginning of servanthood is to know that we are nothing. But our egos are never going to agree to be nothing, claiming to be something but nevertheless being nothing. And we are asking *barakah* from Allah Almighty; as His beloved Prophet (s) said, *"Yad-Ullahi ma'-l-jama'ah, yad-Ullahi 'ala-l-jama'ah."*[199] When Allah Almighty's servants meet, it is an occasion or opportunity to ask, from His endless favors, that He sends to us, to our meeting, from His endless Mercy Oceans, from His endless Favor Oceans, from His endless Knowledge Oceans.

For what? To make us know Him better, because there are endless steps for the ranks of knowledge, and *m'arifat-Ullah*, the knowledge of Allah Almighty, is endless oceans; not only *one* ocean – endless *oceans*, and each ocean is also endless. However far down you may go, you can never find the bottom, and no matter how much you may go around, you can't find any shore –endless oceans with the characteristic that each ocean has no shore, no bottom. *Allahu Akbar wa lil-Lahi-l-hamd!*[200] – everything that pertains to our Lord Almighty is endless, from pre-eternity to post-eternity; yes, eternal. From Your endless Knowledge Oceans we are asking!

---

[199]"Allah's hand is with the congregation [of Muslims], Allah's hand is over the congregation."

[200]Allah is Most Great and His is the praise.

As much as we may know or learn, if you could put all of creatures' knowledge in a single place, in comparison to the Prophet's knowledge about his Lord Almighty, no one can know Allah Almighty as beloved Muhammad (s) knows Him. Allah Almighty gave to him from His divine Knowledge Oceans, and the Prophet's knowledge is itself an ocean.

If all the prophets' knowledges and the saints' knowledges and the scholars' knowledges and the angels' knowledges were to come together, it would be only a little drop from the ocean that the Prophet has been given. All the knowledge of all scholars, all *awliya*, all prophets, is swallowed up by his knowledge. Therefore, the one who knows Prophet Muhammad (s) must be as he is. Understand? Must be like him, another Muhammad; if he is not another Muhammad, no one can know his personality and his greatness in the Divine Presence.

The knowledge of Muhammad (s) was complete knowledge with Allah Almighty, with his Creator. And what did that Prophet teach the sons of Adam? As a summary, he came to teach people how they may respect their Lord, Allah Almighty. That is his job or duty. His duty, his task, is to teach people how they may give more perfect respect to their Lord Almighty, and he was the first and most perfect respecter of Allah Almighty. No one can reach that point!

Now, our respect is going to be according to our knowledge about our Lord Almighty. The more you know about a person, the more respect you give to him. Therefore, when our Prophet, Muhammad (s) was asked, "What is *afdalu-l-a'mal*, the best of deeds?" he said, *"Al-'ilmu bil-Lah*, the knowledge of Allah."

What is this? The Prophet (s) was urging people to gain more knowledge about their Lord Almighty, because, when they asked about deeds, he said, "The knowledge of Allah," since, when we do a deed, it acquires value according to our respect for our Lord. Therefore, don't suppose that the Prophet's *tawhid* (oneness of God) his saying *La ilaha illa-LLah* is like your saying it. If all creatures', all prophets, all angels, all awliya, all scholars and all believers saying *La ilaha illa-LLah* could be put into the balance, only one of the Prophet's *La ilaha illa-Llah* would outweigh them all. His *tawhid* is an ocean, and the *tawhid* of all creatures is only a drop.

You may be surprised by this. Don't be surprised; there is still more than this! You have heard about the Prophet's sayings concerning his *sahabah's*, Companions', virtues. About Sayyidina Abu Bakr alone, may Allah bless him, the Prophet said, "If all the faith of the *ummah* could be balanced against the faith of Abu Bakr, Abu Bakr's faith would be more than the faith of the whole *ummah*," and Abu Bakr was a Companion, not a prophet.

The rank of the Prophet (s) no one can imagine – *no one*! Do you not believe in the Night Journey, when each prophet was placed in his station according to his rank in the Seven Heavens, and have you not heard that Archangel Gabriel was the Prophet's guide up to *Sidrat al-Muntaha*, the limit of created beings? There Archangel Gabriel stopped. Then the command came from the Divine Presence, calling, inviting, Muhammad (s) to come forward, and Muhammad said to Archangel Gabriel, who was the greatest of the angels, "Come with me."

And Gabriel (a) said, "No, I cannot. This is my limit; I cannot pass my limit. No permission for me to move even one hair, one breath further. I can't move from my station." The Prophet (s) was the only one who passed the limit of created beings towards the Creator of the universes, to His Divine Presence. No one may pass except him; the one exception among creatures is for beloved Muhammad (s).

Archangel Gabriel said, "O Muhammad, peace be upon you, if I move even one second's distance from my station, divine lights will burn me, and then no more Archangel Gabriel – finished."

And beloved Muhammad (s) said, "No worry. Let divine lights burn me. I give myself to my Lord. I have no need of anything. I have given myself to Him." And he went into *as-Saraiy at-Tawhid*, the Mansion of Unity in which there is no *ithnainiyah*, duality; finished.

Archangel Gabriel feared that he would be nothing. But the Prophet, beloved Muhammad (s), said, "I agree to be nothing," and went into the endless Oceans of the Greatness of Allah Almighty, went into endless Power Oceans, and went into the endless Beauty Oceans of Allah Almighty, going as a drop into oceans. A drop comes upon the ocean from the skies and when it reaches the ocean, you can't find it. Finished, but endless pleasure.

Do you suppose that the Prophet left that Ocean in the Divine Presence and came back down to earth, when Allah Almighty had taken him up to the highest place in His Presence? If he had come from the Divine Presence, it would have been to the whole earth like its sun. What do you think – if that sun were to come on the earth, could you find the earth? But the sun shines in the skies and the sun also shines on the earth. We are saying that the sun is on earth, but the sun is still there, not on earth. That is from Allah Almighty's mercy, that the sun is in the skies and its rays are on the earth.

You must know our Prophet! We do not know anything. "La ilaha illa-Llah, Muhammadur Rasul-Allah"[201] is written everywhere. That is the divine 'stamp'. If you have these eyes (not like these physical eyes), you may see, even on every atom, "La ilaha illa-Llah, Muhammadur Rasul-Allah"; yes. Therefore, we are asking for more divine knowledge so that we may give our respect to our Lord Almighty, and respect for our Lord passes through respect for the Prophet. He respects His beloved Muhammad (s).

We are respecting beloved Muhammad (s) because his Lord respects him, writing his name in the same sentence, "La ilaha illa-Llah," with "Muhammadur Rasul-Allah" after it. Before the creation, "La ilaha illa-Llah, Muhammadur Rasul-Allah" was written on the Divine Throne, the most honored station; yes. It is written there, and Allah Almighty says, "Wa rafa'na laka dhikrak[202] – We are putting your name with Our name out of respect. I am respecting you, O Muhammad."

---

[201]"There is no deity except Allah, Muhammad is the Messenger of Allah."
[202]"And [have We not] raised high for you [Muhammad] your repute?" (94:4)

Therefore, as much as you are respecting Muhammad (s), you are respecting his Lord Almighty. The Prophet (s) says, "I am nothing, but He is giving honor to me." Yes; Allah Almighty gives honor as He likes. *He gave him honor. Why are you jealous?*

What are people fighting about nowadays, saying *"Shirk!"*[203] to people who are giving respect to Muhammad (s)? If it is *shirk*, Allah has put his name there! Take it away, if you can, so that there is written only *'La ilaha illa-Llah."* But what about the *"Muhammadur Rasul-Allah"* which is written on the Divine Throne? *That is jealousy!*

We are asking forgiveness that we are not giving complete respect to our Prophet (s). If anyone respects your son, you are going to be pleased; if a king sees that people give respect to his crown prince, he is going to be pleased. And Allah Almighty says, *"Inna-Llaha wa malaikatahu yusalluna 'ala-n-nabiyyi. Ya ayyuha-l-ladhina amanu, sallu 'alayhi wa sallimu taslima."*[204]

This is an endless ocean. If we go on with this topic of respect for the Prophet (s), it is not going to end up to the end of this world, and then we can pass on to respect for our Lord. And everyone is giving his endless respects to our Lord Almighty. If we enter Paradise, *Insha'Allah*, there also we will give our endless respects to our Lord by saying, as He says, *"Wa akhira da'ahu any-l-hamdu lil-Lahi Rabbi-l-'alamin."*[205] It is endless, the way in which we are going to give our respects to our Lord Almighty! ▲

---

[203] Ascribing divinity or God-like attributes and authority to someone other than Allah.

[204] "Indeed, Allah and His angels invoke blessings upon the Prophet. O you who believe, invoke blessings upon him and ask for peace [upon him]." (33:56)

[205] "And the last of their call will be, 'Praise be to Allah, Lord of the worlds.'" (10:10)

89: knowledge of the saints

We are in need of the knowledge of *awliya*, not of scholars' knowledge. Scholars' knowledge, even for themselves, is nothing. I was in Alexandria, Egypt. It was the first time I went there and I was waiting for a bus. An *'alim*, scholar, came and said to me, "From where are you coming?"

I told him, "From Damascus."

"O shaykh," he said, "here in this place there are 150,000 scholars from Azhar." You know Azhar, the famous Islamic university in Cairo?

And I told him, "Oh! I am astonished at how there can be 150,000 scholars in a city and so much *fasad*, depravity, in this country." I mean to say, if you see a country in which all the people are ill and they say, "There are 150,000 doctors here," how can it be? If there are doctors, there need be no ill people in that country. *"There are 150,000 scholars here."* Then what is the matter, with all this depravity?

Therefore, as Grandshaykh often said, we are in need of *awliya's* knowledge. Allah Almighty, *ya Rabb*, You send to us from *awliya's* knowledge something to restrain our egos or for protection from the evil of our egos. Yet, although we are asking for something, we are not worthy.

O my Lord, we are asking from Your endless favors, for the sake of beloved Muhammad (s); for the sake of Your beloved people, *awliya*; for the sake of Holy Ramadan: teach us something that will be of benefit to us, that will make us Your obedient servants. O our Lord, we are fed-up with being the servants of our egos – fed-up, but we can't take ourselves away. Our egos are catching us from one side, putting something on our necks, dragging us along. But we are fed-up!

Therefore, we are asking Allah Almighty to make a way to freedom for us. But people are understanding freedom in another way. Yes; they are slaves in themselves but yet they are quarreling to be free people. "What is freedom?" they are asking.

In such countries as this, everything is free, nothing forbidden, but *still* they are asking for freedom. And that is something from Allah Almighty, some inspiration; they are asking for something but yet they do not understand what they are asking. Freedom – there is freedom but *still* they are asking for freedom. That is a secret desire which is appearing in their hearts and their tongues are speaking about it, but yet they are not describing it. People are no longer able to describe what real freedom is.

Real freedom is when you are free from your ego, from your ego's hands. *Then* you are free, free for your Lord and a slave to your Lord; you are free from the hands of your ego and a slave to your Lord Almighty. That person has reached real freedom; otherwise people are slaves, from beginning to end. And that is another purpose of prophethood: to make people free, because people are usually slaves, and prophets came to make them free from the hands of their egos, from their *nafs*.

Nafs is catching people and making them into its servants, while the prophets came to give them freedom. But the surprising thing is that people are running away from the prophets – yes, and throwing stones at them, giving them trouble; every prophet was given suffering by people. The prophets are calling them to freedom but they are fighting the prophets. That is a surprising thing!

And the characteristic of egos never changes, from the beginning up to this day. We are now at the same level. All people are fighting the prophets; they are fighting the Seal of the Prophets, also, the final one, the last one. Yes, because the Prophet (s) came to save people from their egos, and egos are coming in front of all the prophets, saying, 'No! You can't do this! You can't keep my servants from Me! They are *My* servants and I am not giving permission to take My servants.

"To what are you calling people? Who is that?? Their Lord??? *I* am their Lord!" everyone's ego is saying. *"Your Lord, not anyone else!"* Therefore *nafs* says always, *"La ilaha illa ana,* there is no God but Me"; everyone's ego is claiming that. Therefore, as the first step, all the prophets came to say to people, "Say *'La ilaha illa-Llah,'* for truly there is no God except Allah." This is addressed to egos.

What do you think of the prophets? From beginning to end, they were bad people? *Astaghfirullah, astaghfirullah;* may Allah forgive us! They were perfect – perfect in their minds, in their bodily powers and spiritual powers; they were perfect people in everything. How could they be bad? *Hasha, astaghfirullah!* But Abu Jahl, the most bitter enemy to beloved Muhammad (s), would look at the Prophet and say, "I never looked at such an ugly face, I never saw such a bad person!" as if he were looking in a mirror and seeing himself. He was saying it for himself, not for the Prophet.

The Prophet (s) is a mirror. You may look at yourself in it. People like Abu Jahl, who represent evil, may say bad things about the prophets but the prophets are all perfect, and in particular the Seal of the Prophets is the most perfect in his outward form and in his spiritual life. No one may be like him.

Joseph (a), Sayyidina Yusuf, was the most handsome one among all the prophets. When he stood on a balcony and hungry people came and looked at him, they forgot their hunger because of his beauty. From Allah Almighty's Beauty Oceans, one drop was with Sayyidina Yusuf (a). And the Prophet said, "Yusuf was given a *juz,* one part, of beauty. I was given it all"[206] – Muhammad, beloved Muhammad; yes. But Allah Almighty is withholding that because if it were to appear, no one would be able to look.

I mean to say that the prophets were in perfect form both in outward appearance and in inner life. Prophet Muhammad (s) was here [on earth].

---

[206]The Prophet (s) said this as a simple statement of fact, a piece of information which he knew about himself through divine inspiration. No pride or boastfulness is implied by his words.

At the same time, he was in the Divine Presence, as he was during the night of *Mi'raj*, the Night Journey, never leaving that Presence. I am asking scholars, "What about the Prophet – when he went to the Divine Presence, did he come down?" No answer!

The Prophet is still in that Divine Presence, but a shadow or a ray from the Prophet's sun came here into his body and people saw that. He was from Allah Almighty's *nur*, light; *nur Muhammad (s)* – the light of Muhammad from Allah Almighty. When he walked in the sun, he had no shadow. There is still now in existence a hair of the Prophet (s), and it is well-known that when you put your hair in the light, it makes a shadow. But his hair does not make a shadow.

Therefore, people now are running after their egos and they are fighting the prophets; the hardest fighting is in our time. Don't think that in the Muslim world they are going to respect the Prophet as it is necessary, or that others are going to respect him if Muslims do not take care to keep their Prophet's advice to be their Lord's servants; because everyone is claiming to be a *sultan* in himself, and this is the time when people are going along according to their *nafs* – *hawa nafs*, the desires of their egos. People are going by their desires, and everyone's desires are going in millions and millions of directions. You can't keep them in one path.

At the time of the Prophet (s), people ran into the circle of faith and Islam: *'Idha jaa' nasru-LLahi wal-fath, wa raita-n-nasa yadkhuluna fi dini-LLahi afwaja.'*[207] People then ran *into* Islam, but now we are in a time when people are running away from Islam, running out. The Prophet (s) gave the example that, as an arrow leaves its bow, so people will go out of Islam.

Now we are in that time. And we are *ghuraba*, strangers, among people; Muslims feel like hiding themselves. The Prophet described this time, this period, saying that *mumins*, believers, will hide themselves from people and will ask for secret ways, ways where no one is present, to pass, to go to their

---

[207]"When Allah's help comes and victory, and you [Muhammad] see people entering into the religion of Allah in throngs." (110:1-2)

homes, to their businesses, so that not too many people may see them, particularly if they are keeping the dress of the Prophet (s). At the end of time, *mumins*, if they are wearing their 'uniforms,' the Prophet's dress, will hide themselves. It is like a snake: A snake, when it goes out of its hole, always looks for lonely ways to go and catch its prey, and it comes from where no one can see it.

When the Prophet (s) said this, Abu Bakr, may Allah bless him, asked, "Why are you giving the example of such a creature as a snake?" Because unbelievers are looking at *mumins* as people look at snakes, yes; looking at themselves and remembering... undertakers. They are afraid for themselves, being reminded of death, being reminded of Allah Almighty. Unbelievers do not believe in Allah Almighty but they do believe in death. Therefore, when they look at a *mumin*, it is a reminder.

The Prophet (s) informed us about the whole way that Islam would pass through, and this is the most difficult period for believers. And it is going to be ended; it is not too much further now. *"Alhamdulillah,"* we are saying; it is a good tidings that soon the way is going to turn. This period will not go on up to the end of the world, no.

People's eyes are still blinded, but now I am looking and seeing that there is an arrow showing the direction. It is not a long distance. But *tuba*, happiness, the Prophet said, for those who are now keeping to the path of the prophets, riding on their egos and going on.

Now we are asking, as *awliya* are asking, as the Prophet (s) was ordered by his Lord to ask, for more knowledge. We are asking for such knowledge from prophet's and from saint's knowledges which will give us more power to continue. As hard as the conditions around us may be, when we take from *awliya's* knowledge, it makes our way easier. Knowledge is a divine light granted by our Lord to His pure people; pure people have been given a divine light from our Lord Almighty and that light lights our way. There never occurred such a darkness in past times, and we are in need of a knowledge that gives us light so that we may know where we can put our feet.

We hope that something is granted, for the sake of our beloved Prophet (s), by our Lord to our Grandshaykh, by our beloved Prophet to our Grandshaykh, and, by his permission, some of it is coming through our words. And we are thanking our Lord that He is granting us something, and it is enough for us. More than this, we can't carry. ▲

90: miraculous powers

If Allah Almighty helps His servant, everything is going to be easy. If Allah Almighty does not support His servant, no one can support him, and everything is going to be difficult – more difficult, most difficult.

Grandshaykh, may Allah bless him, was always saying – I am still listening to him, also – that Allah Almighty likes His servants when they are humble and recognize that they are nothing, most weak. Therefore, Allah Almighty mentions in His Holy Book, the Glorious Quran, that if anyone feels that he is a strong and rich and powerful and intelligent and very knowledgeable person, every support will be taken away from him and he will be left in his ego's hands. And we are such weak people; for every breath, we are in need of our Lord's help. If our Lord's help does not reach us, we aren't able to breathe. If, in any unit of time, even the smallest, Allah Almighty leaves us alone, everything is going to vanish and finish.

Therefore, the most lovely attribute of servants towards their Lord is to recognize that they are poor and needy and must always be supported by their Lord. Then Allah Almighty supports them and gives His divine help to them. Allah Almighty is angry with those people who look at themselves and think that they possess power or wealth or beauty or knowledge or intelligence. Allah Almighty is very angry with those people who suppose that everything is from themselves, not coming from Him, not a grant from Allah Almighty to them, imagining that *they* possess such an attribute.

The first example is Satan. He thought that everything was from himself; therefore he was proud – of his knowledge, of his worshipping. Therefore, the divine anger fell upon him and took everything away from him, except that Allah Almighty left him with knowledge, and he knew well the Torah, the *Injil*, the Psalms and the Holy Quran. But his pride prevented him from gaining wisdoms from the holy words, the holy verses. Therefore, for the one who sees everything as being from himself and is proud, everything that he has been given will finally go from his hand.

"*Afeta-l-'ilma-n-nasiyan.*"[208] Whoever learns and keeps knowledge and sees it as being from himself, Allah Almighty punishes him by forgetting; he will soon forget. Therefore we must ask from our Lord beneficial knowledge. Knowledge which we may keep with us and that knowledge which will keep us – *that* is beneficial knowledge, and we have been ordered to acquire such knowledge. Therefore, learning is ordered by the Prophet (s), for both *mumins* and *muminahs*. They must learn; everyone must learn.

Learning is not only through writing or reading but through listening; anyone can hear but not everyone *listens*. We must listen. The *sahabah*, the Companions of the Prophet, may Allah bless his *sahabah*, sat and listened. But there were some people who came and heard but did not listen; they heard but it never stayed in their hearts, going away. But the *sahabah* used to sit with the Prophet (s), listening, and they were oceans of knowledge. If one *sahabi* was present in a crowd of people, no one could open his mouth to say anything; they would all listen to that *sahabi*. Because the *sahabah* took the seeds of beneficial knowledges from even one word of the Prophet's, they were an ocean, manifesting knowledge.

But *we* are in need of looking – reading, writing, and then taking into our memory. Therefore, the one who takes by the way of his memory is going to lose it, to forget it, but the one who takes by the way of his soul, by the way of his heart, will never forget it. And "beneficial knowledge" means that it is a power which pushes people towards the Divine Presence, taking them along. Something is in that rocket that pushes it to the skies. If not, nothing can move it from its base.

---

[208]"The calamity of knowledge is forgetfulness." (Sayyidina 'Ali)

All of us have been ordered to jump from *mulk* to *malakut*,[209] from the earth to the heavens. No one comes here to stay on earth; we must prepare ourselves for that day when we may jump from earth to the heavens. We have not come on earth, we never landed on the earth, to stay on it. Rather, we have been invited to return to our stations in the Divine Presence.

We must know this. We have not come here to eat and drink and dance and build and fight, no. Everyone has been offered to reach the station corresponding to his destination, and everyone has been ordered to take care to reach it, also. Everyone has a private destination in the Divine Presence, and we must take care concerning it. Everyone has a *mi'raj*, ascension, so that he may reach the original and private station that Allah Almighty prepared for him, and we must look to that – how we may arrive at or how we may reach that station.

At nighttime we are looking at the stars. Sometimes we may wish to be in the skies, but *safely*; everyone would like to go through space but no one wants to be in a rocket, going up. Perhaps everyone would like to be there with his body, without using any instruments, as they are drawing pictures of Superman, coming and going. It is within the imagination of people to be such a superman, yes? Everyone likes that. That is imaginary, but originally that power is with everyone. *We have that power.*

Superman is an amusement for children. They believe in him; sometimes they think it is true, that there really are some people like this, who go or come like that, yes. If you think like those little boys, it is a way to open to you that extraordinary or miraculous power.

Everyone has miraculous powers in himself, but where is that connection, the thing which will connect everything? If you bring me all the little pieces of this tape, giving them to me to connect them, I can't. Still, that may be relatively easy, but to make a connection within ourselves with our miraculous powers is impossible for an ordinary person to do.

---

[209]From the material to the spiritual plane.

We have been given that, and in order to put a connection within everyone, Allah Almighty sent the prophets to teach people how they may do it. All the prophets are examples for mankind, and the final one is the Last Prophet (s). During the Night Journey, *Isra' wal-Mi'raj*, he demonstrated to all people that they all have such miraculous powers. The one who follows him may acquire that. He may be able to connect with those miraculous powers and go and look at the Heavens.

But where is that person who can follow the Prophet (s)? You can't leave off any *sunnah* of his way; if you leave anything, you will not be complete, you will not be ready to travel to the heavens. Therefore he advised his *ummah* to keep his way; as much you are perfect in keeping his way, traveling to the heavens is going to be easy. If you do not keep it, it is most difficult; you can't even lift your feet one foot off the earth to stand up like this.

You must keep the Prophet's way completely, and the first step is that you must look after the purification of your heart. The way that leads to miraculous powers passes through our hearts; if you can grasp that power, you can grasp it through your heart. Then everything, by divine support, will be easy. If divine support does not come, it is impossible, and divine support comes through the Prophet (s). A transformer gives power, and the transformer for divine powers is the heart of the Prophet (s); it comes through his heart. Whoever is ready to take it, may take.

There are some light bulbs in which the power of electricity doesn't come. What is the reason? Because there is something wrong with them. Those wires are cut, broken and burned; you say the ampoule is broken, the bulb is burned out. If that power does not come in our hearts, you must know that there is something wrong with ourselves – a broken, wire-less bulb. *You* must look after it.

Therefore, even the smallest part in every instrument must be perfect to give perfect results. But in our time, we are interested only in outward things, to make everything excellent from the outside; the inside we are not interested in. In our time, everyone's important concern is to make himself have a good appearance; then – finished. But in the sight of Allah Almighty, the important thing is our hearts.

If our hearts are connected perfectly, we can reach from the earth to the heavens by our spiritual powers in less than the blink of an eye. You may be in safety at the farthest point that you can see in the skies from the earth. Nothing will harm you, however far the distances may be or however much as the heat; even if it is millions of degrees, that will never give you trouble. There may be thousands of times more light than the sun's light, but it will never affect your light because you have been given from divine light; your spirit is composed of divine lights.

Yes; we have been given from our Lord's divine lights, and if the light that everyone has been given appears, all the darkness throughout space up to the stars will be filled with lights. You will not be able to see any dark spot in space if the light of one spirit appears.

Therefore, man is the most important creature in the universe because he is his Lord's deputy, and there must be authority for a deputy to be in every part of the universe. And we are created for the whole universe, not for being only on the earth; the whole universe is to be for us. As our Prophet (s) looked at all the universes on the Night Journey, we may move from the same path.

O readers, our brothers and sisters - believers - time is going too fast. Our lives are going to be ended. And we have been offered to take our spiritual powers for returning to the heavens.

We must take more care of our spiritual life. Now we are giving most of our care for our bodies, for our physical bodies' pleasures, but it is not pleasure, indeed. It is only suffering, not pleasure but suffering.

You may reach pleasure by way of your spiritual life; *that* is pleasure! If you can connect with heavenly pleasures, if you make a relationship from your heart to the heavens, it is endless pleasure, coming from the heavens to your heart.

Therefore, our advice, firstly to myself and then to you, is to take more care of our spiritual life. From our life's most precious time, if we are giving 999 out of 1,000 to our physical bodies' affairs, we are giving only one out of 1,000 to our spiritual affairs, while it is actually right to give 999 for our spiritual lives, and one is enough, and too much, also, for our physical bodies, while if our spiritual life does not support our physical bodies, we quickly become shriveled.

So many people look like that; it comes quickly to a person because there is no spiritual support, because he never takes care of his spiritual life. My Grandshaykh was over one hundred years old, with red cheeks, and his power never declined. Yes, every time; the one who takes more care of his spiritual life gets more pleasure and tastes the sweetness of this life, also, but the one who takes care of his physical body only, every day his ability to taste decreases.

Therefore, my advice to you, and to me also, is to take more care. Now it is the holy month in which we are taking some care of our spiritual life, but we must continue after Ramadan, after the holy month, on the same path, and take more care each day. Therefore the Prophet (s) said that the one for whom two days are equal is a loser. We must take more care each day, and as much as you are taking more care each day, more support comes to you from your Lord.

That is enough for today. And we are asking forgiveness for not giving enough care to our Lord's worship and service, saying, *"Astaghfirullah, astaghfirullah, astaghfirullah...."* And we are giving endless thanks and praise to our Lord Almighty for causing us to listen to such heavenly wisdoms from His prophets and from His *awliya*, and saying, *"Alhamdulillah, alhamdulillah, wa shukru lil-Lah...."*[210] ▲

---

[210] "Praise be to Allah, praise be to Allah, and thanks be to Allah."

91: a present-day miracle of prophet muhammad (s)

It is from the illness of our *nafs* to be *haris*, to be desireful (a new word, "desireful"; you must understand). It is our *nafs'* illness to be desireful, wanting – to like to listen too much and to enjoy through listening but not to enjoy through acting. Action is hard but listening is easy, enjoyable. Therefore, we may listen too much but we are acting less.

And that is all right, also, in our time. We are asking people to attend and to listen because so many prophets did not find people to listen as we are finding now. So many prophets never found anyone to listen and to obey them or to give them their love. Maybe some prophets will come on the Day of Resurrection with only two people; no one else heard, listened, obeyed or accepted their prophethood.

But for the honor of our Prophet (s), *alhamdulillah*, among his nation so many *awliya* are carrying people, and it is from our Lord Almighty's favors to ask and to find in such a country – it is so dark; such a heavy burden on people in London – such a group to listen, giving their love and giving their listening, and asking to obey the orders of their Lord Almighty. That is from the miracles of our Prophet (s), still going on.

Wa min Allah at-tawfiq. And success is only from God.

holy days
of the islamic calendar

The twelve months of the Islamic lunar calendar in chronological sequence, including broadly observed holy days:

Muharram	1st is Islamic New Year; 9th and 10th are days of fasting; 10th is Ashura.
Safar	
Rabi' al-Awwal	12th is the Prophet's birthday, known as mawlid; milad; mawlud; celebrated globally.
Rabi' ath-Thani	
Jumadi al-Awwal	
Jumadi ath-Thani	
Rajab	According to Hadith, the month of Allah. Mi'raj an-Nabi (Heavenly ascension of the Prophet). Superogatory fasting and prayers.
Sha'ban	According to Hadith, the month of the Prophet. 15th is Nifs al-Sha'ban; 7th is Laylat ul-Raghaib. Superogatory fasting and prayers.
Ramadan	According to Hadith, the month of the people. The month of fasting.
Shawwal	1st is Eid al-Fitr, the celebration marking the end of Ramadan, of either two or three days duration.
Dhul-Qadah	
Dhul-Hijjah	The month of Hajj. Standing at Mount Arafat is on the 9th and Eid al-Adha, the celebration commemorating Hajj, is on the 10th.

liberating the soul

Glossary

Abdul-Khaliq al-Ghujdawani – the eleventh grandshaykh of the Naqshbandi tariqat, one of the Khwajagan of Central Asia.

Abu Hanifa – the founder of one of the four schools of Islamic jurisprudence, the Hanafi school.

Abu Yazid Bistami – Bayazid Bistami, a great ninth century wali and Naqshbandi master.

Adhan – the call to prayer.

Ahl al-Bayt – People of the House, that is, the family of the Holy Prophet (s).

Ahl ad-dunya – people of the world, i.e., those who are attached to its life and pleasures.

Ajal – life span, term of life.

Akhirah – the Hereafter, the Eternal Life.

Alhamdulillah – praise be to Allah, praise God.

'Aql – intellect, intelligence, reason, discernment.

Ashhadu an la ilaha illa-Llah wa ashhadu anna Muhammadan wa rasulihu – "I bear witness that there is no deity but Allah and I bear witness that Muhammad is His messenger," the Islamic Shahadah or Declaration of Faith.

'Asr prayer – the late afternoon prayer.

Astaghfirullah – I ask Allah's forgiveness.

A'udhu bil-Lahi min ash-Shaytani-r-Rajim – I seek refuge in Allah from Satan the accursed.

Awwabin – a nafil (superogatory) prayer of six rak'ats, offered in sets of two rak'ats each, after the sunnah of Maghrib prayer.

Awliya (sing., wali) – the "friends" of Allah, Muslim saints.

Barakah – blessings.

Barzakh – the intermediate spiritual state between bodily death and the Resurrection.

Batil – vain or false; falsehood, deception.

Baya' – pledge; allegiance.

Bid'ah – innovation in matters of religion.

Bi-hurmatil-Fatiha – for the sanctity or respect of Surat al-Fatiha, the opening chapter of the Quran.

Bismillahi-r-Rahmani-r-Rahim - "In the name of Allah, the Beneficent, the Merciful," the invocation made at the beginning of every action.

Dajjal – the Anti-Christ or False Messiah foretold in numerous ahadith concerning the End-Time.

Day of Promises – the occasion in the spiritual world when Allah

Almighty called together the souls of all human beings to come and asked them to acknowledge His Lordship and sovereignty (7:172).

Dargah – holy place of Sufi gatherings.

Dhikr (zikr, zikir) – message, remembrance or reminder, used in the Quran to refer to the Quran and other revealed scriptures. Dhikr (or dhikr-Allah) also refers to remembering Allah through repetition of His Holy Names or various phrases of glorification.

Dhuhr prayer – the second of the five daily prayers, observed just after noon up to mid-afternoon.

Dhulm (zulm) – injustice, oppression, tyranny, misuse, transgressing proper limits, wrong-doing.

Du'a – supplication, personal prayer.

Duha prayer – a nafil prayer of between two to eight rak'ats, observed after the sun has risen to shortly before noontime.

Dunya - this world and its attractions, worldly involvements.

Effendi – mister, sir.

Fajr – dawn; specifically, the dawn prayer.

Fana – annihilation, specifically, in Allah.

Fard – obligatory, prescribed.

Fard al-kifiyah – an obligation which suffices to be met by one or a few persons in a community.

Fitna (pl., fitan) – trial, test, temptation,discord, dissension.

Futuhat – openings.

Gabriel (Jibril) – the archangel who conveyed Allah's revela-tions to the prophets, referred to in the Quran as *al-Ruh* (the Spirit), *Ruh al-Quddus* (the Holy Spirit), and *Ruh al-Amin* (the Trustworthy Spirit).

Gharib – strange, foreign, alien, quaint, curious.

Ghusl – the major ablution, consisting of a shower during which water reaches every part of the body.

Grandshaykh – generally, a wali of great stature. In this text, where spelled with a capital "G," "Grandshaykh" refers to Maulana 'Abdullah ad-Daghestani, Shaykh Nazim's shaykh, to whom he was closely attached for forty years up to the time of Grandshaykh's death in 1973.

Hadith – report of the Holy Prophet's sayings, contained in the collections of early *hadith* scholars. In this text, "*Hadith*" has been used to refer to the entire body of his oral traditions, while "*hadith*" denotes an individual tradition.

Halal – lawful, permissible.

Haqiqah – the essential truth or reality.

Haqq – truth, reality, right. Al-Haqq is one of Allah's Holy Names.

Haram – prohibited, unlawful.

Hasan al-Basri – a first century Hijrah scholar and mystic.

Hawa – desires, lusts, passions of the lower self or nafs.

Hidayah/hidayat – guidance.

Hijab – barrier, screen, veil or curtain; the covering of Muslim women.

Himmah – zeal, eagerness, ambition, determination.

Hu – the divine pronoun, He.

Ibrahim – the prophet Abraham.

Imam – leader; specifically, leader of a congregational prayer.

Imam al-Ghazali – the great tenth century mystic and scholar whose voluminous works constitute one of the greatest contribution to Islamic thought of all time.

Iman – faith, belief.

Injil – the original scripture revealed Jesus (a).

Insha'Allah – God willing, if God wills.

'Isa – Jesus (a).

'Isha – night; specifically, the night prayer.

Ishraq prayer – two nafil rak'ats, observed when the sun has fully risen (about fifteen minutes after sunrise).

'Izra'il – the Angel of Death.

Jihad – striving, struggle.

Jihad al-Akbar – the greatest struggle, referring to the inner struggle against ego, Satan, worldly attachments, and the passions of the ego (nafs, Shaytan, dunya, hawa').

Kaffan – burial shroud.

Kafir – a denier or rejector; in an Islamic context, one who denies Allah (an unbeliever or atheist) or does not acknowledge or is ungrateful for divine favors.

Khalifah – deputy, successor, vice-gerent.

Khalifat-Ullah – a deputy or vicegerent of Allah.

Khidr – a holy man, mentioned in the Quran, 18:60-82, whom God has granted life up to the end of the world.

Khutbah – sermon.

Kufr—unbelief, denial of Allah.

La hawla wa la quwwata illa bil-Lah al-'Aliyil-'Adhim – "There is no might nor power except in Allah, the Most High, the All-Mighty." These words are uttered frequently in the daily lives of Muslims to signify total reliance upon Allah.

La ilaha illa-Llah – There is no deity except Allah.

La ilaha illa-Llah, Muhammadu Rasul Allah – There is no deity except Allah, Muhammad is the Messenger of Allah.

Laylat al-Bara'at – the Night of Forgiveness, observed on the night between the 14th and 15th of the month of Sha'ban.

Laylat al-Qadr – the Night of Power, commemorating the first revelation of the Quran to the Prophet in Hira cave, observed during one of the odd-numbered nights of the last ten nights of Ramadan.

Laylat al-Rajab – the night of the Prophet's conception, com-memorated on the first Friday of Rajab.

Laylat al-Wiladah – the night of the Prophet's birth, com-memorated on the night between the 11th and 12th of Rabi' ul-Awwal.

Laylat al-Bara'at ('Isra wal Mi'raj)– the night of the Prophet's Night Journey and Ascension, observed on the night preceding the 27h of Rajab.

Madhhab – school of Islamic jurisprudence, such as Hanafi, Shafi'i, Hanbali or Maliki.

Mahdi – the divinely-appointed guide whose coming at the end-time of this world is mentioned in several authoritative hadiths. He will lead the believers and establish a rule of justice and righteousness for a period of time prior to the events preceding the end of the world and the Last Judgment.

Makruh – something disliked or detested according to the Islamic Shari'ah.

Masha'Allah – as Allah willed.

Masjid – mosque, place of worship.

Mudaraa – roundabout, indirect.

Muazzin (Arabic, muadhdhin)– the one who makes the call to prayer (adhan).

Mumin/muminah – male/female believers in Islam.

Munkar – that which is disapproved, rejected or considered abominable in Islam.

Murid – a disciple or follower of a shaykh.

Musa – Moses.

Muwahhid – one who proclaims the Unity of Allah Almighty.

Nafs – (1) soul, self, person; (2) the lower self, the ego.

Nasihah – advice or counsel, admonition, reminder.

N'imat – favors, blessings.

Qiblah – direction; specifically, the direction of Mecca.

Qisas – retaliation.

Qiyamat/Qiyamah – the Day of Resurrection.

Rabitah – bond, connection, tie, link; in this context, with a shaykh.

Radi-Allahu anhu/anha/anhum – may Allah be pleased with him/her/them, the invocation of blessings upon the Companions of the Prophet.

Rahmah – mercy.

Rak'at – a cycle or unit of the Islamic prayer (salat), which is repeated a specified number of times in each prayer.

Rasul-Allah – the Messenger of God, Muhammad (s).

Sadaqah – charity, good deed.

Sahabah (sing., sahabi) – the Prophet's Companions, that is, the first generation of Muslims who were with the Messenger of God (a) in Mecca and Medina.

Sajdah – prostration.

Salat – the Islamic prayer or worship.

Salat an-Najat – a two-rak'at prayer, observed during the night.

Sallallahu 'alayhi was-salam – the invocation, "May Allah's peace and blessings be upon him," upon the Holy Prophet (s).

Shafa'ah – intercession.

Shahadah – witnessing; i.e., the Islamic declaration of faith, "Ashhadu an la ilaha illa Lah, wa ashhadu anna Muham-madur Rasul-Allah.

Shari'ah – literally, "road"; the Divine Law of Islam established by the Holy Quran and the Sunnah of the Prophet.

Sharr – evil.

Sayyidina 'Ali – the Prophet's cousin and son-in-law, and the fourth caliph of Islam.

Shaykh Sharafuddin – the shaykh of Grandshaykh 'Abdullah ad-Daghistani.

Shaytan – Satan.

Shukr alhamdulillah – thanks of praise be to Allah.

Sohbet (Arabic, suhbah) – companionship, associating together.

Subhanallah – glory be to Allah.

Sultan – king, ruler.

Sunnah - the practice of the Holy Prophet; that is, what he did, said, recommended or approved of in his Companions. In this text, "Sunnah" is used to refer to the collective body of his actions, sayings or recommendations, while "sunnah" refers to an individual action or recommendation.

Tariqah/tariqat – literally, way, road or path. An Islamic order or path of discipline and devotion under a guide or shaykh; Islamic Sufism.

Tariqat tarbiyah – training in the ways of tariqat.

Tasalli – pleasure, amusement.

Taurat – the original scripture revealed to Moses by Allah.

Turbatu-Rasul – the Holy Prophet's grave in Medina.

'Ulama – scholars, specifically of religion.

'Umar – the Prophet's eminent Companion and the second caliph of Islam.

Uns – familiarity.

Wali (pl., awliya) – a Muslim saint.

Wa min Allah at-tawfiq – And success is only from Allah.

Wudu – the minor ablution preceding prayers and other acts of worship.

Ya Allah – O Allah.

Ya Hafidh – O Protector or Guardian.

Ya Halim – O Gentle, Tolerant One.

Yahu – Turkish expression, meaning something like, "My goodness!"

Ya Rabb – O Lord.

Zabur – the original scripture revealed to the prophet David.

Other titles from

Islamic Supreme Council of America

Online ordering now available from www.Amazon.com

Muhammad: The Messenger of Islam

His Life and Prophecy

By Hajjah Amina Adil

ISBN 1-930409-11-7

Retail Price: $21.99

Since the 7th century, the sacred biography of Islam's Prophet Muhammad has shaped the perception of the religion and its place in world history. English biographies of Muhammad – founder of the faith that currently claims 1.5 billion followers, roughly one-fourth of the world's population – have characteristically presented him in the light of verifiable historical authenticity.

Muhammad: The Messenger Of Islam goes one step further in skillfully etching the personal portrait of a man of incomparable moral and spiritual stature, as seen through the eyes of Muslims around the world. Compiled from classical Ottoman Turkish sources and translated into English, this comprehensive biography should be of interest to scholars of Islam and to all who seek to understand the essence of the faith, which is deeply rooted in the life example of its prophet. This esteemed biography not only details Muhammad's life; it also includes mystical secrets that Muslims believe were granted to the prophets who preceded him in the Holy Land and in other regions of the Middle East. This impressive biographical work deftly weaves quotes from authentic religious texts with ancient lore, resulting in a compelling, unforgettable read. Paperback. 608 pp.

The Honor of Women in Islam

Scholars in Islam Series
By Professor Yusuf da Costa
ISBN 1-930409-06-0
Retail Price: $10.99

Relying explicitly on Islamic source texts, this concise, scholarly work elucidates the true respect and love for women inherent in the Islamic faith. It examines the pre-Islamic state of women, highlights the unprecedented rights they received under Islamic Law, and addresses the prominent beliefs and prevailing cultures throughout the Muslim world regarding the roles of women in familial, social service and community development, business, academic, religious, and even judicial circles. In addition, brief case studies of historical figures such as Mary, mother of Jesus and Hagar, handmaiden of Sarah are presented within the Islamic tradition. An excellent resource for academics, policymakers, theologians, laypersons, and service providers. Paperback. 104 pp.

In the Mystic Footsteps of Saints

Sufi Wisdom Series
By Shaykh Muhammad Nazim Adil al-Haqqani
Volume 1 - ISBN 1-930409-05-2
Volume 2 – ISBN 1-930409-09-5
Volume 3 – ISBN 1-930409-13-3
Retail Price: $10.99

Narrated in a charming, old-world storytelling style, this highly spiritual series offers several volumes of practical guidance on how to establish serenity and peace in daily life, how to heal from emotional and spiritual scars, and discover the role we are each destined to play in the universal scheme. Written by Shaykh Nazim Adil al-Haqqani, worldwide leader of the Naqshbandi-Haqqani Sufi Order and a descendant of best-selling poet and Sufi mystic Jalaluddin Rumi. Paperback. Average length 175 pp.

Coming soon from

Islamic Supreme Council of America

Classical Islam
and the Naqshbandi Sufi Order
By Shaykh Muhammad Hisham Kabbani
ISBN 1-930409-10-9

This esteemed work includes an exhaustive historical narrative of the forty saints of the renowned Golden Chain, dating back to Prophet Muhammad in the early 7th century. With close personal ties to the most recent saints, the author has painstakingly compiled rare accounts of their miracles, disciplines, and how for fifteen centuries they have lent spiritual support throughout the world. The Naqshbandi is the most widespread of Sufi orders, with tens of millions of adherents worldwide. In simple terms, the book outlines practical steps to develop stress, anger and time management, and to identify and prioritize what is truly important in life, all of which "awakens" the inner self to a higher dimension of spiritual consciousness.

Classical Islam and the Naqshbandi Sufi Order is a shining tribute to developing human relations at the highest level, and the power of spirituality to uplift humanity from its lower nature to that of spiritual triumph. Paperback. 700 pp.

Liberating the Soul:
A Guide for Spiritual Growth

Sufi Wisdom Series
By Shaykh Muhammad Nazim Adil al-Haqqani
Volume 1 - ISBN 1-930409-14-1
Volume 2 – ISBN 1-930409-15-X
Volume 3 – ISBN 1-930409-16-8
Volume 4 – ISBN 1-930409-17-6

This series focuses on classical Sufi teachings, which open the heart to receive life-altering spiritual powers. *Liberating the Soul* is based on coveted lectures of Shaykh Muhammad Nazim Adil al-Haqqani, the worldwide leader of the Naqshbandi Sufi Order and descendant of best-selling poet Jalaluddin Rumi. Self-improvement and empowerment through spiritual discipline is a running theme. Topics include practical steps to: rid the heart of doubt; build self-confidence in one's unique identity; overcome bad characteristics such as anger, greed, and jealousy; express gratitude for unlimited divine bounty; develop intimate communion with the Creator; learn to respect and appreciate all creation, develop tolerance for others; and much more. Paperback. Average length 300 pp.

The Path To Spiritual Excellence

Sufi Wisdom Series
By Shaykh Muhammad Nazim Adil al-Haqqani
ISBN 1-930409-18-4
Retail: $10.99

This compact volume provides practical steps to purify the heart and overcome the destructive characteristics that deprive us of peace and inner satisfaction. On this amazing journey doubt, fear, and other negative influences that plague our lives - and which we often pass on to our children - can be forever put aside. Simply by introducing in our daily lives those positive thought patterns and actions that attract divine support, we can reach spiritual levels that were previously inaccessible. A transliteration of special prayers and practices is included. This book is an excellent introduction to the classical Sufi teachings that have thrived for fifteen centuries, and would make an attractive addition to the spiritual seeker's resource library. Paperback. 180 pp.

Lightning Source UK Ltd.
Milton Keynes UK
01 June 2010

154961UK00002B/147/A